Read Me First!

A Style Guide for the Computer Industry

SECOND EDITION

PRENTICE HALL
Professional Technical Reference
Upper Saddle River, NJ 07458
www.phptr.com

Sun Technical Publications

Prentice Hall PTR offers excellent discounts on this book when ordered in quantity for bulk purchases or special sales. For more information, please contact: U.S. Corporate and Government Sales, 1-800-382-3419, corpsales@pearsontechgroup.com. For sales outside of the U.S., please contact: International Sales, 1-317-581-3793, international@pearsontechgroup.com.

Editorial/production supervision: *Patti Guerrieri*
Cover design director: *Jerry Votta*
Cover designer: *Anthony Gemmellaro*
Manufacturing manager: *Alexis R. Heydt-Long*
Marketing manager: *Debby vanDijk*
Executive editor: *Ann Sellers*
Editorial assistant: *Brandt Kenna*
Sun Microsystems Press publisher: *Myrna Rivera*

Third Printing

ISBN 0-13-142899-3

Sun Microsystems Press
A Prentice Hall Title

Contents

Tables

Examples

Preface

(i) stands for information, and *Read Me First! A Style Guide for the Computer Industry* provides everything you always wanted to know about documenting computer products, from writing about web sites to legal guidelines, from writing for an international audience to developing a documentation department.

How This Book Is Organized

Read Me First! is organized as described in the following paragraphs.

Chapter 1, "Mechanics of Writing," reviews basic punctuation rules and guidelines, plus other general writing rules and conventions. This chapter also notes exceptions to these rules, guidelines, and conventions.

Chapter 2, "Constructing Text," provides guidelines for tables, cross-references, headings, lists, and other text elements.

Chapter 3, "Writing Style," provides guidelines for writing in a style that facilitates effective communication.

Chapter 4, "Online Writing Style," provides guidelines for writing documentation that is intended primarily for online presentation. Some of these guidelines also apply to online help and web pages.

Chapter 5, "Constructing Links," provides guidelines for using links effectively in online documents.

Chapter 6, "Writing Tasks, Procedures, and Steps," provides guidelines for writing tasks, procedures, and steps in a procedure.

Chapter 7, "Writing for an International Audience," provides guidelines for writing material that is easily understood by readers whose first language is not English and that can be easily translated into other languages.

Chapter 8, "Legal Guidelines," provides guidelines for the proper use of copyrights, trademarks, and proprietary information.

Chapter 9, "Types of Technical Documents," describes the various parts that make up a manual and lists the order in which they appear. This chapter also describes typical types of computer documentation.

Chapter 10, "Working With an Editor," explains how writers and editors work together to produce high-quality documents.

Chapter 11, "Working With Illustrations," describes illustration formats, styles, and types. This chapter also provides guidelines for writing callouts, arranging callouts, using leader lines, and writing captions.

Chapter 12, "Writing About Graphical User Interfaces," explains how to document graphical user interfaces (GUIs). This chapter also provides specific guidelines for writing about web pages and referencing URLs.

Chapter 13, "Glossary Guidelines," explains how to create a glossary for a technical manual.

Chapter 14, "Indexing," explains how to prepare an index for a technical manual. This chapter covers issues such as selecting topics to index, style rules for creating an index, and editing the index.

Appendix A, "Developing a Publications Department," provides information about issues related to a documentation department, including topics such as scheduling, roles and responsibilities, technical review, and printing and production.

Appendix B, "Checklists and Forms," contains sample checklists and forms that you can use at various stages of documentation development, including art tracking, print authorization, and a technical review cover letter.

Appendix C, "Correct Usage of Terms," provides alternatives for terms that you should not use in technical documentation, and terms that you should avoid. This appendix also provides some guidance related to commonly confused words and terms.

Appendix D, "Recommended Reading," presents a list of books, divided by subject headings, that you might want to consult for additional information.

Changes for This Revision

Since the last revision of *Read Me First!*, the globalization of technical products has increased, and online delivery has become a fast-growing means of delivery for technical documentation. *Read Me First!* has been extensively revised in response to these changes. The highlights of this revision are as follows:

- A more logical organization of chapters
- Addition of a chapter on online writing style
- Addition of a chapter on constructing links
- Addition of a chapter on writing tasks, procedures, and steps
- Extensive revisions to the chapters that discuss the following topics:
  - Writing for an international audience
  - Legal guidelines
  - Working with illustrations
  - Writing about graphical user interfaces
- Incorporation of guidelines for easing the translation of documents

Acknowledgments

Read Me First! A Style Guide for the Computer Industry is based substantially on the *Sun Microsystems Editorial Style Guide*.

The people who worked on the fourth edition of the *Sun Microsystems Editorial Style Guide* include Julie Bettis, Maura Burke, Paul Davies, Melanie Doulton, Jeffrey Gardiner, Janice Gelb, Mary Martyak, Jean McVey, Ron Morton, Steve Posusta, PJ Schemenaur, Alysson Troffer, and Linda Wiesner. Janice Gelb was the Project Lead for *Read Me First!*.

Special thanks go to the members of the Sun Microsystems Editorial Forum, who served as primary reviewers and architects of all versions of the *Sun Microsystems Editorial Style Guide*. Bruce Bartlett was instrumental in developing the basis for the chapter on indexing. Thanks also to Andrea Marra, who had the original concept and was the driving force behind the original book. Finally, thanks to Steve Cogorno for invaluable production assistance.

Note – An earlier version of Chapter 7, "Writing for an International Audience," appeared in the *Sun Microsystems Editorial Style Guide* and subsequently in *Solaris International Developer's Guide* by Bill Tuthill (New Jersey: SunSoft Press/Prentice Hall, 1993).

CHAPTER 1

Mechanics of Writing

Error-free writing requires more than just using good grammar. You must also use correct mechanics of writing in your documents. The *mechanics of writing* specifies the established conventions for words that you use in your documentation. *Grammar* reflects the forms of words and their relationships within a sentence. For instance, if you put an apostrophe in a plural word ("Create two file's"), you have made a mistake in the mechanics of writing, not grammar.

The mechanics of writing guidelines in this chapter work well for computer documentation, but other style guides might suggest different rules that are equally effective. In most cases, which rules you follow doesn't matter as long as you are consistent within your document or documentation set. See Chapter 2 for options related to the use of text and graphical elements, such as section headings, tables, and cross-references.

This chapter discusses the following topics:

Capitalization

The chief reason to capitalize a word is that the word is *proper*, not because the word has greater status than other words. A *proper noun* identifies a specific member of a class. A *common noun*, on the other hand, denotes either the whole class or any random member of the class. For example, King Henry VIII (a particular member of a class) was a king of England (the class itself).

Answering the following question can help you determine whether a noun is proper. If the answer is yes, the noun is probably a common noun.

Does an article or other limiting word appear before the noun? Limiting words include "a," "the," "this," "some," and "certain."

Notice the difference between the following sentences:

Use a text editor to change the information in your file.
Use Text Editor to change the information in your file.

In the first sentence, the article "a" makes clear that the writer is not pointing to a particular member of the group of text editors. Therefore, "text editor" is a common noun. But in the second sentence, the absence of an article or limiting word helps to clarify that the writer is pointing to only one member of the group. In that case, capitalize the proper noun "Text Editor."

Note – See Chapter 13 and Chapter 14 for examples of how to capitalize glossary and index entries, respectively.

Use an industry-accepted dictionary or other resource to verify capitalization of computer terms. Refer to "Reference Works" on page 328 in Appendix D for suggested resources.

What to Capitalize

Capitalize the following items:

- Proper nouns
- The letters of many abbreviations and acronyms
- The first letter of the first word in numbered or bulleted lists
- The first letter of the first word in figure callouts (see "Writing Callouts for Illustrations" on page 214)

- The first letter of these terms when they are followed by a letter or number: "table," "figure," "example," "appendix," "chapter," "section," "part," and "step"

  The font style and capitalization in cross-references might differ because these aspects are determined by your template or tool.

  > Go to Chapter 3.
  > See Section 9 in the reference manual.
  > See the following table.

- The Roman numeral that designates the sequence of a part divider in a manual

  > Part III

- The first letter of each term that identifies the name of a key on a keyboard

  > Control-A
  > Escape key
  > the M key
  > Ctrl-Shift-Q

- The first letter of the first word in a sentence, unless the sentence begins with a literal command name or other literal computer term that is not capitalized

  Write in a way that avoids such occurrences.

  > **Incorrect:** `format` enables you to divide the disk into slices.
  > **Correct:** Use the `format` utility to divide the disk into slices.

- The first letter of the first word of a complete sentence following a colon

  > The software saves time: You can now press a single key to accomplish what used to take hours of complex calculations.

  > Select from two options: The Save option stores your changes and the Discard option erases your changes.

- The first letter of the first word in a title or heading, the first letter of all other words in a title or heading *except* conjunctions, articles, prepositions of fewer than four letters, and the "to" in infinitives

  > See "Using the Mouse" on page 11.
  > How to Delete Text With the Cut Function Key

- The first letter of the second element of a hyphenated compound word in a title or heading unless the element is an article, preposition, or coordinating conjunction

  > Installing a Half-Inch Disk Drive
  > Configuring the Audio-in Component

- Figure captions, example captions, table captions, and table column headings, using the same rules as for titles and section headings

- Hardware switch names and buttons

  > Power-On/Off switch
  > Standby switch
  > Power button

What Not to Capitalize

Do not capitalize the following items:

- The word "page" when followed by a number

    Refer to page 45.

- The spelled-out words in most acronyms and abbreviations, even though the words ordinarily appear in a shortened form in capital letters

    field-replaceable unit (FRU)
    direct memory access (DMA)

- The "x" in hexadecimal text, as in "0x8E"
- The "x" in "x86"
- The "x" in dimensions, as in "12x12 inches"
- Any word for the sole reason of emphasizing it (use italic for emphasis)
- The words "release" or "version" unless these words are part of a product name
- Variable names that are used in code examples
- Command and function names
- Words in figure callouts other than the first word, proper nouns, abbreviations, or acronyms
- The first word following a colon if the word begins a text fragment

    This button has only one purpose: to shut down the system.

Contractions

Contractions can potentially cause confusion for localization or nonnative English speakers. When using contractions, follow these guidelines:

- Never use a contraction when you want to emphasize the negative.

    Incorrect: Don't press the Escape key.
    Correct: Do *not* press the Escape key.

- Avoid obscure contractions, nonstandard usage, and regionalisms such as "mustn't," "mightn't," "you'd best," "shan't," "ain't," or "don't" to mean "does not."
- Never create your own contractions.
- Avoid adding "'s" for "is" or "has" to form a contraction (for example, "that's").

    This construction can be confused with possessive constructions.

- Use "it's" and "its" correctly.

  "Its" is the possessive of "it." "It's" is the contraction of "it is."

  If you must use these constructions, make sure that the antecedent is clear.

  > Its features include expanding and contracting list items.
  > It's the correct contraction to use.

The following contractions are not usually a problem for translators: "can't," "isn't," and "don't" (for "do not").

Gerunds and Participles

When you use a gerund or a participle, ensure that the phrase or sentence in which the gerund or the participle is used is unambiguous. A *participle* is based on a verb, ends with "-ing" or "-ed," and functions as an adjective. A *gerund* is also based on a verb and ends with "-ing," but a gerund is used as a noun.

Confusion can arise when a gerund is followed immediately by a noun because the gerund could be misinterpreted as a modifier. For example, the sentence "Moving companies can be a growth opportunity in an economic decline" is ambiguous because you can interpret "moving" in either of the following ways:

> The movement of companies can be a growth opportunity in an economic decline.

> The moving services industry can be a growth opportunity in an economic decline.

Follow these guidelines when using gerunds and participles:

- Rewrite sentences to avoid gerunds that are immediately followed by nouns.

Tip – In many instances, you can avoid ambiguity by preceding the noun with an article or possessive pronoun.

> **Incorrect:**
> Disabling network services prevents IP packets from doing any harm to the system.
>
> **Correct:**
> Disabling the network services prevents IP packets from doing any harm to the system.
>
> The disabling of network services prevents IP packets from doing any harm to the system.
>
> If you disable network services, the IP packets do not harm the system.

- Rewrite sentences to avoid participles that have ambiguous meanings.

  The following sentence is ambiguous because you do not know whether the participle "using" applies to the term "request" or "Document Editor."

  > The Document Editor sends an edit message request using the file name as a parameter for the message.

  You can interpret this sentence in either of the following ways:

  > The Document Editor sends an edit message request that uses the file name as a parameter for the message.

  > The Document Editor uses the file name as a parameter for the message to send the message.

  The following sentence is ambiguous because you do not know whether the participle "used" applies to the term "variables" or "semaphores."

  > Semaphores are almost as powerful as conditional variables used in conjunction with mutexes.

  You can interpret this sentence in either of the following ways:

  > Semaphores are almost as powerful as conditional variables that are being used in conjunction with mutexes.

  > Semaphores are almost as powerful as conditional variables when the semaphores are used in conjunction with mutexes.

Numbers and Numerals

A *number* is expressed by *numerals* (1, 2, 3, 4), by *Roman numerals* (I, II or i, ii), or by words. *Cardinal numbers* use words such as "one, two, three." *Ordinal numbers* use words such as "first, second, third."

In computer documentation, you most often use numerals when numbers are discussed in text.

Spelling Out Numbers

Spell out numbers in the following situations:

- Numbers from zero through nine, unless the number is part of a measurement or is used in standards that are approved by organizations such as International Organization for Standardization (ISO)

  three computers (a count)
  3 MIPS (a measurement)
  XDR fits into the presentation layer (layer 6) of the ISO reference model.

- Common units of time, greater than one second, from zero through nine

  five minutes
  three days

- Approximations

  You can choose from hundreds of applications for your computer.

- The zeroes in extreme values, such as "million" and "billion," but precede these words with a numeral

  3 million instructions per second

- Any number that begins a sentence

  Ten files are required.

- A number that is immediately followed by a numeral

  Print twelve 500,000-byte files.
  Print 12 of the 500,000-byte files.

Using Numerals

Use numerals in the following cases:

- Numbers 10 or greater

- Numbers less than 10 if they are of the same type and appear in the same sentence, paragraph, or bulleted list as numbers of 10 or greater

  The menu offers 11 options, but you use only 4 options.

- Numbers less than 10 if they are used in terms common to standards that are approved by organizations such as International Organization for Standardization (ISO)

  XDR fits into the presentation layer (layer 6) of the ISO reference model.

- Negative numbers

- Most fractions (see "Using Fractions" on page 9)

- All percentages

- All decimals, including the leading zero

    0.15
    1.25

- All measurements (see "Units of Measurement" on page 13)

    6 pounds
    3.5-inch disk drive
    12x12 feet

- Units of time smaller than one second

    5 milliseconds

- Bit and byte references

    4 bytes
    8-bit color

- Chapter, section, page, step, figure, example, and table numbers

    Step 4
    Section 6.2

- Part numbers. Use uppercase Roman numerals, for example, "Part IV"

Punctuating Numbers and Numerals

Numbers and numerals generally require the same punctuation as words. Punctuating numbers and numerals becomes troublesome, however, when the numbers are compounded. Follow these guidelines:

- Do not hyphenate numbers or numerals when they serve as single modifiers.

    Your file contains 500,000 bytes.

- Hyphenate numbers or numerals in compound modifiers.

    Print the 500,000-byte file.

- Do not use a comma in numerals of four digits.

    1028
    6000

- Use a comma in numerals of more than four digits.

    10,000
    600,000

For more information about appropriate use of numbers and numerals, see "Numbers, Symbols, and Punctuation" on page 144.

Using Fractions

The usage of numerals for fractions depends on the context. Sometimes, spelling out the fraction or using decimals is the preferred form. Follow these guidelines:

- Use numerals for fractions in tables and for units of measurement, but spell out common fractions in running text.

  ½-inch tape drive
  half the users in the test

- Use a space between a numeral and its related fraction.

  8 ½ inches

- If a fraction is used in a compound modifier, insert a hyphen between the fraction and its unit of measurement.

  8 ½-inch width

- Use decimals when decimals are the industry standard.

  3.5-inch diskette

- In a table in which you are using a numeric modifier of a fraction to save space, spell out the modifying numeral to avoid confusion.

  In tables: ten ½-inch tape drives (there are ten drives for ½-inch tape)

  In tables: 10 ½-inch tape drive (the drive is for 10 ½-inch tape)

  Preferred in text: 10 tape drives for ½-inch tape

Pronouns

Follow these guidelines for the use of pronouns:

- Avoid the indefinite pronoun or indefinite possessive pronoun, especially at the beginning of a sentence, unless the noun to which the pronoun or possessive pronoun refers is clear.

  A pronoun that forces a reader to search for an antecedent can frustrate or mislead the reader. Pronouns that typically cause this type of confusion include "it," "they," "its," "theirs," "this," "these," "that," and "those."

    Incorrect: It also describes how to install the software.

    Correct: This chapter also describes how to install the software.

    Incorrect: You can use these either individually or together.

    Correct: You can use these two options either individually or together.

    Incorrect:

    The value in this variable is used to determine when to pause during long display output, such as during a software dump. Its value is reset each time the ok prompt is displayed.

    Correct:

    The value in this variable is used to determine when to pause during long display output, such as during a software dump. The variable's value is reset each time the ok prompt is displayed.

- Do not use first person pronouns.

    Incorrect:

    We recommend that you install the custom components only on large systems.

    Correct:

    Install the custom components only on large systems.

    Incorrect:

    We can write a protocol specification that describes the remote version of `printmessage()`.

    Correct:

    You can write a protocol specification that describes the remote version of `printmessage()`.

Technical Abbreviations, Acronyms, and Units of Measurement

Computer documentation requires extensive use of abbreviations, acronyms, and units of measurement, many of which have become generally accepted "words" in the industry language. As with any word in a sentence, use abbreviations, acronyms, and units of measurement accurately and with consistent meaning in your documents. Do not create your own abbreviations or acronyms. Rely on industry definitions for these terms. Reference books of this type include *The New IEEE Standard Dictionary of Electrical and Electronics Terms*, *IBM Dictionary of Computing*, and *Microsoft Press Computer Dictionary*.

Abbreviations and Acronyms

An *abbreviation* is a shortened form of a word or phrase that is used in place of the entire word or phrase. "CPU" for central processing unit, "Btu" for British thermal unit, and "SGML" for Standard Generalized Markup Language are examples of abbreviations. An *acronym* is an easily pronounceable word formed from the initial letters or major parts of a compound term. "GUI" for graphical user interface, "pixel" for picture element, and "ROM" for read-only memory are common acronyms.

Basic Guidelines for Abbreviations and Acronyms

When using abbreviations or acronyms, follow these guidelines:

- Do not use the Latin abbreviations e.g., i.e., vs., op. cit., viz., and etc.
- In most cases, write out the full word or phrase and enclose its abbreviation or acronym in parentheses the first time the word or phrase is used.

  Then, continue using the abbreviation or acronym alone.

  > A local area network (LAN) consists of computer systems that can communicate with one another through connecting hardware and software. Your company probably uses a LAN.

- Do not spell out acronyms and abbreviations that are trademarked terms.
- Avoid using acronyms and abbreviations in the plural form.

  Acronyms and abbreviations in the plural form can potentially cause problems for assistive technologies and for localization.

- If you cite a term only once or twice in a document, show both the abbreviation or acronym and the spelled-out version at each occurrence.

- If an abbreviation or acronym is used often in a document, repeat the spelled-out version at the first appearance in each chapter where the abbreviation or acronym appears.

- When writing out the full word or phrase, do not capitalize any letters unless the letters are capitalized as part of a standard or begin a proper noun.

    floating-point unit (FPU)

    Internet Protocol (IP)

- Do not shorten trademarked terms.

- When using an acronym, ensure that its pronunciation is natural and obvious to a reader.

    The acronym "SCSI," for example, is pronounced "scuzzy." A user who does not know that "SCSI" is pronounceable might expect to see "*an* SCSI port," not "*a* SCSI port." In such cases, provide a pronunciation key when you first use the acronym by itself, as in this example:

    A small computer system interface (SCSI, pronounced "scuzzy") cable connects the disk drive to the SCSI port.

Punctuating Abbreviations and Acronyms

While you usually do not have to add punctuation to abbreviations and acronyms, the following list provides a few exceptions:

- Use periods in abbreviations that look like words.

    U.S. for United States
    no. for number

- Use punctuation marks other than a period in abbreviations or acronyms when that punctuation is standard form.

    I/O for input/output
    3-D for three-dimensional

- Add an "s" and no apostrophe to form the plural of abbreviations or acronyms that contain no periods.

    PCs
    ISVs
    GUIs

- Add an apostrophe and "s" to form the plural of abbreviations or acronyms that use internal periods.

    M.S.'s
    Ph.D.'s

Units of Measurement

When abbreviating units of measurement, follow these guidelines:

- Do not abbreviate common units of measurement, such as inches, pounds, feet, centimeters, and meters, unless space conservation is an overriding concern.

  You may use abbreviations within tables, for example.

- Do not use the # symbol to indicate "pound" or "number," a single quotation mark (') to indicate "foot," or a double quotation mark (") to indicate "inch."

- Use standard abbreviations for units of measurement with great care.

  For example, the difference between Mb and MB is the difference between a megabit and a megabyte. Avoid this confusion by consistently spelling out a term like "megabyte" or by using the less-abbreviated form, "Mbyte."

- Do not add "s" for the plural of units of measurement.

  Abbreviations for units of measurement already account for plurals.

  For example, the abbreviations for 1 kilowatt and 10 kilowatts are written the same way: kW.

- Use periods in abbreviations of units of measurement that look like words.

  in. for inch

  oz for ounce, lb for pound (because "oz" and "lb" are not words)

- Leave a space between a numeral and an abbreviation unless the industry standard for a particular unit of measurement does not include a space or unless the abbreviation resembles a word.

  12 mm

  220V, 10A

- Include the metric or U.S. equivalent of a unit of measurement when appropriate.

  1 in. (2.54 cm)
  0.45359 kg (1 lb)

Punctuation

This section reviews basic punctuation rules and guidelines for American English, notes exceptions, and suggests alternatives. The section is organized alphabetically.

Note – Traditional punctuation marks have specialized meanings in the context of programming languages. A classic example is that of quotation marks in the C shell or Bourne shell. These shells have specialized, nonintuitive meanings for single quotes, double quotes, and back quotes. Watch for these types of specialized usages in your writing and editing.

Apostrophe

Use an apostrophe in the following situations:

- **In contractions.** Use an apostrophe to replace letters that are omitted in a contraction.

    can't
    isn't

- **In place of numerals.** Use an apostrophe to replace omitted numerals. Use this informal construction sparingly.

    Class of '66
    Technology of the '90s

- **For possessives.** Use an apostrophe to denote the possessive case of a noun.

    Add an apostrophe and an "s" to most indefinite pronouns, singular nouns (including collective nouns), and plural nouns that do not end in "s."

    the manager's responsibilities
    someone's system
    the group's privileges
    people's rights

    To form the possessive of singular nouns ending in "s" or its sound, you often add an apostrophe and an "s."

    the mouse's buttons
    the bus's capacity

Add only the apostrophe when the addition of an "s" produces an awkward sound.

    Plirg Systems' employees

In a few cases, however, either is acceptable.

    M. Travis's files
    M. Travis' files

Add an apostrophe to form the possessive of plural nouns that end in "s."

    the Travises' files
    the boards' interrupts

Add an apostrophe and an "s" to the last word of a compound to form the possessive of most compound constructions.

    each other's files
    anyone else's business

The possessive of two or more names depends on ownership. In the first example, ownership is joint. In the second example, ownership is individual.

    Malcolm and Mary's files
    Malcolm's and Mary's files

- **To form plurals.** Use an apostrophe to form the plurals of most numerals and symbols, lowercase letters, and single uppercase letters.

Use an apostrophe to form the plurals of abbreviations and acronyms that use internal periods.

    P's and Q's
    ~'s and #'s
    1's
    Ph.D.'s

The apostrophe is not necessary, although not incorrect, when you are forming the plural of two or more unitary uppercase letters or numerals.

    CPUs
    user IDs
    operating system of the 1990s

Single lowercase letters and single uppercase letters are awkward in the plural possessive form. Rewrite to avoid this problem.

Brackets

Brackets are not substitutes for parentheses. To preserve their unique service as meaningful signals to your readers, construct sentences in a way that minimizes the grammatical need for brackets.

Use brackets in the following situations:

- **Within parenthetic text.** Use brackets to insert a parenthetic word or phrase into material that is already enclosed by parentheses.

  Placing comments within a menu file often makes sense. (See page 154 of *Advanced Skills*, Revision A [May, 1991] for related information.)

- **In optional command-line entries.** Use brackets to set off an optional part of a command line.

  date [*yymmddhhmm*]

Colon

The following sections describe appropriate use of a colon.

When to Use a Colon

Use a colon in the following situations:

- **To introduce a list.** When introducing a list, use a colon if the introduction is clearly anticipatory of the list, especially if the introduction contains phrasing such as "the following" or "as follows."

  Default settings include four secondary groups: operator, devices, accounts, and networks.

  The following options are available from the Diagnostics menu:

  - Test Computer
  - Inspect Computer
  - Upgrade Software

  If the introduction is complete in itself, use a period. See "Capitalizing and Punctuating Lists" on page 39for other guidelines to use when punctuating lists.

Ensure that any introductory text that ends in a colon is a complete sentence or a noun phrase. Avoid sentence fragments for introductory text that ends in a colon.

Incorrect:

For example, in your startup script, set:

Correct:

For example, in your startup script, set the following parameters:

When the introduction to steps in a procedure is a complete sentence, the use of a colon is optional. If numbered steps immediately follow the statement, you can generally use a colon. If numbered steps do not immediately follow the statement, use a period.

Learn how to send a message by following these steps:
Follow the steps in this section to send a message.

- **Before explanatory text.** Use a colon to indicate that the initial clause will be further explained or illustrated by information that follows the colon.

  The colon serves as a substitute for phrases such as "in other words," "namely," or "for instance."

  Notice in the next example that the first word following the colon is capitalized. Capitalize the first word of the statement if the statement is a complete sentence. Do not capitalize the first word if the statement is a sentence fragment.

  This software project was bad from the start: Customer requirements were never defined, management was not committed to the project, and the deadlines were unrealistic.

- **After an introduction.** Use a colon after an introduction to a statement or question.

  Here is the choice: Do you want to save the file or delete it?

  Remember this cardinal rule: Never reboot your system until you have saved all of your files.

- **Before "for example" and similar expressions.** Use a colon before expressions such as "for example," "that is," and "namely" when the expression causes a major break in the flow of the sentence.

  Take precautions to preserve your data: For example, the best precaution that you can take is to save your files often.

- **With the name of a disk drive.** Use a colon after the name of a specific disk drive.

  Insert the diskette into drive A: and press Return.

When Not to Use a Colon

Do not use a colon in the following situations:

- **To introduce a figure or a table.**

    Figure 3–2 shows the relationship between servers and clients.
    Table 4–7 lists the features and their corresponding UNIX® commands.
    The following figure shows the parts of the editing window.

- **When referring to screen elements in text.** When a field name, menu option, or any element on the screen is followed by a colon, omit the colon in text.

    The Printers menu (even though the on-screen label is "Printers:")
    The Hosts option (even though the on-screen label is "Hosts:")

- **To introduce headings.**

    Incorrect:

    <Level2Head>Preinstallation Checklist

    Before you begin the installation, verify several things about your system:

    <Level3Head>Check the Configuration

    Correct:

    <Level2Head>Preinstallation Checklist

    Before you begin the installation, verify several things about your system.

    <Level3Head>Check the Configuration

- **At the end of a procedure heading.**

    Incorrect: To Configure Your System:
    Correct: To Configure Your System

- **In a list that is introduced by "includes" or "are" within a sentence.**

    Incorrect:

    The base colors that are used in four-color printing are: cyan, magenta, yellow, and black.

    Correct:

    The base colors that are used in four-color printing are cyan, magenta, yellow, and black.

Comma

The following sections describe appropriate use of a comma.

When to Use a Comma

Use a comma in the following situations:

- **In a series.** Use commas to separate the items in a series of three or more words, phrases, or clauses.

  > Among your hidden files are `.cshrc`, `.defaults`, `.login`, and `.mailrc`.

  Using a comma before the conjunction that joins the last two items in a series prevents confusion regarding whether the last two items in a series are related.

  The following sentence is confusing because the final job opening could be read as a single field ("advertising and public relations").

  > Current job openings include positions in programming, technical writing, advertising and public relations.

  If an independent clause already contains a comma, consider using a list to separate the items in a series.

  > **Incorrect:**
  > The window has a menu bar, which lists available menus, a palette, which shows graphics tools, and a working area, where you draw.

  > **Correct:**
  > The window contains the following items:
  > - Menu bar, which lists available menus
  > - Palette, which shows graphics tools
  > - Working area, where you draw

- **To separate independent clauses in a sentence.** Use a comma to separate independent clauses that are joined by the coordinating conjunctions "and," "but," "yet," "for," "nor," and "or."

  Place the comma before the conjunction.

  > You do not have to back up your files, but doing so is prudent.
  > She lost all of her work, yet she still does not back up her files.

- **To separate a subordinate clause or long introductory phrase at the start of a sentence from the main clause.**

  > If you have not deleted a marked file, you can restore it.
  > Using a text editor, change the last line of the file.

- **After a dependent adverbial clause or prepositional phrase that starts a sentence.**

  By recording transactions and automating billing, the financial software saves time and prevents costly errors.

  In such cases, hosts assume that destinations are not accessible.

  Do not include the comma if the phrase appears in its normal order in the sentence.

  Because this feature automatically updates system files, it saves time.
  This feature saves time because it automatically updates system files.

- **To separate an introductory modifier from the rest of the sentence.**

  Hopefully, he entered the personnel office.
  Confident that she had saved her work, she logged out.

- **With nonrestrictive phrases.** Use a comma to set off nonrestrictive clauses or phrases.

  The mail icon, which looks like a mailbox, flashes.

  Writers often refer to this book, which is a style guide for the computer industry.

- **With parenthetic text.** Use commas to set off short parenthetic material.

  The software, with its simple interface, decreases input time by 50 percent.

- **In addresses.** Use commas to set off components of an address when the address appears in a sentence or on one line.

  Write to Plirg Systems, Inc., North Bay Village, Florida.

- **With appositives.** In most cases, use commas instead of dashes to set off a single appositive.

  The monitor, hardware that looks like a television set, has only one function.

- **In dates.** Use commas to separate components of a date.

  The comma is optional, however, with only two components.

  She was hired on January 1, 1996, and left six months later.
  She was hired in January 1996.

- **With "for example" and similar expressions.** Use commas to set off expressions such as "for example," "that is," and "namely."

  Enter the date in MMDDYY format, for example, 110798.

Precede such expressions with a comma only for minor breaks in continuity. For major breaks in continuity, divide the sentence into two sentences.

Incorrect:

The database lists existing objects; however, it does not include objects created since the previous session.

Correct:

The database lists existing objects. The database does not include objects created since the previous session.

When Not to Use a Comma

Do not use a comma in the following situations:

- **In a series of adjectives that is used as one modifier.**

  Click the small black button at the top of the window.

- **Between two short independent clauses.**

  Back up your work or you are fired.
  Save your changes and quit the text editor.

- **If a dependent adverbial clause or prepositional phrase appears in its normal order in the sentence.**

  Because this feature automatically updates system files, it saves time.
  This feature saves time because it automatically updates system files.

Dash (Em Dash)

Using an em dash for explanatory purposes can result in sentences that are difficult for readers to understand because the sentences contain more than one main idea. When possible, divide a sentence in which em dashes are used for explanatory purposes into two sentences.

Incorrect:

After a context is established between two peers—say, a client and a server—messages can be protected before being sent.

Correct:

After a context is established between two peers, messages can be protected before being sent. An example of two peers is a client and a server.

Em dashes are sometimes used before and after an appositive series.

Three vital pieces of hardware—the keyboard, the system unit, and the monitor—are packed in the largest carton.

Dash (En Dash)

Use an en dash in the following situations:

- **To indicate ranges.** Use an en dash, without surrounding spaces, to indicate a range.

    Refer to pages 16–24.
    Place the machines 12–16 inches apart.

    However, if a book uses chapter-by-chapter page numbering, use the word "to" to indicate a page range.

    Refer to pages 2-15 to 2-19.

- **To indicate negative numbers.** Use an en dash as the minus sign for numbers that are less than zero.

    Do not operate this equipment in temperatures lower than –10° C.

- **In lists.** In a bulleted list, you can use an en dash to separate an introductory word or phrase from its explanation.

    When you use this list format, put a space before and after the en dash. If the text following the introductory word or phrase is extensive, use a period instead of an en dash.

    The word processing software includes the following features:

    - **Automatic save** – Saves changes every two minutes
    - **Automatic backup** – Creates a backup file when you exit
    - **Automatic recall** – Tracks the last 20 transactions

- **In table, figure, and example numbers.** Most authoring tools automatically provide the table or figure number in table and figure cross-references.

    If you have to type a table or figure number, use an en dash between the two numbers.

Ellipsis Points

Ellipsis points are made up of three dots. Avoid the use of ellipsis points except when showing truncated text within a code fragment. Do not include the ellipsis points shown in a menu item when mentioning the item in running text.

Exclamation Point

Do not use exclamation points except where they have some technical significance. For example, the ! operators in programming and scripting languages have technical meaning.

> **Incorrect:** Configure the system manually!
> **Correct:** Configure the system manually.

Hyphen

Because the computer industry has developed unique terminology, the use of hyphens has become troublesome. Computer documents are often littered with unnecessary hyphens. As a general rule, hyphenate a multiword expression that is used as a modifier. Do not hyphenate a multiword expression that is used as a verb or noun.

the check-in procedure	check in the material
the direct-access password	if you have direct access
the end-user application	writing for end users
the look-up table	look up the definition

When to Use a Hyphen

Use a hyphen in the following situations:

- **In compound modifiers.** With some exceptions, use a hyphen to form a compound modifier when the modifier is used before the noun.

    An exception is open compound nouns used as modifiers, as described in "When Not to Use a Hyphen" on page 25.

    > Review the context-sensitive help.
    > This menu-driven application provides all possible options.

    Use hyphens with numerals in compound modifiers.

    > Print the 500,000-byte file.

    Note the difference in meaning between "end-user control" and "end user control." If you do not intend to abolish the user's control, use a hyphen to avoid ambiguity.

    Hyphenate a compound modifier when it appears before a noun. When a modifier appears after a noun, do not hyphenate a compound modifier.

    > An easy-to-remember mail alias is a person's first initial and last name.

    > A mail alias that is easy to remember is a person's first initial and last name.

- **To prevent ambiguity.** Use a hyphen to clarify ambiguous text.

  Ed owns a small-doll shop.   Ed owns a small doll shop.

  He recovered the sofa.   He re-covered the sofa.

- **With some prefixes and suffixes.** Use a hyphen in most cases between a prefix or suffix and a root word when the combination results in double letters.

  re-enable
  co-organizer
  shell-like

  When in doubt, use the guidelines in a standard dictionary. For example, the following words do not use the general rule:

  reentry
  unnumbered
  misspell

  Use a hyphen to join numbers and proper nouns or modifiers with the following prefixes. However, these prefixes are usually joined without hyphens to common nouns and modifiers.

  mid-
  neo-
  non-
  pan-
  pro-
  un-

  Almost without exception, hyphens join the following prefixes with the main word of a compound:

  all-
  ex-
  self-

- **With two words that precede and modify a noun as a unit if one of the words is a past or present participle.** A participle functions as an adjective and is formed by the addition of "-ing" (present participle) or "-ed" (past participle).

  file-sharing protocol
  write-protected device
  user-defined functions

- **In fractions.** Use a hyphen to separate the components of a spelled-out fraction.

  The resulting file will occupy nearly one-third of your disk.

- **In key combinations for some product lines.** Unless the platform that you are documenting indicates another style, use a hyphen to join simultaneous keystrokes.

  Control-A
  Ctrl-Shift-Q
  Meta-A

  For more information about punctuation for key combinations, see "Documenting Multiple Keystrokes" on page 62.

- **In variable names.** Use a hyphen to separate words of a variable name that is two or more syllables long except *userid*, *username*, and other variable names that are short and easy to read as one word.

  Do not use a space or underscore in variable names. Reserve underscores for their designated use in code.

  directory-name
  system-name
  hostname
  mount-options

Note – Some authoring environments consider a hyphen to be a line-break character. However, some hyphenated terms should stay on the same line, for example, Control-Q. Talk to your tools support person to find out how to indicate a nonbreaking hyphen.

When Not to Use a Hyphen

Do not use a hyphen in the following situations:

- **For industry-accepted terms.** Do not hyphenate compound words that are generally accepted as single words.

  online
  database
  email

- **To construct nouns.** Do not hyphenate two words that are used as a noun even if those same words are hyphenated when they are used as a compound modifier.

  Writing documentation for end users is different from writing the end-user application.

  If you have direct access, you can use the direct-access password.

- **To construct verbs.** Do not hyphenate two words that are used as a verb even if those same words are hyphenated when they are used as a compound modifier.

  Check in the book only after reading the check-in instructions.
  Look up the value in the look-up table.

- **With open compound nouns used as modifiers.** Do not hyphenate open compound nouns used as modifiers except to avoid ambiguity or to comply with industry standards, such as the terms "cathode-ray tube" or "CD-ROM drive." An open compound noun is a combination of separate nouns that are so closely related as to constitute a single concept. When using open compound nouns, do not create noun strings longer than three words.

  data interchange format
  device driver interface
  disk storage device
  domain name address
  file name extension
  file server specifications

  For more information, see "Use Modifiers and Nouns Carefully" on page 141.

- **With a compound modifier (adverb) ending in "ly."** Never hyphenate a compound modifier that includes an adverb that ends in "ly."

  An easily remembered mail alias is a person's first initial and last name.

- **By itself in suspended form.** When you have successive compound adjectives with a common component, do not omit the component and leave the hyphen suspended.

  Incorrect: 8- and 7-bit characters
  Correct: 8-bit and 7-bit characters

- **With numerals as single modifiers.** Do not hyphenate numerals or numbers when they serve as single modifiers.

  The file requires 500,000 bytes of disk space.

- **With some prefixes.** Do not hyphenate a word that is listed as unhyphenated in a standard dictionary and that uses a common prefix.

bi-	multi-	pre-
inter-	non-	sub-
meta-	over-	un-
micro-	post-	under-
mini-		

- **To indicate a range.** Use an en dash (with no space before or after it) instead of a hyphen to indicate a range.

> Refer to pages 16–24.
> Place the machines 12–16 inches apart.

However, if a book uses chapter-by-chapter page numbering, use the word "to" to indicate a page range.

> Refer to pages 2-15 to 2-19.

- **With trademarked terms.** See "Proper Use of Trademarks" on page 157 for exceptions.

Parentheses

Avoid parenthetical statements that distract from the main idea of a sentence. Consider rewriting a sentence that contains a parenthetical statement as two sentences. If the parenthetical statement is a definition, move the term and text to a glossary and create a cross-reference.

Incorrect:

The configuration file that is created by Create Action is written to *home-directory*/`.dt`/`type`/*action-name*`.dt`. The `action_file` (the executable file with the same name as the action) is placed in your home directory.

Correct:

The configuration file that is created by Create Action is written to *home-directory*/`.dt`/`type`/*action-name*`.dt`. The `action_file` is placed in your home directory. The `action_file` is the executable file with the same name as the action.

Note – Do not use "(s)" after nouns to indicate singular or plural. Either use the plural alone or insert the phrase "one or more" before the plural.

When to Use Parentheses

Use parentheses in the following situations:

- **In lists.** Use either two parentheses or one parenthesis to set off letters or numerals that designate items that are listed within a sentence.

> Choose from (a) keyboard entry, (b) mouse entry, and (c) voice entry.
> Choose from a) keyboard entry, b) mouse entry, and c) voice entry.

- **To enclose an entire sentence.** Parenthetical sentences can occasionally hinder clear writing by causing the reader to pause. Where possible, consider rewriting a parenthetical sentence without the parentheses. Occasionally, you might want to use parentheses to enclose an entire sentence that is relevant to information presented in the paragraph, yet dispensable to the paragraph's meaning. When an entire sentence is enclosed in parentheses, place the final parenthesis after the sentence's final punctuation mark.

Whole paragraphs should never be parenthetic.

> Position the pointer on the top scrollbox and click the left mouse button. (For detailed instructions on scrolling windows, see page 586.)

- **With first occurrences.** Use parentheses to enclose special keyboard symbols, abbreviations, and acronyms when they first appear in text.

> The operating system inserts a tilde (~) when a file name is too long.

> The software package tracks maintenance on your heating, ventilating, and air conditioning (HVAC) systems.

- **When providing the metric equivalent of a U.S. measure.**

> 3 in. (76.2 mm)

Period

Use a period in the following situations:

- **To end a sentence.** Use a period to end a declarative or imperative sentence.

> Computer documentation is always grammatically precise.

- **In file and directory names.** Use a period as part of a file name to separate the file name from a file extension.

When used in technical terms, a period is called a "dot."

> The procedures are in the `howto.doc` file.
> The `ls -a` command lists `.cshrc` and `.orgrc` among your hidden files.

In the UNIX operating system, a period also serves as an abbreviation for the current directory.

> To copy a file into the current directory, you would type the following command:
>
> `cp ~/work/budget .`

- **With abbreviations.** A period is used with some abbreviations, and always with those abbreviations that would look like a word otherwise.

> a.m.
> U.S.

- **In lists.** In a bulleted list, you can use a period to separate an introductory word or phrase from its explanation. If the text following the introductory word or phrase is brief, use an en dash instead of a period.

Quotation Marks

Use quotation marks in the following situations:

- **For quotes.** Quotation marks indicate that material was taken verbatim from another source.

  Do not enclose verbatim commands, system messages, file names, and so forth in quotation marks. In some cases, a reader can be misled into thinking that the quotation marks are an integral part of text that is to be typed.

- **For multiple-paragraph quotations.** If the quotation has multiple paragraphs, put an open quotation mark at the beginning of each paragraph and a final quotation mark at the end of the last paragraph.

  If the paragraphs are indented as a block quotation, do not use any quotation marks.

- **Around chapter titles and section headings.** Use quotation marks to enclose titles of chapters and headings of sections in a book.

  "Sending Mail" on page 42 describes how to send an email message.

- **For emphasis.** Use quotation marks to emphasize a word or phrase when it is used in an uncommon way or when it is the subject of discussion.

  Use the `tee` command to take a "snapshot" of your keystrokes.

  The word "menu" is often used in technical writing, but not the word "restaurant."

- **Around single letters.** Use quotation marks to surround single letters.

  The letter "x" denotes the version number.

No single rule governs the placement of quotation marks that are next to other punctuation marks. Whether the final quotation mark follows or precedes another punctuation mark depends on context, as explained here:

- **With commas and periods.** Place the final quotation mark *after* commas and periods, no matter how long or short the quoted material is.

  "Yes," he replied, "the program is written."

- **With colons and semicolons.** Place the final quotation mark *before* a colon or semicolon unless the colon or semicolon is part of quoted text.

  Remember the cardinal rule for taking a "snapshot": Use the recommended palette.

- **With question marks.** Place the final quotation mark *after* a question mark when the question is part of the quoted material.

  The system prompts, "Do you want to continue?"

  The user's guide answers the question, "What can I do with this product?"

Place the final quotation mark *before* a question mark that is not part of the quoted material.

How do I display a list of files that are "hidden"?

Semicolon

Avoid using semicolons. Semicolons are often misused and are difficult to read online. For conjoined sentences, consider rewriting the text as separate sentences.

Incorrect:

The redirects contain the link-layer address of the new first hop; separate address resolution is not necessary.

Correct:

The redirects contain the link-layer address of the new first hop. Separate address resolution is not necessary.

Semicolons are sometimes used to separate short independent clauses joined by conjunctive adverbs such as "however" or "therefore."

Both methods are acceptable; however, the direct access method is preferred.

For serial semicolons, consider rewriting the text as a vertical list.

Incorrect:

The Reply menu provides the following options: Reply (all), include; Reply, include; Reply (all); and Reply.

Correct:

The Reply menu provides the following options:

- Reply (all), include
- Reply, include
- Reply (all)
- Reply

Slash

Do not use a slash in running text. Slashes can be confusing for translators due to the multiple meanings of this symbol, which can mean "or" ("and/or"), "and or" ("open/close"), and "divide by" ("36/6").

Use a slash for fractions.

1/2

3/4

CHAPTER 2

Constructing Text

This chapter provides information about the use of text and graphical elements, such as section headings, tables, and cross-references. Many acceptable ways exist to present these elements. The design, layout, and writing style that you choose will help make your document unique.

The style and writing conventions in this chapter include suggestions that have worked successfully in published computer documents. You might decide to adopt these conventions or to adapt them to your company's documentation. Whatever convention you choose, make sure that the format is easily recognized and understood by readers. Use the style guidelines consistently throughout your document.

This chapter discusses the following topics:

Headings

Headings describe the material that follows them. The appropriate placement of a document heading depends on the content and flow of information. For example, several pages of material might fit well in the context of a single first-level heading, while a few sentences might require a fourth-level heading. Use first-level headings for the broadest summaries, and become more specific as you progress to fourth-level headings. Do not go beyond fourth-level headings. If you have additional topics to cover beyond fourth-level headings, restructure the text. Try to have at least two headings at each level.

For more information about writing headings for online documents, see "Write Meaningful Headings and Subheadings" on page 96. For more information about writing procedure headings, see "Use Procedure Headings Appropriately" on page 125.

Writing Section Headings

Section headings group topics in a chapter and provide points of reference for a reader. Headings are hierarchical. Build headings and text in a logical and understandable progression.

When writing headings, follow these guidelines:

- Avoid ambiguous headings such as "Overview."
- Make sure that the heading summarizes the specific information that is discussed in a section.

   Incorrect: Introduction
   Correct: Sun Fire V880 Features

   Incorrect: Front Panel
   Correct: Front Panel Features

- Reflect the reader's perspective rather than your own.

   Incorrect: Authentication
   Correct: Administering System Authentication Options

- Keep headings short but as meaningful as possible.

   Concise headings are easier to scan in text and in the table of contents.

   Incorrect: ChorusOS 4.0 Supported Features
   Correct: ChorusOS 4.0 Features

- Place the most important words first.

  Incorrect: Elements of Netra High Availability
  Correct: Netra High Availability Features

- Try to use parallel construction when writing headings at the same level.

  If a heading level includes gerunds (for example, "Opening," "Installing"), try to write all other headings in the chapter at that same level using gerunds.

  Incorrect:

  Restoring the Operating System, Disaster Recovery With Autochanger, Recovery With a Standalone Drive

  Correct:

  Operating System Disaster Recovery, Autochanger Disaster Recovery, Standalone Drive Disaster Recovery

- Repeat the subject in the first sentence of the paragraph following a heading, rather than using a pronoun to represent the subject.

  <Level2Head>Remote Digital Loopback Test

  Incorrect: This tests the system's ability to...

  Correct: The remote digital loopback test examines the system's ability to...

  <Level2Head>cd

  Incorrect: Use this to change directories.

  Correct: Use the cd command to change directories.

- Avoid starting headings with articles or with a technical term that begins with a lowercase letter.

  One exception is when the only text used in the heading is a computer term such as a command, function, or class name.

- Do not repeat the exact text of higher-level headings in subheadings, or the text of chapter titles in section headings.

- Include some text before the initial first-level heading in a chapter.

- Some documentation groups add qualifiers to headings and subheadings to identify the type of information that is contained in a section, such as overviews, tasks, and reference material.

  If you use qualifiers, do so consistently within the documentation set.

  Booting a System (Overview)
  Shutting Down a System (Tasks)

Using Fonts in Headings

The font conventions that you use for text in a heading are the same as the conventions that you use for the text in a paragraph. For punctuation and spaces, use the default font. See Table 2–1 for typographic conventions.

Capitalizing and Punctuating Headings

Follow these guidelines for punctuation and capitalization of headings:

- Use no punctuation at the end of a heading except for a question mark or quotation mark when needed.
- Capitalize the first letter of the first word and the first letter of all other words *except* conjunctions, articles, prepositions of fewer than four letters, and the "to" in infinitives.

Numbering Section Headings

Unnumbered headings are generally used in documents that are designed for end users. *Numbered headings* are reserved for hardware installation manuals, technical references, and service manuals.

Numbered section headings use a digit for each heading level. The numbers start with the chapter number. The digits are separated by a period.

The section number 4.2.3.1 tells readers that the text is in Chapter 4, the second first-level heading, the third second-level heading, and the first third-level heading. These sections are numbered in this way:

```
4.2
    4.2.1
    4.2.2
    4.2.3
        4.2.3.1
        4.2.3.2
```

Lists

Lists are used to extract information from the paragraph format and to structure the information into an easier-to-read format. Lists must include at least two items. Be sure that lists are unmistakably lists. You do not want the reader to confuse a list with steps, which denote actions. Use secondary entries only if you cannot avoid them. Complex entries defeat the easy-to-read format of a list.

Use *unnumbered (bulleted) lists* when the entries are not dependent on the sequence in which you present them. When the entries are dependent on sequence, use *numbered lists* with numerals and letters to build the hierarchy.

Use running text when you have up to four one-word items that have equal weight and no order. Incorporate the items in a sentence in which the items are separated with serial commas. You can also put the items in a list if you want to call particular attention to the items.

Use lists in the following situations:

- When you have a list of five or more items
- When you have a list of two or more items in which any of the items consists of two or more words
- When you have a list of two or more items in which any of the items is a link

Introducing Lists

Introduce a list with one of the following constructions:

- A complete sentence
- A paragraph
- A sentence fragment or noun phrase

   A *sentence fragment* contains a verb, for example, "Use File Manager:"

   A *noun phrase* does not contain a verb, for example, "Functions:"

List Introduction Guidelines

Follow these guidelines for constructing list introductions:

- Do not insert a list between the beginning and the end of a sentence.

  Incorrect:

  The calculator can be used for the following operations:

  - Addition
  - Multiplication
  - Subtraction
  - Division

  and has a large, easy-to-read display.

  Correct:

  The calculator has a large, easy-to-read display and can be used for the following operations:

  - Addition
  - Subtraction
  - Multiplication
  - Division

- When introducing a list, do not construct the list items so that they complete a sentence.

  List items should be grammatically complete.

  Incorrect:

  Use App Builder if you:

  - Are not an expert Motif programmer
  - Are not familiar with desktop services
  - Want to build your application interface quickly

  Correct:

  Use App Builder in the following situations:

  - If you are not familiar with desktop services
  - If you are not an expert Motif programmer
  - When you want to build your application interface quickly

- Do not end an introductory phrase with a preposition.

  Incorrect:

  Entities are useful for:

  - Referencing a common string of text
  - Using the same text among different authors
  - Preventing entry errors

  Correct:

  Entities are useful in the following situations:

  - Referencing a common string of text
  - Using the same text among different authors
  - Preventing entry errors

- When introducing a list, use a colon if the introduction clearly anticipates the list, especially if the introduction contains phrasing such as "the following" or "as follows."

  If the introduction is complete in itself, use a period.

  For example, you could use either of these statements to introduce the same list:

  > Send a mail message in any of the following three ways:
  > The system provides three convenient ways to send a mail message.

- When you use a complete sentence or a phrase with a colon to introduce an unnumbered list, be sure that the syntax of the items in the list agrees with the syntax of the introduction.

  Incorrect:

  You can use Mail Tool to:

  - Compose a new message
  - Replied to a message sent to you
  - Forwarding a message to another person

  Correct:

  You can use Mail Tool to perform the following tasks:

  - Compose a new message
  - Reply to a message that was sent to you
  - Forward a message to another person

List Introductions and Verbs

Avoid ending the introduction to a list with a verb. Ending the introduction to a list with a verb usually causes problems for translators and nonnative English speakers.

- Do not end an introductory phrase with the word "to" as part of infinitives in the list.

    Incorrect:

    This section explains how to:

    - Prevent unauthorized users from gaining system access
    - Protect shared servers
    - Create user names and passwords

    Correct:

    This section explains the following tasks:

    - Preventing unauthorized users from gaining system access
    - Protecting shared servers
    - Creating user names and passwords

- Do not end an introductory phrase with a modal verb.

    Modal verbs include "can," "could," "may," "might," "must," "should," "will," and "would."

    Incorrect:

    To do complete print integration, your application must:

    - Provide a print action
    - Use all the environment variables for desktop printing

    Correct:

    Your application must meet the following requirements to do complete print integration:

    - Provide a print action
    - Use all the environment variables for desktop printing

- An introductory phrase can end with an imperative verb.

    In the login screen, type:

    - Your system name
    - Your user name
    - Your password

Capitalizing and Punctuating Lists

For consistency, follow these guidelines when you construct the items in lists:

- Capitalize the first word of each entry in all lists.
- Use punctuation at the end of each item in a list of complete sentences.
- Use no punctuation at the end of each item in a list of sentence fragments.

Avoid mixing complete sentences and sentence fragments in the same list. If you must have a mixed list, add periods at the end of every list item.

To make the list items parallel, a sentence in a mixed list might be preceded by a fragment that describes or introduces the sentence. The fragment ends with a period. The following examples illustrate this recommendation.

Incorrect:

- Fragment
- Fragment
- This item is a complete sentence.
- Fragment

Better:

- Fragment.
- Fragment.
- This item is a complete sentence.
- Fragment.

Best:

- Fragment.
- Fragment.
- Fragment. This item is a complete sentence.
- Fragment.

Writing Bulleted Lists

Use bulleted (unnumbered) lists when the sequence of the entries is not important.

- Make sure that the items in a bulleted list are similar in value.

    Incorrect:

    The workstation that you purchased comes with the following hardware:

    - System unit
    - Monitor
    - Keyboard and mouse
    - Maybe a CD-ROM drive
    - Maybe a modem

The last two entries in the example are not similar to the first three entries because they are options, not standard equipment.

Correct:

The workstation that you purchased comes with the following hardware:

- System unit
- Monitor
- Keyboard and mouse

After setting up your workstation, you can add several options, such as a CD-ROM drive or a modem.

- Use an introductory phrase for each entry, when needed.

Lists sometimes begin with a summary word or phrase, followed by an explanation. Present the summary word or phrase in bold. The text that follows the summary word or phrase is in the same font as the document's body text. Use a period after the summary word or phrase if the related text is extensive. Use an en dash after the summary word or phrase if the related text is brief. This style is often referred to as a *bold lead-in*. This structure works well when you have explanatory text for each entry.

The workstation that you purchased comes with the following hardware:

- **System unit.** This unit houses the main components of the computer.
- **Monitor.** This monitor is a 19-inch color monitor.
- **Keyboard and mouse.** These input devices are part of the computer package.

Writing Numbered Lists

Use numbered lists when the order of the entries is important. However, exercise caution. Many readers are impatient to complete tasks and could mistake numbered lists for procedures. Follow these guidelines:

- Write the text for numbered lists in a style that differs from the style of instructional steps in a procedure.

Do not assume that a reader will notice any format differences between numbered lists and numbered steps.

- Avoid using verbs in the imperative form.

  Using an imperative verb could lead a reader to believe that the numbered lists are procedures. Use gerunds or participles instead.

  Incorrect:

  To create a file with the `vi` editor, you need to perform the following basic operations:

  1. Start `vi`.
  2. Add text to the file.
  3. Write the file to save its contents.
  4. Quit `vi`.

  To avoid possible misinterpretation, introduce the list clearly and do not use imperative verbs.

  Correct:

  Creating a file with the `vi` editor involves the following basic operations:

  1. Starting `vi`
  2. Adding text to the file
  3. Writing the file to save its contents
  4. Quitting `vi`

Writing Jump Lists

A *jump list* is a bulleted list of cross-references that serves as a table of contents for a portion of a book, usually a chapter. Jump lists are useful navigational tools for a reader. These lists also provide you with a good test of the integrity of your document structure. If your document is online and hypertext is available, include links to the selected sections.

Note – If your document is going to be presented in a specific online display, check whether jump lists are generated automatically as part of the navigational system.

When constructing jump lists, follow these guidelines:

- Try to keep the text of a jump list short enough to fit on one page.
- Try to use jump lists consistently in your document.

  If you use a jump list at the beginning of one chapter, try to begin every chapter with a jump list.

- List headings for topics that might be of particular interest to a reader.

  You do not need to include only first-level headings, but be consistent throughout a book.

Tables

Tables are an ideal format for presenting statistical information or facts that you can structure uniformly. Information that is conceptual or explanatory is best written in running text rather than presented as a table.

Writing Text for Tables

Tables typically include a number, caption, column headings, and table text. Use spaces and rules (vertical and horizontal lines) to format the table text, when necessary.

Table Introductions

If you need to introduce the context of a table to your readers, follow these guidelines:

- Use a complete sentence when introducing a table, not a phrase ending in a colon.
- Refer to the table's position on the page in the document flow, for example, "The following table describes the compatible applications."

  In subsequent references to the same table, use "preceding" or "following" as appropriate.
- Refer to the table number only if the table is not close to the introductory text.
- Do not insert a table between the beginning and end of a sentence.

  Incorrect:

  Add the following utilities from the installation CD

Utility	Description
Tutorial	Includes step-by-step introductory procedures to help you get started
Templates	Common business document structures that you can customize
Spelling checker	An interactive spelling checker

  and their related help files.

Correct:

Add the following utilities and their related help files from the installation CD.

Utility	Description
Tutorial	Includes step-by-step introductory procedures to help you get started
Templates	Common business document structures that you can customize
Spelling checker	An interactive spelling checker

Table Captions

When you construct table captions, do the following:

- Use formal tables with numbers and captions except when the context of the tables is so clear that the numbers and captions are redundant.
- Capitalize table captions.

  Match the table caption style to the figure captions and section headings in your document.

- Decide how you can indicate when table text runs onto more than one page in the printed document.

  "Continued" usually appears in a caption on the second and subsequent pages. For longer tables, you might indicate how many pages the table runs and the current page in that sequence, for example, "Sheet 3 of 8." Your authoring environment might insert this wording for you.

Table Column Headings

Table column headings concisely summarize information in a column. To create table column headings, follow these guidelines:

- Avoid starting a column heading with an article.

  For example, write "Alternative Backup Schedule" rather than "An Alternative Backup Schedule."

- Do not use end punctuation, except a question mark.
- Capitalize column headings as you do section headings.

  Capitalize the first letter of the first word and the first letter of all other words *except* conjunctions, articles, prepositions of fewer than four letters, and the "to" in infinitives.

Table Text

The table text is the main body of information, formatted into rows and columns. To construct table text, follow these guidelines:

- Use parallel construction, capitalization, and punctuation.

  - For better readability, use an initial capital for only the first word in a table cell unless a reason exists to capitalize other words in the text.

  - Use a period at the end of each entry in a column when one or more entries are complete sentences. Try to use either all phrases that do not require periods or all sentences that do require periods.

- Write table text as concisely as possible.

- You may use abbreviations or symbols in tables when you need to conserve space.

  Some common space savers include "no." for "number" and "%" for percentages.

- Avoid bold in table text, but use the typographic conventions established for the document.

- For footnotes in a table, use numerals when possible.

  When numerals might be confusing due to numbers in the table text, use these symbols in the following order:

  - Asterisk (*)
  - Section mark (§)

Determining the Type of Table to Use

Tables present information in concise categories. The way that you design a table depends on the information that you need to present. The following is an example of a standard table with columns and rows separated by spaces.

EXAMPLE 2–1 Standard Table

Specifier	Value of the Variable	Data Type for the Variable
ACCESS	'DIRECT SEQUENTIAL'	CHARACTER
BLANK	'NULL' 'ZERO'	CHARACTER
IOSTAT	Error number	INTEGER
OPENED	.TRUE.	LOGICAL
	.FALSE.	

The following table uses horizontal lines to group information into rows.

EXAMPLE 2–2 Horizontal Lines Table

Name and Address	Corporate Office	Sales	Service
ABC Corp. 624 Main Street Chelmsford, MA 01824	+1-617-555-9731	+1-617-555-1632	+1-617-555-4932
DEF Corp. 90 Columbia Avenue Los Angeles, CA 940434	+1-213-555-8413	+1-415-555-5940	+1-415-555-3662
GHI Corp. Colorado Springs, CO 80920	+1-719-555-8842	+1-719-555-9013	+1-719-555-4701

The following table uses horizontal and vertical lines to separate information.

EXAMPLE 2–3 Horizontal and Vertical Lines Table

Command	Syntax	Options
at	at *time* at [*options*] *job-ids*	-l List current job -r Remove specified job *time* Specify the time when commands will run
chown	chown *owner filename*	-h Change ownership of symbolic link
find	find *filename*	-print Print names of files found -name *filename* Find file with cited name

The following table uses side and top headings to create a grid. Both the top and side headings are bold. A vertical line separates the side headings from the table text.

EXAMPLE 2–4 Side and Top Headings Table

Permission	User	Group	Others
Read	4	4	4
Write	2	0	0
Execute	1	1	1
Total	7	5	5

The following table uses a two-column format. You can use this format as an informal table without a number or a caption. Two-column tables are often used for command options and their descriptions. In some authoring environments, this format might be a list rather than a table.

EXAMPLE 2–5 Two-Column Table

`-a`	List hidden files
`-l`	Include date and size information in the file list
`-r`	List the files in reverse alphabetical order

Code Examples

Code examples are portions of computer programs that you include in a document to help explain a topic. Code examples can include the dialogue between a user's input and the computer's responses. Examples can also include only the code that a person enters into the computer.

Because programming code is precise, you must reproduce the exact code, even if the code contains language errors in spelling, grammar, or punctuation. If you have the opportunity, bring the error to the attention of the person or group supplying the code so that the error can be corrected in the source.

If you want to include a code example in a List of Code Examples in the front matter, add a caption. Capitalize and punctuate the caption as you would any other caption, title, or heading.

Note – If you are presenting lengthy programs, put them in an appendix and cross-reference to them unless the entire book mainly consists of long code examples.

For information about legally protecting information in code examples, see "Protecting Information That Appears in Examples" on page 167.

Error Messages

When documenting error messages, follow these guidelines:

- Reproduce the exact message text.

  Use monospace font for the error message text.

- Format error messages in a way that differs from paragraph text.

- Always follow an error message with text describing why the message is displayed and what a reader can do to correct the problem.

- If you are documenting numerous error messages, consider compiling them into an appendix or even into a separate book.

The following examples show ways that you can format error messages in text and in a table, depending on your needs and your authoring environment.

EXAMPLE 2–6 Error Message Formatting as Text

`Current working directory,` *directory*`, not a valid install area`

> **Cause:** You are running the install program from a directory other than where the `install` package was installed.
>
> **Solution:** You must change to the directory in which the `install` package was installed and run the `install` package again.

EXAMPLE 2–7 Error Message Table

Message		Cause	Solution
6000	`Signal to Noise ratio too low on` *name*`, SNR =` *number* `db, Min SNR =` *number* `db (`*text*`)`	■ Loopback cable missing or faulty ■ Audio hardware problem (usually consistent failures) ■ System software problem (usually intermittent failures)	Contact system administrator for assistance.
8000	`Must be superuser to execute. The user does not have superuser privileges.`	User does not have superuser privileges	Contact system administrator for superuser privileges.
8012	`Invalid audio device` *device-name* `for Crystal test`	Crystal test not supported on system audio	Provide required equipment.

Cross-References

Cross-references identify additional information about a specific topic that is available in the document or in a different source. To be useful to a reader, cross-references must be specific and accurate. Include all details that can help a reader find the information easily.

For information about how to write links for online documents, see Chapter 5.

Several formats are acceptable for cross-references. These formats often depend on the location of the cited information, the length of the reference, and your authoring environment. The cited information can be in your document, another document produced by your company, or a third-party document.

Do not use a cross-reference in the following situations:

- When the information is vital for a reader to understand the discussion

  Instead, provide the vital information. If the information is extensive, you can summarize it and also include a cross-reference to the source.

- When the additional information is brief and you can just as easily repeat it

- When you cite safety information that describes how to protect a person, hardware, or software

  For safety information, use Caution text. For more information, see "Writing Cautions" on page 54.

Formatting Cross-References

The punctuation, capitalization, and fonts that are used for cross-references might be determined by your authoring environment. Otherwise, follow these guidelines:

- Use italic for the title of a book, journal, multivolume work, or magazine.

- Use quotation marks or commas around a chapter title or section heading.

  See "Setting Administrative Options" on page 97.

  See Chapter 4, "System Board and Component Replacement," in the *Plirg 5763 System Service Manual*.

- Capitalize "chapter," "appendix," "part," "section," "table," "figure," "example," or "step" when these terms are followed by a number or letter.

  See Chapter 6.
  This process is shown in Section 3.5, "Null Modem Cabling."

- Do not capitalize the word "page" when it is followed by a number.

  Refer to page 42 for further information.

Writing Cross-References

Cross-references break the flow of your discussion. Therefore, write cross-references so that a reader easily recognizes when you have given a reference.

- Make sure that you introduce cross-references with clear phrases.

    Incorrect: To reboot, see Chapter 4.
    Correct: For instructions on how to reboot, see Chapter 4.

- If cross-references are brief, include them within sentences.

    Use the `diff` *filename1 filename2* command to compare two files (see "Working With Text Files" on page 86).

    If the cross-references require lengthy text references, put the cross-references in separate sentences.

    Use the `diff` *filename1 filename2* command to compare two files. See Chapter 2, "Working With Text Files," in *UNIX Simplified*.

- Do not provide the title of your document as part of the cross-reference.

- Do not cross-reference to a figure, table, or example that appears adjacent to the paragraph text.

    Instead, provide the relative location, for example, "The following figure shows the File menu."

- For a cross-reference to a third-party book, include the title and author, with the publisher and year in parentheses.

    One of the reference books used in preparation of this document was *The Deluxe Transitive Vampire* by Karen Elizabeth Gordon (Pantheon Books, 1993).

    The title is sufficient for subsequent references in the same chapter.

Endnotes, Footnotes, and Bibliographies

Sometimes, you need to provide complete cross-references to other sources. You can include these references in *endnotes* at the end of a chapter, in *footnotes* at the bottom of a page, or in a *bibliography* at the end of a document. You also can use endnotes and footnotes as a place to add comments about a discussion.

Writing Endnotes and Footnotes

Endnotes and footnotes provide complete information about the source, including author, title, place of publication, and page number in the source where readers can find the information. A *footnote* provides the reference at the bottom of the page. An *endnote* groups all references cited in a chapter at the end of the chapter.

When writing endnotes and footnotes, follow these guidelines:

- If an online presentation or authoring environment restricts the use of footnotes to tables only, do one of the following:
  - Fold the footnote information into the text.
  - Put the footnote information in an endnote.
- Use consecutive superscript numerals in the main text to indicate the endnotes or footnotes.

  Place the numeral at the end of the sentence, phrase, or quotation for which you are providing a reference. Do not include a period after the superscript numeral. The numeral appears after punctuation marks, except for a dash.
- Do not use lettered subnotes, such as 4a and 4b.
- Do not place endnote or footnote numerals in chapter titles or section headings, or in figure, table, or example captions.
- Keep the text of the footnote on the same page as its superscript numeral unless your authoring tool determines the placement for you.
- Introduce the text of the note with the corresponding numeral, followed by a period if the numeral is not a superscript.

  Use consistent alignment of the numerals and text. Use single-spacing for the text of each note.
- When repeatedly referring to the same source document, you can abbreviate the information.

  Include only the author's last name, the book title, and the page number.

The following examples show the content and style of endnotes and footnotes.

1. Skillin, Marjorie E., Robert M. Gay, and other authorities. *Words into Type*, 3d ed. Englewood Cliffs, N.J.: Prentice-Hall, 1974, p. 150.

2. Burnett, Rebecca E., *Technical Communication*, 2d ed. Belmont, Calif.: Wadsworth Publishing Company, 1990, p. 36.

3. *The Chicago Manual of Style*, 14th ed. Chicago: University of Chicago Press, 1993, p. 701.

4. Skillin, *Words into Type*, p. 16.

Writing Bibliographies

A bibliography lists all sources to which you refer in your document. Bibliographies appear at the end of the document, after the appendixes and glossary and before the index.

The format for bibliographies varies, depending on the number and type of resources that are cited. These resources might include books, journals, articles, and so forth. *The Chicago Manual of Style* provides a lengthy discussion on text and formats used in bibliographies. That discussion is summarized in the next few sections, followed by guidelines describing how to cite and format electronic source material.

Citing Books

When citing a book, provide the following information:

- Name of the person or institution credited as author, which could be single or multiple authors, editors, or institutions
- Full title of the source, including any subtitle
- Title of the series, and its volume and number if the book is part of a series
- Volume number if the book is part of a multivolume set
- Edition of the book if not the original edition
- City where the book was published
- Publisher's name
- Date of publication

Citing Articles

For an article in a periodical, provide the following information:

- Name of the author
- Title of the article
- Name of the periodical
- Volume or issue number of the periodical
- Date of the periodical
- Page numbers where the article is found in the periodical

Formatting Bibliographies

Two examples of ways to format text for bibliographies follow. The first example wraps each line flush left, while the second example provides a two-column format.

Atre, Anand. *Performance Tuning Guide for Sybase SQLserver on Solaris*. Palo Alto, Calif.: Sun Microsystems, Inc., 1995.

Yram, Kaytram.   *Upgrading Your System With Multimedia*. Acton, Mass.: New Look Publishing, 1995.

Citing Electronic Sources

When citing electronic source material, provide the following information:

- Name of the author, plus the author's email address if available
- Title of the work or the title line of the message
- Title of the list or site, as appropriate
- Volume or issue number of a digest if applicable
- Date of the message or the date on which the source was accessed

Formatting Electronic Sources

Suggested ways to format various types of electronic sources are shown here:

- Database online

  Joe User, "Citing Electronic Material," in REFSTUFF [database online] (Silicon, Calif.: REFSTUFF, 1986) [updated 9 January 2002; cited 31 February 2002], identifier no. Q000307, [52 lines].

- Email message

  Joe User [juser@macland.org], "Citing Electronic Material," private email message to Sys Admin [sadmin@funix.com], February 21, 2002.

- FTP site

  Joe User [juser@macland.org], "Citing Electronic Material," [ftp://ftp.macland.org/pub/local/reference/cites.txt], February 2002.

- Internet article based on a print source

  VandenBos, G., Knapp, S. & Doe, J. (2001). "Selection of Resources by Psychology Undergraduates" [electronic version]. *Journal of Bibliographic Research, 5*, 117–123.

- Article in an Internet-only journal

  Fredrickson, B.L. (2001, November 7). "Cultivating Positive Emotions." *Prevention & Treatment 3*, Article 0001a. Retrieved March 20, 2002 from http://www.journals.apa.org/prevention/pre11010001a.html

- Listserv message

    Joe User [juser@macland.org], "REPLY: Citing Electronic Material," in GRAMR (Digest vol. 6, no. 8) [electronic bulletin board] (Dubuque, Iowa, 1995) [cited February 21, 2002]; available from [gramr@miskatonic.edu]; INTERNET.

- Material from an unknown author

    GVU's 8th WWW user survey. (n.d.) Retrieved April 8, 2002, from http://www.cc.gatech.edu/gvu/usersurveys/survey2002-04

- World Wide Web

    Joe User, "Citing Electronic Material," [http://www.macland.org/cites.html], accessed February 21, 2002.

Notes, Cautions, and Tips

Notes, Cautions, and Tips provide important information that diverges from the topic under discussion.

A *Note* usually provides information that is related to the text. A Note might contain an explanation, a comment, a reinforcement of the text, or a short expansion of the concepts in the text. A Note might also contain a statement that is intended to catch the reader's attention.

A *Caution* is mandatory text that you *must* provide to protect the user of equipment from personal injury or to protect hardware or software from damage. Precede the text of a Caution with the appropriate graphical symbol specified by the International Organization for Standardization (ISO).

A *Tip* describes practical but nonessential information that does not otherwise fit into the flow of the text.

Try to limit the number of Notes and Cautions to approximately two on a page. The inclusion of many Notes might indicate an organizational problem in the text.

Writing Notes

Few constraints exist on the text or format you can use in a Note. Consistency in both writing style and format is important so that a reader learns to recognize a Note that is interjected into the text.

When writing Notes, follow these guidelines:

- Use a Note to extract related, reinforcing, or other "special" information.
- Keep your Note short and relevant.
- Never use a Note to cite safety information.
- If your text requires many Notes, consider reorganizing the text to reduce the number of Notes that are required.

An example of a Note and its format follows.

Note – Keep the text short and relevant.

Writing Cautions

Unlike a Note, a Caution is not optional. You must provide a Caution in the following situations:

- When you describe a situation that has the potential to cause injury to a person, or when there is a risk of irreversible destruction to data or the operating system
- When you describe anything that has the potential to cause damage to equipment, data, or software

When writing or formatting Cautions, follow these guidelines:

- Be direct when writing a Caution.

  First describe the potential hazard to data, equipment, or personnel. Then, describe the actions that are required to avoid the hazard.
- Insert the Caution before the information that might cause the potential hazard.

The following symbols are commonly used in technical documentation:

- Use the "lightning bolt" symbol when there is danger of physical harm to a person or damage to equipment due to an electrical hazard.
- Use the "heat" symbol when there is risk of personal injury from a heat source.
- Use the "exclamation point" symbol when there is risk of personal injury from a nonelectrical hazard or risk of irreversible damage to data, software, or the operating system.

Examples of Cautions and their common graphical symbols follow.

Caution – Lithium batteries are not customer-replaceable parts. Do not disassemble them or attempt to recharge them.

Caution – Software hazard is present. Before copying data from a disk from an outside source, check the disk for viruses. Otherwise, you could contaminate the data on your hard disk.

Caution – Irreversible destruction can occur to data or the operating system. Follow the instructions carefully.

Caution – Electrical hazard is present. Leaving the side panel off the computer exposes you to dangerous voltage and risk of electrical shock. Do not leave the side panel off while you are operating the computer.

Caution – Hot surface. The surface of the CPU chip can be hot and could cause personal injury if touched. Do not touch this component.

Writing Tips

A Tip describes practical but nonessential information that does not otherwise fit into the flow of the text. Examples include a keyboard shortcut or an alternative way to perform a step in a procedure.

When writing Tips, follow these guidelines:

- Keep the text short and relevant.
- Do not introduce new topics or elaborate on conceptual material in a Tip.

An example of a Tip and its format follows.

Tip – You can also minimize a window by pressing Alt-F9.

Part Dividers

A lengthy book might require *part dividers* to group similar chapters in the document. Because readers often merely glance at the part divider page, keep the text on the divider page minimal and succinct. Never include any information on the divider that is essential to the topics that are discussed in the chapters. For example, instructions to turn off power before proceeding with tasks are not appropriate on the divider.

When you prepare part dividers, follow these guidelines:

- Make sure that there are at least two parts.
- Provide a number (Part I, Part II, Part III, and so on) and the part title.
- Include only text or text with graphics.

  For example, you could use graphics on the front of the part divider with text on the back, or a combination of text and graphics on the front with text continuing on the back.
- List, if helpful, the chapter titles on the divider to orient a reader.

  For online documents, include a hypertext jump list of the chapter titles.
- If your authoring tool enables you to choose, do not include a page number on the part divider page.

  Although a page number does not appear on the part divider, the divider is counted in the total number of pages of the document.

Typographic Conventions

Typographic conventions help a reader distinguish special uses of fonts. The following table shows elements used in technical documentation and some recommended typographic conventions for them.

To provide consistency in typographic cues for readers, use the following conventions in your document.

Note – The point size of the font for monospace elements should match the point size of the text within which they appear, including a heading, paragraph, table, or caption.

TABLE 2–1 Typographic Conventions

Text	Specification	Examples
Arrow keys	Lowercase	Press the up arrow, then the left arrow.
Book titles	Italic	See the *DeskSet Reference Guide*.
Chapter titles or section headings	Initial capitals in quotation marks	See Chapter 1, "Getting Started."

Code examples	Monospace	`struct inode  {`
		`struct inode *i_chain[2];`
		`struct vnode i_vnode;`
		`struct vnode *i_devvp;u_short i_flag;`
		`};`

Collection titles of online documents	Initial capitals	PlirgSoft User's Collection
Command field names	Monospace	Look at the `Flags` field in the output.
Command names or options	Monospace	Type `ls -a` to list all files.
Database files	Monospace	`bootparams.dir, hosts.byaddr.dir`
Database names	Initial capitals	Tmark
Directory, file, or path names	Monospace	Delete all `.bak` and `core` files from the book directory in `/docs/work`.
Diskette names	Initial capitals	Insert the first Update diskette.
DOS commands	Monospace, all capitals	`RENAME, FDISK`
Driver names	Monospace	`asy, ata, dnet`
Email addresses	Monospace	Send questions to `editgroup@plirg.com`.
Emphasized or new words	Italic	You *must* delete your old files. These options are called *class* options.
Environment variables	Monospace, all capitals	`PATH, PROMPT, TMPDIR, TERM`
Error messages, when you know the exact wording	Monospace	`stty: No such device or address.`
Field names in text	No colon or ellipsis points	[Field name appears as Tag Type: _____] Type the name of the tag in the Tag Type field.
File format names	Monospace	`mif, mpeg, java`
File names, generic	Default font	When you use makefiles, additional swap space might be required.

TABLE 2–1 Typographic Conventions *(Continued)*

Text	Specification	Examples
File permissions	Monospace	To make the file readable and writable by the file owner and readable by everyone else, change the permissions to u+x.
File system names	Monospace	/usr, /opt, /var
File system types in text	Default font, all capitals	UFS, NFS, HSFS
Flags	Monospace	The flag THR_NEW_LWP is passed to the function thr_create() to create LWP.
Function calls	Monospace	abs(), ctermid()
IP addresses	Monospace	10.255.255.255
Key names[1]	Initial capitals	Press the Control key.
Keystrokes, consecutive	Join with a plus sign	Ctrl+A+N. Press the first key, release it, then press subsequent keys.
Keystrokes, simultaneous	Join with a hyphen	Shift-F1. Press the first key while you press subsequent keys.
Keywords in files (see also "reserved words")	Monospace	netmask
Machine names	Monospace	newstop, dickens
Macros	Monospace, all capitals	MAX(), MIN()
Menu items, menu names	Initial capitals, no colon or ellipsis points	Choose Go To from the Page menu. [Option appears as Insert Markup on screen.] Choose Insert Markup from the Markup menu.
Parameters	Monospace	foo(x, y) (x and y are parameters for foo())
Partition names, the PC disk partition fdisk	Monospace	Reformat the SOLARIS partition.
Port names in text	Default font, all capitals	COM1, LPT3
Print services	Default font	LP print services
Programming constructs	Monospace	The names of classes, exceptions, fields, and interfaces in a programming context

[1] See "Key Name Conventions" on page 60.

TABLE 2–1 Typographic Conventions *(Continued)*

Text	Specification	Examples

Prompts	Monospace, unless from a GUI	%, $, #
		 `system123%`
		 `system123$`
		 `system123#`
		 `>`
		 `ok`

README files, generic	Default font, all capitals	See the README file in `/tmp`.
README files, specific file name	Monospace	See the `README.html` file.
Reserved words, or keywords (see also "keywords in files")	Monospace	`if`, `else`, `int`, `float`
Return values	Monospace	The function `open_max()` returns `TRUE`. A value of `-1` is returned.
Routines	Monospace	The `time()` routine computes time.
Settings in windows	Initial capitals	Check the Pair Kern setting.
System calls or subroutines	Monospace	`read()`, `open()`, `_lwp_info()`
System error codes	Monospace, all capitals	`EINVAL`, `ENOENT`, `setErr()`
System names	Monospace	Move the file to the `plirg1` system.
System types	Monospace	`sun4u`
System variables	Monospace	The system variable in `set maxusers=40` is `maxusers`.
Tool names	Initial capitals	Nametool, Mail Tool, BugTraq
URLs	Monospace	`http://www.plirg.com`
User input in running text or procedures	Monospace	Type `ls -a` to list all files. **1. Type** `teh` **in the Find text field.**
User input contrasted with computer output or with a prompt in code examples	Monospace, bold	`system123%` **`su`** `Password:` `#` **`tar -xvf`** *filename*
User names and IDs	Monospace	User `davemc` has a user ID of `1001`. User `root` destroyed the system.
Utilities	Monospace	`grep`, `sed`, `vi`, `appletviewer`

TABLE 2–1 Typographic Conventions *(Continued)*

Text	Specification	Examples
Variables, command-line placeholders	Italic	Name the file *filename* `TOC.doc`.
		Sun StorEdge A5*x*00
		Go to `/`*hostname*`/docs/work`
		`% chmod 600` *filename*
Web site names	Monospace	For more details, go to `www.plirg.com`.
Window button names	Initial capitals	Click Apply to save your changes.

Key Name Conventions

A *key name* indicates which key on a keyboard to press to obtain a desired action. Follow these guidelines when referring to the names of keys unless the product you are documenting specifies other requirements:

- Capitalize the name of a key that is a letter.

  Press the A key
  Press Stop-A

  However, if you type a letter as part of a procedure, use lowercase monospace font.

  1. Type n **for no.**

- Include the Shift key when instructing users how to obtain a capital letter, symbol, or punctuation mark that appears on the upper half of a keycap.

  Press Control-Q Shift-P to include an en dash in a FrameMaker document.
  Press Shift-8 to type an asterisk.

- Use initial capitalization for each term in a key name.

  Press Caps Lock

- Use the short form for key names when three keystrokes are required to perform one action, as shown in Table 2–2.

  Ctrl-Alt-Del

  Notice that the accepted way to refer to some keys is in abbreviated form.

  Num Lock (the Numerical Lock key)
  Sys Req (the System Request key)

Use the previous guidelines and the format of key names in the following table if the product assigns different names to keys. For example, if F7 is renamed Pick Copy, this key name would appear as two words with initial capitals.

Referring to Keys

The following table shows how to refer to common names of keys. Even if Ctrl, CONTROL, or CTRL appears on your keyboard, for example, refer to that key as the Control key. Use the short form when noting three simultaneous or consecutive keystrokes or when using the key names in tables.

TABLE 2–2 Key Name Conventions

Standard Name	Short Form	Standard Name	Short Form
Again		left arrow (no caps)[1]	
Alt		Meta (for <>)	
Alt Graph		Num Lock	
Backspace		Open	
Backtab		Page Down	PgDn (no space)
Break		Page Up	PgUp (no space)
Caps Lock		Paste	
Compose		Pause	
Control	Ctrl	Print Screen	PrtSc (no space)
Copy		Props	
Cut		Return	
Delete	Del	right arrow (no caps)[1]	
down arrow (no caps)[1]		Scroll Lock	
End		Shift	
Enter[2]		spacebar (no caps)	
Escape	Esc	Stop	
F1 to F10 or F12		Sys Req	
Find		Tab	
Front		tilde (no caps) (for ~)	
Help		Undo	
Home		up arrow (no caps)[1]	
Insert	Ins		

[1] If an arrow key is used in a keystroke combination, use initial capitals, for example, Shift-Down Arrow.

[2] When writing about personal computers, use Enter, not Return.

Documenting Multiple Keystrokes

Use the following conventions to describe multiple keystrokes unless you are documenting Microsoft products:

- Use a hyphen to join *simultaneous keystrokes*.

  Press the first key while you press subsequent keys.

  > Control-A
  > Ctrl-Shift-Q
  > Meta-A

- Use a plus sign to join *consecutive keystrokes*.

  Press the first key, release it, then press subsequent keys.

  > Ctrl+A+N
  > F4+Q

If you are documenting Microsoft products, follow these conventions:

- Use a plus sign to join simultaneous keystrokes with no spaces around the plus sign, as in "press Control+F."

- Use a comma and a space to separate each key name in consecutive keystrokes, as in "press Alt, F, N."

Follow alternative key name conventions as appropriate for your audience.

CHAPTER 3

Writing Style

If *content* is *what* you communicate, then *style* is *how* you communicate. Writing style is determined by all the decisions that you make while creating a document, such as the type and tone of information you present, choice of words, language and format consistency, use of technical terms, and so forth. In the literary world, style is judged in part on artistic grounds, which might be highly subjective. In the field of technical documentation, however, experience and practice have provided objective criteria for evaluating style.

This chapter presents some guidelines for writing effectively. It discusses the following topics:

Why Is Style Important?

Good style is synonymous with effective communication. Documents that communicate effectively reduce costs and increase customer satisfaction. Style that responds to the requirements of readers results in fewer revisions, fewer calls to customer support, reduced training needs, and easier translation. Customer satisfaction increases when accurate and functional documentation enables customers to use a product quickly and efficiently.

Stylistic Principles

Keep in mind a few stylistic considerations when writing computer documentation: simplicity, accuracy, and consistency. Two principles underlie stylistic considerations:

- **Time is a valuable commodity.** Readers of computer documentation are generally in a hurry. Readers turn to documentation to find answers to problems and are impatient to get on with the task at hand. Write in a style that aids the customer's speedy understanding of the product.
- **Readers are worldwide.** International markets are a significant source of revenue. Documentation is being translated more frequently than ever before.

For more information about style and internationalization, see Chapter 7.

Write Simply, Directly, and Accurately

People most often read technical manuals to find answers to problems that they are having with software or hardware. They need their questions answered concisely and accurately. Concise writing means readers do not have to contend with unnecessary technical jargon. Write simple and direct sentences. Use short, familiar words, but respect the reader's level of technical knowledge and competency. Simple, direct, and accurate writing makes a document more usable and easier to translate.

Be Consistent

Readers project some significance onto every change in tone, language, or typographic convention. A consistent style enables readers to internalize the language and text conventions of a document. As a result, understanding occurs more easily and significant points stand out more clearly. Consistency is one of the most valuable aspects of good style.

Some Basic Elements of Style

At every level of writing, you must make stylistic decisions, from word choice to paragraph structure. The following sections discuss a few aspects of these style decisions.

Avoid Jargon

Writers frequently incorporate jargon associated with the subject matter into their documentation. Jargon can be difficult for the "uninitiated" to understand. In addition, jargon can be very difficult to translate.

In the following example, a writer uses the specialized phrases of the computer industry in a hardware manual:

> Powering down a system means turning off the power. To avoid losing data, shut down the system before powering down. For details on how to shut down a system, see the previous section.

The writer introduces the phrase "powering down," while admitting that the phrase only means turning off the power. The writer further confuses the reader by introducing "shut down" immediately after the term "powering down."

Rewrite: Using common English shortens the preceding example and permits the writer to be more specific and helpful.

> To avoid losing data, follow the shutdown procedure that is described in the previous section *before* turning off your computer.

When you have to use computer terms, introduce them in italic, explain them, include them in a glossary, and use them consistently.

Use Active Voice and Passive Voice Appropriately

Always try to write in the active voice, but do not fear the correct, thoughtful use of the passive voice. Writing entirely in the active voice is nearly impossible to achieve, so know when to use the passive voice.

Because writers in the computer industry often insist on using the active voice, the writer of the following example introduces a message with this sentence:

> As soon as the application completes, the following message displays.

Rewrite: A message does not display. Rather, a message appears or is displayed by the system. The passive voice can indicate that the subject is the receiver of the action rather than the performer.

> As soon as the application is finished, the following message is displayed.
>
> Or
>
> When the application finishes, the following message appears.

Make your writing active by concentrating on the activity of your subject. Use the passive voice when it is unavoidable because the performer of the action is either unimportant to the reader or unidentifiable.

Use Present Tense and Future Tense Appropriately

Readers use technical documents to perform tasks or gather information. For readers, these activities take place in the present. Therefore, the present tense is appropriate in most cases. Only use the future tense when necessary.

Incorrect:

If you attempt to copy a directory without using this option, you will see an error message.

Correct:

If you attempt to copy a directory without using this option, you see an error message.

Use Sentence Structures That Enhance Understanding

Convoluted sentences or sentences densely packed with information cause confusion, slow the reading process, and are difficult to translate. Any sentence that attempts to convey too much information is too long, regardless of its word count. Use punctuation, rhythm, and clarity of meaning to regulate sentence length and to attain a style that is easy to understand.

Write as if you were talking to a person, rather than formulating a law or theorem. Consider the following example:

To scroll directly to a relative location in the document, move the pointer into the bar at the point that represents the relative location of the text in the document.

Comments: A person would never speak that sentence. The sentence is grammatically correct, but it is stiff and formal. Ask yourself, "Does this sound like me responding to a question?"

To get a response such as the previous example, a person would have had to ask, "How can I scroll directly to the relative location of text in my document?" More likely the person would ask, "If what I want to read is way up or way down in the document, how can I get to it without scrolling through every line?"

Rewrite: Respond naturally to the reader's question. Remember that the reader is a person who wants to do something.

If the text that you want to read appears elsewhere in the document, guess where it is. Then, move the pointer to that spot in the scroll bar, and click mouse button 1.

Avoid Complex, Conjoined Sentences

A long, complicated sentence that contains several concepts is difficult to translate and to understand. Try to keep sentences to one topic. Rewrite the sentence or divide the sentence into several shorter sentences.

Incorrect:

The descriptions in this chapter follow the flow of data through an organization, starting with the back-end data repositories and working through them to the user-access layer provided by the web server, making the assumption that these components are connected by a reliable, available, and scalable network infrastructure.

Correct:

The descriptions in this chapter follow the flow of data through an organization. The flow begins with the back-end data repositories. Data then works through the repositories to the user-access layer provided by the web server. In these descriptions, the components are connected by a reliable, available, and scalable network infrastructure.

Also, a sentence that contains more than two uses of "and" or "or" can be difficult for readers to understand. Readers have difficulty with such sentences when multiple conjunctions join more than one main idea.

Incorrect:

From the addresses tab, you can add or delete networks, and add or delete IP addresses individually or in blocks.

Correct:

From the addresses tab, you can perform the following operations:

- Adding or deleting networks
- Adding or deleting IP addresses individually or in blocks

Separate Independent Clauses Appropriately

Readers can parse simple sentences more easily than compound sentences. Therefore, avoid combining independent clauses with "and." Instead, write two separate sentences.

Incorrect:

The Motif program uses Motif Version 2.1, and the old shared library uses Motif Version 1.2.

Correct:

The Motif program uses Motif Version 2.1. The old shared library uses Motif Version 1.2.

Limit Subordinate Clauses

Readers can have difficulty parsing sentences that contain a number of subordinate clauses. Limit subordinate clauses, such as "She said that Kathy said that she updated the file."

Use Positive Constructions

Negative constructions can cause confusion. Use positive constructions to state advice or instructions.

Incorrect:

You cannot reconnect to the server without restarting your computer.

Correct:

Restart your computer to reconnect to the server.

Use Parallel Structure

When you use "and" or "or" to link phrases, the reader expects parallelism on both sides of the conjunction. Be sure that your linked phrases are of the same type, for example, noun phrase or verb phrase.

Incorrect:

You can use Mail Tool for composing and to send messages.

Correct:

You can use Mail Tool to compose messages and to send them.

Differentiate Between Restrictive Clauses and Nonrestrictive Clauses

Make sure that you distinguish between restrictive and nonrestrictive clauses. Consider the differences in meaning for the following two sentences:

Check the LED that is on the front panel. (restrictive)
Check the LED, which is on the front panel. (nonrestrictive)

In the first sentence, the reader is told to check the LED specifically on the front panel, not the one on the side panel or back panel.

In the first part of the second sentence, the reader is told merely to check the LED. The second part of the sentence also states that the LED happens to be on the front panel. This clause implies that no other LED exists anywhere else. The minor difference in meaning could confuse translators or nonnative speakers of English.

Make sure that you include the word "that" when introducing a restrictive clause.

Incorrect:

This chapter provides the information you need to install the software.

Correct:

This chapter provides the information that you need to install the software.

Divide nonrestrictive clauses that are associated with a relative pronoun into separate sentences. This separation can help the translator to understand the meaning.

Unclear:

This topic describes how to write makefiles that take full advantage of CodeManager and InstantMake, the make utility that is included with the PlirgWare release.

Clear:

This topic describes how to write makefiles that take full advantage of CodeManager and InstantMake. InstantMake is the make utility that is included with the PlirgWare release.

Write Concise Paragraphs

Always write concisely. Avoid paragraphs that are so dense with information that the reader must struggle to understand the information. For instance, the reader struggles to make sense of the following paragraph:

With Gizmo, users of standard mail programs, such as a window-based mail tool, can transparently exchange electronic messages with users of private or public mail systems that conform to X.400 and ISO protocols. Users can reach this broader community without affecting their current electronic-mail routines. Gizmo is both a gateway and a message relay (message transfer agent, MTA, in CCITT terminology). The gateway translates standard mail messages conforming to DoD Simple Mail Transfer Protocol (SMTP) specifications to and from the format specified by X.400. The MTA provides full message analysis and routing. Gizmo builds the Gizmo OSI foundation for messaging over a local area network, and Gizmo OSI combined with Gizmo X.25 for use over packet-switched data networks.

Comments: The paragraph attempts to deliver too much information. Almost every sentence in the example conceals a smaller bit of information, which in turn conceals an even smaller bit of information, and so on.

Even the reader who understands all of the technical language faces the chore of sorting and retrieving all the information. Count the facts and concepts presented in each sentence. Do not count repeats.

- **First sentence: 12** – Gizmo, users, standard mail programs, window-based mail tool, transparently exchange, electronic messages, private mail systems, public mail systems, conform, X.400, ISO, protocols
- **Second sentence: 2** – Broader community, current electronic-mail routines
- **Third sentence: 5** – Gateway, message relay, message transfer agent, MTA, CCITT
- **Fourth sentence: 6** – Translates, standard mail messages, conforming, DoD, Simple Mail Transfer Protocol (SMTP) specifications, format
- **Fifth sentence: 2** – Full message analysis, routing
- **Sixth sentence: 5** – Gizmo OSI foundation, local area network, Gizmo X.25, packet-switched, data networks
- **Total: 32**

The reader's burden is to receive, translate, comprehend, or otherwise deal with one technical fact or technical concept every seven words.

The issue is clarity, not space.

Look at each paragraph that you write. If the paragraph looks too long, it *is* too long. Present general information at the beginning of the paragraph. Add details in descending order of importance toward the end. Use as much space and as many paragraphs as you need to make sense.

Rewrite: Divide some sentences into two sentences. Divide the example into several paragraphs.

Gizmo enables users of standard mail programs to exchange electronic messages with users of other mail systems. Gizmo works with systems that conform to X.400 and ISO protocols.

With Gizmo, users of mail programs, such as a window-based mail tool, can reach this broader community without affecting their current electronic-mail routines.

Gizmo is both a *gateway* and a message relay. In CCITT terminology, the relay is called a *message transfer agent (MTA)*.

- The gateway translates mail messages that conform to DoD Simple Mail Transfer Protocol (SMTP) specifications. The messages are translated to and from the format specified by X.400.
- The MTA provides full message analysis and routing.

Gizmo builds the Gizmo OSI foundation for messaging over a local area network. Gizmo also combines the OSI with Gizmo X.25 for use over packet-switched data networks.

Writing for the Reader

As a writer, you research, organize, and communicate information for the reader, who depends on you. In your relationship with the reader, you are the expert. Keep this point in mind when you make decisions about what information to present and how that information addresses the reader's questions.

Make Decisions for the Reader

Often a product provides several different ways to accomplish a single task. You might decide that you owe the reader an explanation of each method. However, remember that the reader is more interested in using the product than in understanding all options. Choose the best method for most of your audience, and tell the reader to use that method.

After you commit to the best course of action, you might explain to the reader that other methods exist. Tell the reader where to find your descriptions of those methods. Also, tell the reader why and in what situations options A, B, and C are useful.

For example, the writer of a user's guide for a DOS application included all of the possibilities in this text:

The system then displays the following message:

```
Accept the path C:\GIZMO? (y/n)
```

Type y to accept the default path C:\GIZMO, or n to designate a different path.

Comments: The writer reveals consequences but no guidelines. The details seem to be there, but the entire passage is ambivalent. The writer does not tell the reader why the choice exists. The reader is left to decide without guidance.

Watch for words that could lead to unguided choices. Avoid ambivalent words and phrases, such as the following:

- It is possible to
- Maybe
- Perhaps
- Either, or
- If you want
- Should, would

When you write these words or phrases, or similar ones, make sure that you are prepared to explain the benefits of the choices.

Rewrite: The writer recognized that the passage was ambivalent because the passage did not guide the reader. The rewritten passage guides the reader with this explanation.

The system displays the following message:

`Accept the path C:\GIZMO? (y/n)`

If you keep all your applications in a particular directory, or if you want to store `GIZMO` on a different hard disk, type n to specify your own path.

If you want to create the default `C:\GIZMO` path, type y.

Anticipate the Reader's Questions

One of the most important contributions a writer makes is to anticipate the reader's questions and provide appropriate answers. A writer must anticipate questions about related topics as well and provide cross-references to where those questions are answered. As the subject matter expert, a writer can create a climate of understanding that is far more significant than merely recounting facts about the product.

For example, when you review a procedure in your document with the reader's perspective in mind, ask these questions:

- What assumptions have I made about what the reader knows?
- Do steps follow in a logical sequence? Are there any gaps in the instructions?
- Are even the simplest words used precisely? For example, did I write "any" when I meant "all"?
- Did I define all technical terms?
- Have I incorrectly put conceptual and explanatory material within steps, rather than in paragraph text?
- Did I structure each step so that the condition is stated before the action?

  Write, for example, "If the card's I/O address conflicts with another device, remove the card and change the I/O address according to the manufacturer's instructions." Do not write "Remove the card and change the I/O address according to the manufacturer's instructions if the card's I/O address conflicts with another device." State conditions before actions unless this practice needlessly restricts you.

Anticipate Questions

In the following example, the writer of a tutorial clearly explains the function of the clipboard. However, the writer realizes that the explanation might lead to a question: "What happens if I cut or copy another selection?" By anticipating this question, the writer is ready to answer the question in a Note.

When you cut or copy text, the text is put aside for you on the clipboard, a temporary text storage facility. When text is on the clipboard, you have the option of pasting the text back into the file in any location you choose.

Note – As soon as you cut or copy text again, the most recently cut or copied selection replaces the text previously on the clipboard.

Use Cross-References to Address Anticipated Questions

A lack of cross-references can cause the reader great frustration. Often the reader of technical manuals skips important sections. You can presume, therefore, that the reader has not read anything in the book other than the current topic of the current paragraph.

For example, the reader has a question about the file system hierarchy. The reader opens the manual, finds the topic in the table of contents, turns to the page, and reads:

> As mentioned above, the file system directory hierarchy is a part of the "landscape" that you want to become familiar with.

Comments: No reference to either the hierarchy or the "landscape" appears above this sentence. The sentence dooms the reader who has not read everything. The writer presumes that the reader has carefully read everything before the statement that the hierarchy or "landscape" has already been mentioned. Consequently, the reader who goes directly to this section must search for the information.

When using cross-references, do not use the words "above" and "below" to refer to items that are *literally* above and below. Remember that something that appears "above" in today's draft could be "on the previous page" in tomorrow's draft, and these terms are even more problematic in online documents. Using the words "next," "following," "previous," and "preceding" is acceptable if the item referenced is nearby.

Do not write phrases like "As stated in a previous chapter." This reference is too far away to use "previous." Chapters have numbers and names, sections have names, and pages have numbers. Find the location of the information. Cite the location in a specific cross-reference. If the information is not too long or complex to repeat, repeat it.

Rewrite: Cite the specific location of the information:

> As explained in detail in "Issues" on page 2, the file system directory hierarchy is a part of your computer's "landscape."

Style That Could Offend the Reader

At times, stylistic considerations must go beyond issues of preference. You must also be aware of writing style that could offend the reader. Though offending the reader is not your intention, the use of humor and sexist linguistic conventions can offend. Humor and, especially, sexism are inappropriate in technical writing.

You can also offend the reader by being unintentionally condescending. In keeping your message clear, do not mistake economy of expression for simplicity. Do not underestimate the technical sophistication of the reader.

Avoid Humor

A great temptation for writers of computer documentation is to inject a note of levity into the text. Resist this temptation. Even genuinely humorous commentary is a distraction and becomes annoying on subsequent readings. Likewise, humor that descends into user-friendly chumminess never works. A sympathetic reader might forgive you for trying to "lighten up" the text, but another reader might resent a chummy tone.

For example, this humor was injected into a tutorial:

> You can use a mouse (one without fur) in conjunction with the window system of your computer.

Comments: The phrase "one without fur" detracts from the content of the sentence and distracts the reader. The goal of the sentence was to tell the reader that the mouse is related to the window system. The apparent goal of the humor was to reassure the reader that the mouse is "friendly."

Rewrite: The following revision pursues those goals in a direct, conversational tone:

> The mouse is a versatile tool that you use with the window system of your computer.

Humor is difficult, if not impossible, to translate successfully. Humor is usually cultural. What might be funny to an American could be offensive to readers in another country.

Avoid Sexist Language

Regarding the issue of sexism in language, appearances count.

In many cultures, language has developed so that "men" often refers to "men and women," and "he," "him," and "his" are regarded as gender-neutral words. In decades past, this sentence might have been perfectly acceptable:

Ask your system administrator for his advice.

Today, this usage of "he" and "his" is far less acceptable. These pronouns assume too much about the gender of an individual. Writers who defend the use of such pronouns must contemplate the following: Many readers could interpret a writer's intentions negatively and could consciously or subconsciously reject the work.

Use Acceptable Methods to Achieve Common Gender

To achieve common gender, use the following methods:

- Use plural antecedents and plural pronouns as often as possible.

   Awkward: Tell each user to shut down his machine.
   Better: Tell the users to shut down their machines.

- Eliminate the possessive as much as possible when you are writing in the third person.

   Awkward: Ask your system administrator for his advice.
   Better: Ask your system administrator for advice.

- Use the word "you."

   Awkward: If the user decides he wants to change the settings, he should follow these steps.

   Better: If you want to change the settings, you should follow these steps.

- Instead of using a personal pronoun, repeat its antecedent when doing so does not sound unpleasant or unnatural.

   Awkward:

   If a system administrator installed the software, wait until he can help you.

   Better:

   If a system administrator installed the software, wait until the system administrator can help you.

Use the following suggestions carefully:

- Give names to "third persons."

  This technique does not work for all types of documentation, but this technique can be effective in a tutorial or other type of user's guide. Consider using names, male or female, to humanize your writing and eliminate the "he" or "she" clumsiness.

  For example, if you want to tell the reader how to copy a file from someone else's directory, try this approach:

  > Before you can copy a file from someone else's directory, Sally Smith's directory for example, you need permission. Ask Smith to set her file permissions to grant you access. After she has changed permissions, you can copy the file.

- Create your own techniques.

  Keep in mind that the writing should sound natural, be taken literally, and inform.

Avoid Unacceptable Methods to Achieve Common Gender

Eliminating the appearance of sexism by writing poorly, ungrammatically, or self-consciously is not a good solution. Keep the following guidelines in mind:

- Never write "s/he."
- Use "their" with a plural antecedent.

  For example, "ask your system administrator for their advice" is incorrect.

- Try to avoid "his or her," which is grammatically correct but awkward.
- Even in pursuit of the goal of eliminating perceived sexism, never dehumanize people with the pronoun "it."

Respect the Reader

A "naive reader" is not unsophisticated. Treat the reader as a peer.

Unintentionally, this sentence is condescending:

> Don't be afraid to play with the computer. The computer won't bite you.

Comments: The sentence belittles the reader's anxiety. In an effort to reassure the naive user, the writer seems to belittle the reader's genuine fear of doing something wrong. Of course, the computer will not "bite" the user, and of course the reader can see the writer's point. But the writer makes this point as though writing for a juvenile. A reader might find the tone condescending and insulting.

Remember that the reader might be naive only in relation to the particular computer technology you are documenting. Credit even the least experienced computer user with intelligence and life experience. Show respect for this person when you write.

Rewrite: Get directly to the point, and be positive rather than negative.

> Experimenting with your computer is a great way to learn, and you can quickly undo almost any error.

Common Writing Problems to Avoid

This section identifies words, phrases, constructions, and practices that often lead to abstract or unclear meaning, disjointed cadence, or unnatural and improper language usage.

Anthropomorphisms

Anthropomorphisms attribute human motivation, characteristics, or behavior to inanimate objects. Anthropomorphisms often creep into technical writing. Avoid using anthropomorphisms. Follow these guidelines:

- Do not ascribe human qualities to nonhumans, or machine qualities to humans.

  Use similes or words within quotation marks instead. For example:

  > The program differentiates among remote procedure calls and acts on one type as though it recognizes its unique "voice."

  The example combines simile ("…as though…") with the ironic use of a word set off within quotation marks ("voice").

- Keep in mind that no computer has feelings or thinks. No computer holds opinions, "wanting" one thing, "disliking" another.

  Instead, the computer "accepts" only certain things. Software does not "look" at a directory, but software might "check" one.

- Be sure to use the prepositions "in" and "on" correctly.

  No person can ever be "in" a text editor or "in" any of its modes. A person might be using a text editor, or the text editor might be in insert mode. A person cannot "move around in a file," but the pointer position might move, or the screen display might change. No person is ever "on" a server, but the system might be on one.

- Do not use "We recommend" or "It is recommended that..."

  A company does not recommend, or hope, or advise. Instead of saying "We recommend that you remove the cover first," just go ahead and tell the reader to do so. Or start out with the benefit of the behavior. Instead of saying "It is recommended that you set the cache to 512 Kbytes," say "Setting the cache to 512 Kbytes makes the system run faster."

- Rewrite anthropomorphisms whenever you can.

  However, there might be occasions when an anthropomorphism is an industry standard. For example, you might say the system "listens" to a network to determine when the network is free.

Commands as Verbs

Command names are only names. Command names are never verbs.

Incorrect: First cd to the new directory.
Correct: First change to the new directory by using the cd command.

Redundancies

You create redundancies when you fail to consider the literal meanings of the words that you choose. Some common examples of redundancies and alternatives are listed in the following table.

TABLE 3–1 Common Redundancies and Alternatives

Redundancy	Alternative
Accidental mistake	Mistake
Add additional	Add
Add on	Add
Already exists	Exists
At this point in time	At this point, at this time
Basic fundamentals	Fundamentals
Boot up	Boot
Check to be sure	Check, ensure, make sure
Close proximity	Close, near, nearby
Connect together	Connect

TABLE 3–1 Common Redundancies and Alternatives *(Continued)*

Redundancy	Alternative
Create a new	Create
Dial up	Dial
Edit an existing	Edit
Existing conditions	Conditions
First create	Create
Group together	Group
Necessary prerequisites	Prerequisites
Print out	Print
Specific requirements	Requirements
Start up	Start
Still pending	Pending
Time out	Time
Whether or not	Whether, if

Test the usefulness of each modifier you choose. If the modifier does not help the construction, for example, if it does not amplify, clarify, or intensify the meaning of the word that it modifies, do not use it. If the modifier's meaning is equal to the meaning of the word that it modifies or if the phrase or clause is a virtual restatement of a point previously made in the sentence, do not use it.

Well-used "intensives," however, often add emphasis to the sentence. For example, "turn on your system for the very first time" might appear redundant at first glance. Something cannot be any more "first" than first. But the intensive, "very," makes clear that the ensuing description happens only once in the system's life. Use this technique sparingly.

Ways to Improve Your Style

An effective writing style is learned, not inherited. You can improve your style through study, practice, and constructive criticism.

Study Good Writing

One way to learn good style is to analyze examples of effective technical writing. Appendix D lists books worthy of your professional attention. Study the literature in your area of specialization and ask yourself what works, what doesn't, and why.

As you analyze examples of effective technical writing, you will see that writers of effective technical prose present material as follows:

- At the point the reader needed the material and in a logical progression
- At the place the reader expected to find the material
- In a tone and diction that the reader could immediately understand
- In a consistent form that the reader could easily interpret

Work With an Editor

If you are fortunate enough to work at a site with an editorial staff, take every opportunity to have your work edited. A good editor is an invaluable partner in producing effective documentation. An editor can often assist you in determining the best way to present information to the customer and to international readers. Your editor is also the expert in your company style.

A good editor is often familiar not only with other documentation produced at your company but also with other documentation in your field. An editor relates to a document as an advocate for the reader and as a professional who can critique your work. An editor is often the first "customer" to read your document.

For further discussion of the partnership between writers and editors, see Chapter 10.

Attend Classes and Training

Technical writing is a recognized profession. An excellent way to improve your style is to attend classes offered by other professionals in the field. Classes are also often available through the following avenues:

- Colleges and university extension programs
- In-house training services
- Commercial seminars and tutorials

CHAPTER 4

Online Writing Style

Online writing presents special challenges for writers. Online documents have characteristics that distinguish them from their printed counterparts. For example, online documents have the capability of linking to related information. However, they also have screens that are less easily read than printed pages. Because readers can view only one window of text at a time, they cannot easily visualize the size or complexity of an online document.

When writing for online presentation, you must provide context for your readers to avoid disorientation. You also must balance the reader's dislike of scrolling and excessive linking with the need to provide sufficient and relevant information.

This chapter discusses the following topics:

About These Guidelines

The guidelines in this chapter focus on online text that is intended to be read in a web browser. This chapter does not discuss software tools, web browsers, screen design, graphics, or document delivery methods. Underscores before and after link text show where to place links in the text.

The online writing guidelines in this chapter do not apply to the following types of documents:

- PDF documents
- PostScript™ documents

This chapter uses the word "page" to refer to an online page or web page. A "page" is equivalent to an online file or web file. When "printed" precedes the word "page," the reference is to hard copy.

Note – For single-source document writers: If you encounter a conflict between online and print writing guidelines, follow the guidelines for your primary delivery mode.

Solving Online Writing Problems

The following table summarizes the problems that are unique to online writing and presents possible solutions.

TABLE 4–1 Online Writing Problems and Solutions

Problem	Solution
Online readers cannot easily envision the size or complexity of an online document or the relationship among various topics.	Create an effective document structure that is obvious and easy to navigate. See "Creating an Effective Document Structure" on page 83.
Many people do not like reading online text and become frustrated when they cannot quickly find what they want.	Write short, self-contained topics and construct simple, scannable text. Both strategies help reduce information overload and make it easier for readers to find quick answers to their questions. See "Writing Short, Self-Contained Topics" on page 92 and "Constructing Scannable Paragraphs, Headings, and Lists" on page 93.
Text is more difficult to read online.	Construct simple, scannable text. See "Constructing Scannable Paragraphs, Headings, and Lists" on page 93.

TABLE 4–1 Online Writing Problems and Solutions *(Continued)*

Problem	Solution
Most readers go directly to a topic to find information. Because they have no context from earlier reading, they can easily become disoriented.	Preserve context to keep readers from becoming lost or disoriented in a document. See "Preserving Context in Online Documents" on page 98.
Links can be annoying, especially when the content and value of the material located at the link destination is unclear.	Construct effective links that enable readers to make their own decisions about how to access information. Avoid distracting or disorienting readers by overlinking or by providing insufficient context for links. For more information about links, see Chapter 5.

Creating an Effective Document Structure

Readers cannot easily visualize the size or complexity of an online document because they view only one window of text at a time. Both the absence of hard copy to reveal the document's general dimensions and the small window size also create challenges for readers. These challenges combine to make it difficult for readers to see how various topics are related.

Readers who must retrace their steps or move forward with no clear idea of where they are going are easily frustrated. To reduce the risk of reader disorientation, help readers visualize the structure of your online document.

To create an effective document structure, do the following:

- Determine how much control to give readers.

  When planning your online document, decide how much control readers should have over the sequence of topics or the paths that they can follow. Consider the purpose of your document, the scope and complexity of your technical content, and the skill level of your audience with online media.

- Provide links that anticipate readers' needs.

  Provide links that are embedded in the text and that point to other relevant content in the document. Also provide links in a jump list. See "Use Jump Lists" on page 97 and "Writing Jump Lists" on page 41. For guidelines on writing link text, see Chapter 5.

- Use an easy-to-follow, meaningful structure.

  If your document requires many clicks to find the information readers seek, rethink its structure.

Note – Do not describe how to navigate in your online document unless it has truly unusual features or you anticipate that many inexperienced online readers will use your document.

Use an Easy-to-Follow, Meaningful Structure

The following table suggests ways to structure an online document. These structures are not mutually exclusive. You can use these high-level and low-level organizational strategies together in the same document.

TABLE 4–2 Ways to Structure an Online Document

Structure	When to Use
Hierarchy	Use for a large number of layered topics that are linked together. This structure organizes content at the *section* level.
Inverted pyramid	Use for text within individual sections. This structure organizes content at the *paragraph* level and *sentence* level.
Table	Use when each topic contains the same subtopics. This structure typically organizes content at the *paragraph* level.
Flow diagram	Use for high-level overviews to show how topics or groups of tasks or procedures are related.
Task map	Use for task-based information to give users quick access to step-by-step instructions.

Organize Text by Hierarchy

In an online document organized by hierarchy, high-level generalities and overviews offer a preview of what lies below. Levels within hierarchies can be based on importance, frequency of use, or complexity.

Be careful not to create too many hierarchical levels that bury important information. You must balance the need to divide text into short, self-contained topics against the risk of creating valueless intermediate screens.

In a technical manual that is organized by hierarchy, the top three levels serve as a clickable table of contents from which readers can jump to various topics. Within the text of the document, readers can jump to related material, both in and out of the document, through links.

In the following example, a plus sign indicates that a topic contains hidden subtopics. The underscores indicate links.

EXAMPLE 4–1 Organizing Text by Hierarchy

Workstation Reference Manual
+ __Preface__
+ __Back Panel Connectors__
__Media Independent Interface (MII) Connector__
     + __Twisted-Pair Ethernet (TPE) Connector__
     + __SCSI Connector__
     __Audio Ports__
     __Audio Specifications__
+ __Modem Setup Specifications__
__Identifying Jumpers__
     __Flash PROM Jumpers__
     __Serial Port Jumpers__
+ __System Specifications__

Organize Text by Inverted Pyramid

When organizing by inverted pyramid, you place the conclusion and a short summary of the main ideas at the beginning of the topic. The details follow in decreasing order of importance. Readers can digest the main points even if they stop reading before reaching the end of the document.

The inverted pyramid structure, typically used in newspaper writing, is also appropriate for long narrative text in online technical documents. Use this structure to organize paragraphs and sentences within a section of narrative text.

To create an inverted pyramid structure, follow these guidelines:

- Use clear, meaningful headings or lists at the beginning of a topic.
- Create separate paragraphs or topics to emphasize important points.
- Do not bury your main point in the middle of a paragraph or topic.

The following text begins by defining "device driver optimization." The text then provides links to sections that describe three types of optimization guidelines: general, transmit, and receive. Details appear later in three separate subsections. If long enough, each section could be divided into one or more separate pages.

EXAMPLE 4–2 Organizing Text by Inverted Pyramid

<Level1Head>Optimization Guidelines for Network Device Drivers
Optimization in a device driver means that the software interacts directly with a hardware device and mainly fields asynchronous interrupt events.

To assist you in the design of network device drivers in the kernel, this document provides three types of optimization guidelines:
- __General__
- __Transmit__
- __Receive__

This document assumes that you have some knowledge of kernel and device driver programming. For a tutorial that covers network device drivers, see `http://www.plirg.com/drivers/tutorial/index.html`.

<Level2Head>General Optimization Guidelines
Some guidelines are universal:
- Use tail calls for stack frame creation.
- Avoid deeply nested automatic variables.
  Compilers can do a better job of register allocation when the scope of automatic variables is limited.
- More guidelines.

<Level2Head>Transmit Optimization Guidelines
The transmit path requires attention from a driver writer to keep machine performance from being affected under heavy load. To avoid problems, follow these guidelines:
- Queue only when necessary.
- Keep packets in order when queuing.
- More guidelines.

<Level2Head>Receive Optimization Guidelines
Receive is the most difficult path to tune because many factors are outside the driver's control. For example, packet size and arrival are determined by the remote machine, and the behavior of the protocol stack plays a much greater role than it does on transmit. Follow these guidelines:
- Copy small packets.
- If you must drop a packet, do not tail drop.
- More guidelines.

Organize Text by Table

Tables are an effective way to compare facts and enhance reader comprehension. However, tables with many rows and columns can be difficult to read and display online. Make online tables short and simple to improve online readability and reduce load time.

If readers are likely to print a table for future reference, make sure that the table does not run off a printed page.

To simplify tables, follow these guidelines:

- Limit the number of columns and rows so that the entire table can fit inside a typical web browser.

  For example, you can divide long, wide tables into several short tables.

- Use few words within table cells.

  Use phrases rather than sentences to eliminate unnecessary text. Use abbreviations as necessary. However, do not omit articles where they are needed.

- Consider using a table instead of a bulleted list for long lists with repeating elements.

When formatting tables, leave room for the expansion that can occur during translation. For more guidelines on constructing tables, see "Tables" on page 42.

In this example, the table helps readers make decisions about tasks that they need to perform and provides links to additional information.

EXAMPLE 4–3 Organizing Text by Table

Installation Status	Procedure	For More Information
Before software is installed	1. Deselect the `QInstall` package. 2. Create and run a `finish` script that creates a file named `plirginst`.	*__PlirgSoft Advanced Installation Guide__*
After software is installed	1. Use the `instremove` command to remove the `QInstall` package. 2. Add the `plirginst` file in the `utilities` directory.	*__Chapter 21, Software Administration (Tasks)__* *__PlirgSoft Advanced Installation Guide__*

Organize Text by Flow Diagram

Use clickable flow diagrams to direct readers through related topics. For instance, you can use flow diagrams to lead readers through a complex task consisting of multiple procedures. Links can take readers to step-by-step instructions for each procedure.

If the product you are documenting lends itself to a high-level overview, you can use a flow diagram to show how groups of procedures are related. This strategy can help give readers the "big picture" of the product.

When formatting flow diagrams, leave room for the expansion that can occur during translation.

In the following example, a clickable flow diagram with four links helps users troubleshoot the workstation in reference to the OpenBoot™ PROM report.

EXAMPLE 4–4 Organizing by Clickable Flow Diagram

```
┌─────────────────────┐
│ Hold down the F7 key│
│ for 10 seconds while│
│ powering on the     │
│ appliance.          │
└─────────────────────┘
         │
┌─────────────────────┐  Y   ┌──────────────────────┐
│ Is the screen garbled or│──────│ Replace the __DIMM__ │
│ partially garbled?  │      │ and retest.          │
└─────────────────────┘      └──────────────────────┘
    │ N
┌─────────────────────┐
│ The __OpenBoot PROM │
│ report__ is displayed.│
└─────────────────────┘
         │
┌─────────────────────┐
│ Compare the OpenBoot│
│ PROM report with what│
│ is known about the  │
│ __workstation       │
│ configuration__.    │
└─────────────────────┘
         │
┌─────────────────────┐  Y   ┌──────────────────────┐
│ Is there any discrepancy│──────│ For each discrepancy, go│
│ between the OpenBoot │      │ to the respective section│
│ PROM report and the │      │ of this manual to remove│
│ workstation         │      │ and check the FRU. See │
│ configuration?      │      │ __Block Diagram__.     │
└─────────────────────┘      └──────────────────────┘
    │ N
┌─────────────────────┐
│ Conditions are normal.│
│ Power off the appliance│
│ and continue with the │
│ next flow diagram.  │
└─────────────────────┘
```

This example shows a flow diagram with eight links. The diagram is intended to help users get started with the system and its preinstalled software.

EXAMPLE 4–5 Organizing a Complex Task by Flow Diagram

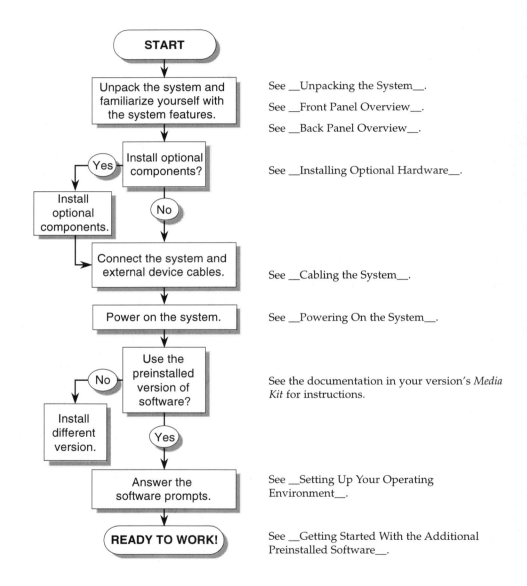

See __Unpacking the System__.

See __Front Panel Overview__.

See __Back Panel Overview__.

See __Installing Optional Hardware__.

See __Cabling the System__.

See __Powering On the System__.

See the documentation in your version's *Media Kit* for instructions.

See __Setting Up Your Operating Environment__.

See __Getting Started With the Additional Preinstalled Software__.

Organize Text by Task Map

Task maps organize task-based information for users who need fast access to procedures. You can organize individual tasks into a task map that lists either of the following:

- Required, sequential procedures related to a complicated task
- Optional procedures related to a particular topic, such as "Maintaining a Printer"

Links to each procedure create a clickable task map. A link to overview information directly before or after each task map enables readers to view overview material only if they want to do so.

A task analysis can help you determine which tasks are best grouped. Ideally, include on your analysis team users who perform these tasks.

See also "Using Task Maps to Organize Tasks" on page 120.

The following task map provides links to procedures and high-level descriptions for quick reference. Tasks are numbered because they must be performed in sequential order. Note the link to overview information that follows this task map.

EXAMPLE 4–6 Organizing Text by Task Map

Task	Description
1. __How to Configure a File System for Quotas__	Edit the /etc/vfstab file to activate quotas each time the file system is mounted. Then, create a quotas file.
2. __How to Set Up Quotas for a User__	Use the edquota command to create disk quotas and inode quotas for a single-user account.
3. (Optional) __How to Set Up Quotas for Multiple Users__	Use the edquota command to apply prototype quotas to other user accounts.

For an overview of managing quotas tasks, see __Managing Quotas (Overview)__.

Writing Short, Self-Contained Topics

Write topics that minimize screen readability problems and that help readers find needed information quickly. Follow these guidelines:

- Divide text into self-contained, linked topics.
- Keep topics short.

  Online topics can be quite short. However, just one or two short sentences probably do not justify splitting off the text into a separate topic.

- Focus on the structure of content, not on how formatting renders online.
- Include transitions within each topic.

Divide Text Into Self-Contained, Linked Topics

Divide each document into self-contained, linked topics. Ideally, each topic explains its content without making assumptions about previous topics. Links to overviews or other explanatory information can help readers who need more background.

To determine how much information to put in a topic, consider the complexity of the information and your audience's knowledge and experience.

Make each topic clearly focused and coherent so that it answers one question about one subject for one purpose. Try writing a single question that the topic is meant to answer. Then, judge whether the content in that topic fully answers that question.

Also, repeat contextual information within each topic when needed. Contextual information helps orient readers so that they know what the current topic is and how it fits within the larger document structure. See "Preserving Context in Online Documents" on page 98.

Focus on the Structure of Content

Short topics and the frequent use of subheadings might at first appear undesirable from a visual design standpoint, depending on the display tool and the reader's browser preferences. If the document is single-sourced and also delivered in print, so many subheadings might appear cluttered on the printed page.

However, many subheadings make text more scannable for readers scrolling through a document. Subheadings also help readers more easily locate specific information in a clickable table of contents. Instead of being concerned about how the formatting is rendered in print and online, focus on the structure of the content. Divide text into short, self-contained topics. Then, label the topics with meaningful headings and subheadings.

Constructing Scannable Paragraphs, Headings, and Lists

Readers expect online text to be succinct and directly relevant. They are also goal oriented and scan for information rather than read long blocks of text thoroughly. Make online documents scannable to help readers locate information quickly.

To construct scannable paragraphs, headings, and lists, do the following:

- Write clearly and simply.
- Keep paragraphs short.
- Condense text.

  Write concisely and eliminate unnecessary material. However, be cautious about condensing text too much. See "Condense Text Carefully" on page 96.
- Use links to make text seem shorter.

  Text seems shorter because readers use links to select only the topics of interest. See "Use Links to Make Text Seem Shorter" on page 107.
- Replace text with tables, charts, and figures, when possible.
- Write meaningful headings and subheadings.
- Use bulleted lists and jump lists.
- Emphasize key words and phrases in bold.

Write Clearly and Simply

Short, uncomplicated sentences are especially important online because reading text on a screen is slower than reading printed text. To present information clearly and simply, follow these guidelines:

- Use simple declarative and imperative sentence structures.
- Use active voice, present tense, and concrete, meaningful words.

  For suggestions on improving your technical writing style, see Chapter 3.
- Use terms consistently.

  When you use terms consistently, readers do not have to recheck different topics to grasp the meaning of the material.

EXAMPLE 4–7 Writing Clearly and Simply

Incorrect:

It is recommended that virtual memory limits be set high so that these limits can never be reached under normal operating circumstances. However, the virtual memory limit can also be used to place a limit over the entire database server in order to stop a failing database with a memory leak from spilling over to other databases or workloads on the system.

Correct:

Set virtual limits high so that they are never reached under normal circumstances. However, you can use the virtual memory limit to place a limit over the entire database server. This strategy prevents a database with a memory leak from affecting other databases or workloads on the system.

Keep Paragraphs Short

Short paragraphs offer visual breaks and are easier to scan and read online. To keep paragraphs short, follow these guidelines:

- Limit each paragraph to one idea.
- Make the topic sentence the first sentence in each paragraph.
- Emphasize main points.

  Set off each main point in its own sentence or short paragraph.

- Keep paragraphs from three to five sentences long.
- Limit paragraphs to 75 words or fewer.

EXAMPLE 4–8 Keeping Paragraphs Short

Incorrect:

There are two methods for setting device attributes. The first method is to call the `xil_device_create(3)` and `xil_device_set_value(3)` functions before creating the device image with the `xil_create_from_device(3)` function. The second method is to call `xil_device_set_value(3)` after calling `xil_create_from_device(3)`. Certain attributes require that they be set with the first method (such as `DEVICE_NAME`) and are documented as such in the following sections.

Correct:

You can use one of these methods to set device attributes:

- Call the `xil_device_create(3)` and `xil_device_set_value(3)` functions before creating the device image with `xil_create_from_device(3)`
- Call `xil_device_set_value(3)` after calling `xil_create_from_device(3)`

Certain attributes, such as `DEVICE_NAME`, must be set with the first method. __Device Attribute Descriptions__ documents these attributes.

Eliminate Unnecessary Material

To determine what material is unnecessary, you need to know not only what readers need, but what they do not need. To reduce word count, follow these guidelines:

- Do not include unnecessary definitions and explanations, or information that is too technical for readers' needs.

  Consider creating a glossary for your document. A glossary condenses text by moving definitions out of the main text.

- Eliminate "nice to know" or overly detailed information.

- Avoid flowery language, such as "great" and "amazing," buzzwords, and unsupported claims.

- Eliminate introductory text that repeats the content in the headings.

- Avoid writing introductions to figures or tables that repeat the figure or table caption.

  In this example of text that introduces a figure, the figure caption reads as follows: "Figure 8–4 Work Item Statistics Page."

  Incorrect:

  When you click the Statistics tab and then the Find Statistics on Work Items link, the Work Item Statistics page is displayed. Use this page to request a statistics report for all work items for one or all applications that are initiated or modified within a given time period. The following figure shows the Work Item Statistics page.

  Correct:

  When you click the Statistics tab and then the Find Statistics on Work Items link, the Work Item Statistics page is displayed, as shown in Figure 8–4. Use this page to request a statistics report for all work items for one or all applications that are initiated or modified within a given time period.

- Omit redundant figure callouts.

  Eliminate callouts for buttons or other screen features that already have a self-explanatory name. For example, you probably do not need a callout for the Delete or Copy button.

- Do not duplicate instructions on how to use a graphical user interface (GUI).

  If the instructions are available in online help, do not repeat them in other online technical documentation.

  For guidelines on writing GUI instructions, see Chapter 12. See also "Use One Method in a Single Procedure" on page 126.

- If possible, perform informal usability testing to see how readers use the online document and whether you can eliminate certain types of content.

  If you have control over document navigation, also perform usability testing to improve its design. A good design helps you avoid wasting time and words writing text that attempts to resolve navigational flaws.

Condense Text Carefully

Do not make text so short that it seems "dumbed down," choppy, abrupt, confusing, or incomplete. You do not want to sacrifice content, readability, quality, tone, or flow.

Most importantly, do not remove content that readers need to complete necessary tasks. Also, if topics can be read in any order, you might need to link to or repeat some information to provide sufficient context for readers. See "Preserving Context in Online Documents" on page 98.

Remember that online writing does not always have to be short. Drastically condensing text can disappoint readers who are seeking very detailed information online. Readers prefer documents that fully answer their questions on a topic. For in-depth answers, readers are likely to print the document anyway.

Write Meaningful Headings and Subheadings

Write headings and subheadings as short, precise abstracts of their associated content. Headings are often displayed out of context in a search results list or bookmark menu. Sometimes only the first few words are displayed, or the words in the middle of the heading are truncated and replaced with ellipsis points.

Even when headings are displayed with their associated content, the small amount of information visible on a computer screen is difficult to interpret at a glance.

To construct scannable headings, follow the guidelines in "Headings" on page 32.

Use Bulleted Lists

Bulleted lists are ideal for online documents because they emphasize information in a concise format that encourages scanning. Key facts within list items are easy to identify. Bulleted lists also help hard-to-read screen text and provide white space that gives the eyes a visual break.

To facilitate scanning, follow these guidelines:

- Use bulleted lists to break up long paragraphs.
- Use more lists online than you would on a typical printed page.
- Avoid having more than nine items in a list.

  If a list has more than nine items that can be logically broken up, divide the list into two or more lists.
- Use concise phrases.

  Concise phrases are easier to scan than complete sentences. Also, lines are less likely to wrap in a browser window when you use phrases.

- Write the first sentence as a concise summary if a list item consists of two or more sentences.

  Provide explanatory information in a new paragraph, as shown here.

For more guidelines on constructing lists, see "Lists" on page 35.

EXAMPLE 4–9 Using a Bulleted List

Incorrect:

You must choose a user name for each user account that you create. User names must be unique within your organization, which could span multiple domains. They must also contain from two to eight letters and numerals. (The first character must be a letter and at least one character must be a lowercase letter.) Lastly, they cannot contain an underscore or a space.

Correct:

You must choose a user name for each user account that you create. User names must adhere to the following criteria:

- They must be unique within your organization, which could span multiple domains.
- They must contain from two to eight letters and numerals.

  The first character must be a letter. At least one letter must be lowercase.
- They cannot contain an underscore or a space.

Use Jump Lists

A jump list provides a clickable list of topics that helps readers scan and navigate in an online document. Use a jump list so that readers can easily scan and link to the following:

- The contents within a chapter or section
- All procedures, including those that are part of a long, complex task
- A list of related topics that are typically cross-referenced in print documents

When you create a jump list, consider briefly explaining the content of each list item so that readers can decide which links to traverse. Annotating links is not necessary if the link text clearly describes the link destination.

For more guidelines on constructing jump lists, see "Writing Jump Lists" on page 41.

EXAMPLE 4–10 Using a Jump List

You can perform the following optional procedures to maintain user and group accounts:

- __Modifying a Group__
- __Deleting a Group__
- __Disabling a User Account__

EXAMPLE 4–11 Using a Jump List With Annotations

This chapter explains the proper design and building of a computer room.

- For recommendations about flexibility and planned redundancy, expansion, room layout and planning, and access issues, see __Designing the Room__.
- For recommendations about floor height, support grids, tile construction, load and fire ratings, and supplemental bracing, see __Designing the Floor__.
- For recommendations about preparation and materials selection, see __Building the Room__.

Preserving Context in Online Documents

Online readers create their own transitions as they move through a document. Through traversing links, both associative and navigational, readers choose their own path by deciding where to go next.

This freedom to jump around online has a down side. Sometimes, context is lost and readers can become confused or disoriented. To preserve context, online documents must support nonlinear and incomplete reading. Follow these guidelines:

- Make few assumptions about reading order.
- Offer contextual cues.
- Give the precise location of related information.
- Use pronouns carefully.

    The antecedents of "this" and "it" are often unclear, especially online. Pronouns that are too vague also cause problems for translators.

Make Few Assumptions About Reading Order

In an online environment, you usually do not know how readers come to your document or a section of it. They might arrive through a table of contents or a search engine. They might click on a cross-reference that leads them there. They could just be scanning links.

When you make few assumptions about reading order, you are better prepared to offer readers the necessary contextual cues.

Offer Contextual Cues

Contextual cues help readers understand where the information belongs within the larger structure of the document.

If you do not provide sufficient context, readers have to figure out how the sections are related. You need to help readers make these associations meaningful. For example, you could indicate to readers that a certain topic is part of a broader topic.

For instance, to indicate that information under a third-level heading is a subtopic of a second-level heading, you could write the subtopic heading to reflect this relationship. Or, you could include introductory text to this effect.

If sequential order is important, give readers a sense of what comes before and after a topic. For example, if a complex task is logically divided into several short subtasks or procedures, tell readers what comes before and after each procedure. A list of prerequisites before a procedure and a "Where to Go From Here" section after a procedure would suffice here.

Give the Precise Location of Related Information

The words "above" or "below" have no meaning in a document that is not read linearly. Instead, use one of these strategies:

- Use "next," "following," or "previous" if the information is contained in the same topic.
- Name the item.

  For example, instead of using the text "in the following section," you can name the section by using the text "Modifying a Group."
- Link to the information.

EXAMPLE 4–12 Preserving Context in Online Documents

Incorrect:

<Level2Head>Demo Programs

You can find demo programs in C:\Demos. See the README file for detailed information about them.

<Level2Head>Related Documentation

For more information about this, see the Application Builder help volume and the *__Application Builder User's Guide__*.

Correct:

Previous Topic: Developing an Application

<Level2Head>Application Builder Demo Programs

You can find the Application Builder demo programs in the C:\Demos directory. See the README file for detailed information about these programs.

<Level2Head>Application Builder Documentation

For more information about Application Builder, see the Application Builder help volume and the *__Application Builder User's Guide__*.

Next Topic: Designing and Maintaining Portable Applications

Note – Explicitly state Previous Topic and Next Topic only if your document display tool does not automatically generate this information.

CHAPTER 5

Constructing Links

A *link* consists of the link text and the link destination. Links enable readers to jump to related information with a single click. Links are one of the advantages of online reading because they enable readers to make their own decisions about how to access information.

However, links pose challenges for writers. Too many links clutter text and can distract readers. Too few links mean readers might have difficulty finding the supplemental information that they need when looking at a screen of text, which lacks the context of a printed page.

This chapter discusses the following topics:

- "About These Guidelines" on page 101
- "Where to Place Links" on page 102
- "General Linking Strategies" on page 103
- "Guidelines for Writing Link Text" on page 110

About These Guidelines

The guidelines in this chapter focus on online text that is intended to be read in a web browser, such as technical documentation on a Web site. This chapter does not discuss software tools, web browsers, screen design, graphics, or document delivery methods. Underscores before and after link text show where to place links in the text.

The online writing guidelines in this chapter do not apply to the following types of documents:

- PDF documents
- PostScript documents

This chapter uses the word "page" to refer to an online page or web page. A "page" is equivalent to an online file or web file. When "printed" precedes the word "page," the reference is to hard copy.

Note – For single-source document writers: If you encounter a conflict between online and print writing guidelines, follow the guidelines for your primary delivery mode.

Where to Place Links

When considering which links to create, anticipate paths that your readers are likely to take. Which associations would benefit them? Let your readers' needs, expectations, and interests guide you. Create links that support good decision making.

When readers must follow a certain sequence through your content, for example, when following a procedure, limit their choices by reducing or eliminating links. At the least, guide readers with additional explanatory text.

Except for such instances, your goal is to provide readers with opportunities, not to order them around. However, do not make these opportunities endless. You must set priorities in your documents and point your readers in relevant directions.

The following list suggests ways to use links in online documents.

- **Tables of contents.** If your writing tool does not generate a clickable table of contents for you, include one as the entry point into your online document. If your writing tool can expand and collapse entries for tables of contents, use this feature.

- **Summaries.** To reduce the amount of information that readers see, briefly summarize content and then link to supporting details. For example, you can link to long examples and to overview, background, reference, detailed, or supplementary information.

  If you organize your document by hierarchy, you can present general overviews that link to increasing levels of details. See "Organize Text by Hierarchy" on page 84.

- **Lists.** Online readers interpret links more easily in bulleted lists rather than links embedded in paragraphs. A jump list can serve as a short table of contents or a brief summary of the content if it is placed at the beginning of a chapter or main section of a document.

  For more information, see "Use Jump Lists" on page 97 and "Provide Links in a List" on page 108.

- **Tables.** Tables with links to related information provide scannable content and quick access to more details. See "Organize Text by Table" on page 87 and "Tables" on page 42.

- **Cross-references.** Cross-references to other sections, chapters, or manuals typically become links embedded in the text. Consider clustering cross-references to headings or titles under a "See Also," "Related Topics," or similar heading.

  Capitalize and punctuate cross-references by following the rules in "Formatting Cross-References" on page 48.

- **Code examples.** Consider placing long blocks of programming code in a separate text file. Then, link to the text file from your document. This strategy eliminates the formatting cleanup that is often necessary when a user cuts and pastes code from documents displayed in a web browser.

- **Glossary terms.** Wherever the prominent use of a glossary term appears, link to the document's glossary if the document has one. In determining the prominent use of the term, consider the reader's likely path through the document. Remember that too many links can distract readers. Balance the desire to provide helpful links to the glossary against the risk of overlinking.

- **Reader comments.** Include an online feedback mechanism on every page of your online document if you have control over this information design feature. Direct comments to the appropriate group, not, for instance, to the webmaster if your document is displayed on the Web. Also, let users know if they should expect a response to their comments.

- **Reference lists.** A document such as a white paper can link to a reference list that is contained in a separate page. In print, the reference list would be contained within the body of the paper.

- **Other relevant web sites.** For web documents, links to material on other sites enable you to take advantage of what others have produced. For information about policies for linking to third-party Web sites, see "Third-Party Web Site References" on page 162.

General Linking Strategies

Links stand out by virtue of being underlined and displayed in color, so think of them as emphasized words. Because the scanning eye notices only two or three words at a time, emphasized or not, make the link text short but informative. In addition, be sure that the links on a page collectively offer context about what that page contains, not just where each link leads.

When constructing links, use these general strategies:

- Create links that anticipate readers' likely paths.

  See "Where to Place Links" on page 102.

- Avoid overlinking.

- Prevent reader disorientation.

- Include links that answer readers' questions.
- Use links to condense the amount of information readers see.
- Provide links in a list when possible.
- Place links at the end of a topic when possible.
- Provide URLs only when needed.
- Test the validity of links.

Avoid Overlinking

Be careful about filling text with distracting links. Too many links dilute the message on a page and can confuse readers with irrelevant digressions. You need to guide readers and filter their choices.

Links also disrupt the narrative flow of text by inviting readers to go elsewhere. Unless that is your goal, link sparingly. Also, remember that too many links can involve too much maintenance and that they are hard to read on a cluttered screen.

The following sections suggest ways to avoid overlinking.

Avoid Interrupting Readers

If you do not want to interrupt the reader at a certain point in the text, do not put a link there. Ask yourself: Is the information at the link destination relevant to the audience, purpose, and content of this document?

Do Not Link the Same Text Repeatedly

- Do not repeat a link wherever the link text occurs.

  Identifying a link once per topic is sufficient.

  Incorrect:

  PlirgSoft uses __file folders__ to organize your files. These __file folders__ can contain only graphic and text files.

  Correct:

  PlirgSoft uses __file folders__ to organize your files. These file folders can contain only graphic and text files.

- Do not link to an online feedback mechanism more than once on a page.
- Avoid making explicit cross-references if they create redundancy.

  Incorrect:

  If you used __Wrap To Fit__, the Save dialog box includes an additional choice about handling line endings (see __Wrap To Fit__).

  Correct:

  If you used __Wrap To Fit__, the Save dialog box includes an additional choice about handling line endings.

Minimize the Number of Clicks

Do not add a link if you can succinctly present the information in the current topic.

In the following incorrect example, readers need to click twice to access the *Application Builder User's Guide*. The first click, __click here__, takes readers to the list of related documentation. The second click, which is not shown in the example, takes readers to the user's guide. In the correct example, readers need to click only once to access the user's guide.

Incorrect:

For related documentation on Application Builder, __click here__.

Correct:

For related documentation on Application Builder, see the Application Builder help volume and the __*Application Builder User's Guide*__.

Limit Internal Linking

- Especially if a page is short, do not link to other destinations on that page.

  Readers typically expect links to take them to another page. If a link takes readers only a few lines down, readers can become disoriented.

- When a table, figure, or example immediately follows a textual reference to it, do not include a link.

  The unnecessary link can disorient and frustrate readers, especially if clicking on the link renders an entirely new web browser that contains only that structure.

  In the textual reference to the table, figure, or example, use the word "following" to indicate the structure's location. For example, you might begin the sentence with the text "The following figure shows."

Prevent Reader Disorientation

Ensure that readers remain fully oriented and in control as they navigate through an online document. Readers are properly oriented when they can identify the content presented, the location of the content within the larger body of information, and the navigational options.

The following techniques can help prevent disorientation:

- Reserve link formatting for links only.

  Never use your link formatting convention for any other purpose. Links are usually identified by underlining and a certain color.

- Label navigational icons.

  Label navigational icons if you have such control over them. Some users are visually oriented while others are text oriented. A combination serves all users.

- Provide sufficient context.

  Sufficient context helps readers decide whether to follow the link. Explain what information is located at the link destination and how it relates to the present topic. See "Provide Context in Link Text and Surrounding Text" on page 110.

- Warn readers about unexpected link destinations.

  Let readers know when a link might take them to an unexpected destination. For example, tell readers when clicking on a link does the following actions:

  - Opens another document
  - Opens another application
  - Takes them to another site
  - Leads to a large file with a long download time
  - Requires them to register or enter a password to access the destination

  If you carefully word a link and its surrounding text, readers know when the link takes them away from your document.

In the following example, links to "VI" and "Emacs" take readers away from the tutorial. The correct version clearly indicates that clicking on either link takes readers to another site.

EXAMPLE 5–1 Preventing Reader Disorientation

Incorrect:

Pico is probably the easiest of the three editors to use. If you are curious about how to use the other editors, however, see the reference cards for __VI__ and __Emacs__.

Correct:

Pico is probably the easiest of the three editors to use. If you are curious about how to use the other editors, however, see their reference cards:

- __VI Reference Card__ from Dalhousie University
- __GNU Emacs Reference Card__ from www.geek-girl.com

Include Links That Answer the Reader's Questions

One reason for providing links is to answer the reader's questions, such as "How do I compress a file?" Ideally, write link text so that it corresponds to the reader's search tasks.

Incorrect:

Bug voting provides another channel for feedback and for establishing priorities. You can cast a vote on the bugs that frustrate you the most. Your votes are viewed by engineering. If you want to vote, __click here__.

Correct:

Bug voting provides another channel for feedback and for establishing priorities. You can __cast a vote__ on the bugs that frustrate you the most. Your votes are viewed by engineering.

Use Links to Make Text Seem Shorter

Your online document might be lengthy. However, with links, your text can appear shorter to readers without sacrificing depth of content.

- Link to in-depth information.

  Use summaries and link to supporting details. See "Summaries" in "Where to Place Links" on page 102.

- Link to, rather than duplicate, information.

  For example, if a procedure is basic and frequently used as part of other more complex procedures, do not repeat the steps of that basic procedure. Instead, put the steps for the basic procedure in one section and link to it from other places.

  Also, do not duplicate background or overview information. Include this material in one place and link to it from other places, as needed.

- Link to basic information.

  Link to basics so expert users do not stop reading. Novice users can access the material if they are interested.

Note – Avoid dividing long, linear text into multiple pages with Next links, which is known as "electronic page turning." If this method seems like the only way to present the material, consider providing a printer-friendly version for offline reading or a PDF file that readers can download.

Provide Links in a List

- Try to use a list of links instead of links embedded in the text.

  Searching a list of links rather than a paragraph with embedded links reduces the mental processing demands of online reading and link interpretation.

  Incorrect:

  The installation of the application server is affected by the following resource issues: __unique network ports__, __shared directory configuration trees__, __shared environment__, and __login__.

  Correct:

  The installation of the application server is affected by the following resource issues:

  - __Unique network ports__
  - __Shared directory configuration trees__
  - __Shared environment__
  - __Login__

- Carefully craft the link text, and annotate each link, when necessary, to ensure that readers can easily decide which links to follow.

Place Links at the End of a Topic

To encourage readers to stay with a topic, place links at the end of a topic, when possible. Readers might read all or at least some of the content before moving on.

In the following incorrect example, the link text falls in the middle of the paragraph. In the correct example, the link text falls at the end of the topic.

Incorrect:

You can install the application server by using `setup.exe` or `ezSetup.exe`. The ezSetup method provides an easy installation without requiring various inputs. For more information, see __Using ezSetup__. However, this section covers the `setup.exe` installation options: Express, Typical, and Custom installations. The Typical option is the default.

Correct:

You can install the application server by using `setup.exe` or `ezSetup.exe`. This section covers the `setup.exe` installation options: Express, Typical, and Custom installations. The Typical option is the default.

For an installation that does not require various inputs, use the __ezSetup method__.

Provide URLs Only When Needed

Use URLs in the following instances:

- When readers are likely to print the page and then later retype a URL on that page in a web browser
- When your online document is also available in print
- When your goal is to raise awareness of a site

  Reserve this usage for short URLs only, because readers are unlikely to remember long URLs.

Make references to URLs as simple and as direct as possible. For suggestions on how to introduce URLs in text, see "Referencing URLs" on page 228.

Test the Validity of Links

Testing the validity of links ensures that links in your document lead where they promise. Test the validity of both internal and external links.

Guidelines for Writing Link Text

When writing link text, apply these guidelines:

- Provide context in link text and surrounding text.
- Weave link text into sentence structure.
- Choose key words or phrases for link text.
- Choose an appropriate length for link text.
- Write scannable link text.
- Make link text conceptually similar to titles or headings of link destinations.
- Do not use quotation marks around link text.

Provide Context in Link Text and Surrounding Text

Readers use links as guideposts when scanning, so take full advantage of them and word your link text accordingly. Effective link text also creates adequate context for readers and reduces the likelihood of readers becoming disoriented.

- Choose your link text carefully, as well as the text that surrounds the link text.
- If possible, supply explanatory text before the descriptive link.

    This additional information helps readers understand where each link leads and why it was chosen.

    Incorrect:

    __Appendix F__ identifies the system components.

    Correct:

    For a list of the Plirg 5763 system components, see __Appendix F, Illustrated Parts Breakdown__.

    Incorrect:

    The combination of hypertext and the global Internet started a revolution. In __this article__, published in *Scientific American,* Jon Bosak and Tim Bray tell how a new tool, XML, is poised to finish the job.

    Correct:

    The combination of hypertext and the global Internet started a revolution. Jon Bosak and Tim Bray tell how a new tool, XML, is poised to finish the job. See the *Scientific American* article, __XML and the Second-Generation Web__.

Weave Link Text Into Sentence Structure

- Make the text of the link meaningful and part of the natural syntax of the sentence.
- Do not make the link text refer to the mechanism of the online display tool, as in "click here" or "go here."

    One exception is when readers need to see the URL of a web document. See "Provide URLs Only When Needed" on page 109.

    Incorrect: __Click here__ for more information about Plirg File Manager.

    Correct: For more information, see __Plirg File Manager__.

Note that using a list of links is almost always preferable to embedding links in the text. Placing links at the end of a topic is also preferable.

Choose Key Words or Phrases for Link Text

Choose key words or phrases in text that best represent the content of the destination.

Incorrect:

1. __How do you__ set Netscape™ Messenger to use the POP protocol?
2. __What are__ known problems with the Netscape Communicator for Plirg products?
3. __Netscape Communicator 4.*x* Frequently Asked Questions__

In the correct example, the wording of the third question in this example has changed. The reworded text removes the long, unbroken line of link text and presents two different link destinations. Readers now have two link choices instead of one.

Correct:

1. How do you __set Netscape™ Messenger to use the POP protocol__?
2. What are known __problems with the Netscape Communicator__ for Plirg products?
3. __Netscape Communicator 4.*x* Frequently Asked Questions__ from Netscape's site _help.netscape.com_

Choose an Appropriate Length for Link Text

A link that is the length of a complete sentence is too long and difficult to read. One to three words usually works best, as long as those words are context-rich. Using more words is acceptable if they provide helpful context.

Incorrect:

Plirg 5763 System:

- __Plirg 5763 Installation Guide (Download)__
- __Plirg 5763 Maintenance Manual (Download)__
- __Plirg 5763 Parts List (Download)__

Correct:

For the Plirg 5763 system, you can download the following information:

- __Installation Guide__
- __Maintenance Manual__
- __Parts List__

Write Scannable Link Text

Write links as though your reader were scanning only the links on the page. As the eye processes a page, it jumps to the links, so make them self-explanatory and scannable.

Incorrect:

There will be a moderated online chat on the PlirgSoft API for XML Parsing (PAXP) on Tuesday, April 25, at 11:00 a.m. Pacific Daylight Time. The guests are Wallace Gromit, Plirg architect–XML technologies, and XML parser guru Laurel Hardy. To join the chat, go __here__.

Correct:

Join the __online chat__ on PlirgSoft API for XML Parsing (PAXP) on Tuesday, April 25, at 11:00 a.m. Pacific Daylight Time.

The guests are as follows:

- Wallace Gromit, Plirg architect in XML technologies
- Laurel Hardy, XML parser guru

Make Link Text Conceptually Similar to Titles or Headings

Check that the text of all or most of the links in a topic are conceptually similar to the title or headings of their associated link destination.

Also, use consistent wording for link text that leads to the same link destination, if possible. For example, if you have a __Feedback Form__ link at the top of your multipage document, do not use the link text __feedback page__ elsewhere in the same document.

Do Not Use Quotation Marks Around Link Text

Quotation marks around link text unnecessarily clutter the text.

Incorrect: See "_Knowledge Management Center_."

Correct: See _Knowledge Management Center_.

CHAPTER 6

Writing Tasks, Procedures, and Steps

The purpose of many technical documents is to explain how to use a product to accomplish specific tasks. In such documents, detailed instructions on how to accomplish tasks are often provided in the form of procedures and steps.

This chapter discusses the following topics:

- "Understanding the Relationship Among Tasks, Procedures, and Steps" on page 115
- "Developing Task Information" on page 116
- "Writing Procedures" on page 123
- "Writing Steps" on page 127

Note – This chapter mainly discusses how to write procedures for software documentation. Some information about writing hardware procedures also appears.

Understanding the Relationship Among Tasks, Procedures, and Steps

This chapter uses these task-related terms as follows:

- **Task.** An overall topic of what specific work is to be done and why the work needs to be done. A task includes instructions for completing the work. A task also can include prerequisites and examples.

  A task can be short and simple, even just one action to complete. A task can also be long and complex. A long, complex task might need to be broken up for greater user understanding.

- **Subtask.** A small, short component of a larger task. A subtask might be one action or one set of actions to complete. A subtask can include prerequisites and examples. If a subtask is long and complex, that subtask can also contain subtasks.

  To complete a task, a user might need to complete or choose from multiple subtasks. Some subtasks might be *optional* or *conditional*. Such tasks might not always have to be completed, depending on the user's situation or the desired outcome. Make certain that you clearly identify any optional or conditional subtasks as being alternatives.

- **Procedure.** One step or an ordered set of steps that explains how to accomplish a task or subtask. If a task or subtask is not complex, the task or subtask might be just one action.

  A procedure can be optional or conditional. A procedure also can include prerequisites and examples.

- **Step.** An instruction that explains how to perform a procedure or part of a procedure. A short, simple procedure might require only one step. Two or more steps are ordered and are numbered to show the sequence of actions.

  A step can be optional or conditional. A step also can include prerequisites and examples.

A short task, such as backing up a system, might require performing one simple procedure. In such instances, you might not use all of the guidelines in this chapter.

Developing Task Information

A task is work that needs to be done for a particular purpose. If a task does not correspond to a sequence of steps that are performed in real time, it can still be presented as task oriented. An application programming interface (API) task is one example of a task that is presented in a way other than as a procedure.

Task orientation is useful for all technologies. Task orientation is as important for a developer's guide as it is for a user's guide or an administrator's guide. When identifying tasks, do not become distracted by the interface. The interface, be it a graphical user interface (GUI), application programming interface, or command-line interface, is how to accomplish the task. The interface is not what needs to be done to accomplish the task.

To develop and write task information, follow these guidelines:

- Perform an audience analysis and a user task analysis.
- Provide only what is necessary to complete the task.
- Organize related, optional, and conditional tasks.
- Use continuous prose to write some task instructions.

Perform an Audience Analysis and a User Task Analysis

Before you start writing tasks, identify the audience and perform a user task analysis.

An *audience analysis* identifies the readers and the readers' skills. From the audience analysis, you can determine the amount of detail to provide in the tasks that you write.

Product managers and engineers can tell you who the audience is for a particular document. The audience might be end users, developers, or operators, for example. Subject matter experts can tell you the audience's level of experience and training.

A *user task analysis* identifies all possible uses of a product or products or what a user does with the product. A user task analysis can help you determine whether to write about one task or to divide the task into subtasks. From the user task analysis, you can determine which tasks to divide into subtasks and which tasks to group together. You can also determine whether tasks and subtasks are required, optional, or conditional. Consult with subject matter experts as needed.

Provide Only Necessary Information

When writing a task, provide only the information that is necessary to complete the task. In particular, limit any overview information to information without which the user cannot complete the task.

To provide just the relevant information, include the following information in a task:

- An explanation of what the task is
- The reasons why readers need to perform the task
- Prerequisites for performing the task
- Instructions on how to perform the task
- Examples that illustrate how to perform the task

For most tasks, the instructions on how to complete the task are in the form of a procedure. For guidelines on how to write procedures, see "Writing Procedures" on page 123.

Some tasks are not suitable for being explained as a procedure. Such tasks might not correspond to a sequence of steps that a user performs in real time. For example, tasks that are associated with an API are not suitable for being explained as a procedure. For examples of writing a task other than as a procedure, see "Use Continuous Prose" on page 122.

Including Prerequisites

Include any prerequisites that users must consider before users perform a task. The risk of users performing an action out of sequence is particularly high with online documents because users can enter a task from various points.

For a task that is written as continuous prose, place prerequisites in an introductory paragraph.

For a task that is written as procedures, follow these guidelines:

- If users must perform a prerequisite step or procedure, make the first step the prerequisite step or a cross-reference to the prerequisite procedure.

   1. If the system is not already shut down, type shutdown.

- If some readers are novice users, include a cross-reference to a basic procedure.

   1. If a web browser is not already running, start a browser.

   See "To Start a Web Browser" on page 8.

- If prerequisites apply to all procedures in one section, include the prerequisites after the section heading and before the first procedure.

Providing Examples

Consider including one or more examples whenever doing so can help readers. Do not provide an example if the task is self-evident or long and cumbersome.

A command-line example shows the commands and the resulting output. A continuous prose example shows all of the function calls and other code that are required to complete the task.

Note – Most examples in this chapter show command-line information for software procedures.

When providing an example, follow these guidelines:

- If the example requires clarification, include text with the example.
- Keep the example short, showing only the necessary elements.

   If output is lengthy or used only for verification, show just the first lines, last lines, and pertinent intervening lines. Use vertical ellipsis points to indicate any missing lines that readers do not need to see.

For example:

```
$ eject -n
 .
 .
 .
rmdisk0 -> /vol/dev/rdsk/c4t0d0/clik40     (Generic USB storage)
cdrom0 -> /vol/dev/rdsk/c0t6d0/audio_cd    (Generic CD device)
zip1 -> /vol/dev/rdsk/c2t0d0/fat32         (USB Zip device)
zip0 -> /vol/dev/rdsk/c1t0d0/zip100        (USB Zip device)
jaz0 -> /vol/dev/rdsk/c3t0d0/jaz1gb        (USB Jaz device)
```

The following example shows how you could provide an example in a procedure.

EXAMPLE 6–1 Installing the Driver Package (Example of Procedure)

After you download the SUNWdrvr.tar.Z package to the tmp directory, install the driver:

```
$ cd tmp
$ uncompress SUNWdrvr.tar.Z
$ tar xf SUNWdrvr.tar
$ su
Password:
# ./install.drvr
```

Note – Be careful when providing examples of code or screen captures. Make sure that each name that you use for a URL, computer, IP address, and network domain can be made public. See "Protecting Information That Appears in Examples" on page 167 for details.

Organize Related, Optional, and Conditional Tasks

Consider including jump lists, task maps, or flow diagrams in a document to help readers understand the organization of tasks. The tasks can be related, optional, and conditional, as explained here:

- **Jump lists.** Use jump lists if you want to provide cross-references to simple, related tasks.
- **Task maps.** Use task maps if you want to provide a tabular summary of related, optional, and conditional tasks.
- **Flow diagrams.** Use flow diagrams if you want to provide a graphical representation of related, optional, and conditional tasks.

Using Jump Lists to Organize Tasks

A *jump list* is a bulleted list of cross-references that serves as a table of contents for a chapter or section of a document. By using a jump list, readers can quickly go to a particular task within the list of related tasks.

See "Writing Jump Lists" on page 41 for information about constructing a jump list.

Using Task Maps to Organize Tasks

A *task map* organizes tasks in tabular format. A task map lists the subtasks that relate to an overall task. A task map also points to instructions for completing those tasks. When writing a task map, do not provide step-by-step instructions.

To create a task map, follow these guidelines:

- Provide a brief introduction to the task map.

  If users must perform the tasks in a specific order, say so. You can also cross-reference related overview or supplementary information.

- If users are to perform the tasks in sequential order, number the individual tasks.

- Identify any optional and conditional tasks that appear in a task map for sequential tasks.

  For an example of an optional task and a conditional task, see Task 3 and Task 5, respectively, in the example that follows.

- Cross-reference each task to its related instructions.

  The cross-reference is usually to a book, chapter, or section.

EXAMPLE 6–2 Task Map

The following table shows a task map for setting up a custom QuickStart installation. Perform the tasks in sequential order.

Task	Description	For Instructions
1. Make sure that the system is supported.	Check the hardware documentation to see if the system is supported.	*PlirgSoft Hardware Platform Guide*
2. Make sure that the system has enough disk space for the PlirgSoft software. Also, consider the disk space requirements for any additional third-party software you might want to install.	Determine which software group to install. The disk space must accommodate a minimum of five file systems. (Optional) Check that the disk space for third-party software is adequate.	Chapter 2, "Planning Disk Space"
3. (Optional) Preconfigure system installation information.	Use the `plgconfig` file or the name service to preconfigure installation information, for example, the `locale`. Then, you are not prompted to supply that information during the installation.	"To Preconfigure System Installation Information" on page 26
4. Prepare the system for a custom QuickStart installation.	Create a QuickStart directory. Creation involves doing the following: ■ Adding rules to the `rules` file ■ Creating a profile for every rule ■ Testing the profiles ■ Validating the `rules` file	Chapter 6, "Preparing Custom QuickStart Installations"
5. *For network installations only.* Set up the system to install the software over the network.	To install from a remote CD image, set up the system to boot. Install the software from an install server or a boot server.	Chapter 9, "Preparing to Install PlirgSoft Software Over the Network"

Using Flow Diagrams to Organize Tasks

A *flow diagram* organizes related, optional, and conditional tasks in a graphical format. If a task is complex and requires a high-level overview, you can use a flow diagram to lead readers through the task. A flow diagram can also provide cross-references to instructions for completing each task or subtask.

To find more information about flow diagrams and to view an example, see "Organize Text by Flow Diagram" on page 88.

Use Continuous Prose

If a task is not suitable for being explained in a procedure, use continuous prose to write the instructions. The following two examples show task-oriented material that is written as continuous prose.

EXAMPLE 6–3 Task Written as Continuous Prose

8.4.1 Verifying the Result of an Asynchronous Operation

To enable your application to perform different actions depending on whether an asynchronous operation succeeds, verify the result of the operation. For example, verify the result of an asynchronous operation to notify the user or to perform another recovery action if the operation fails.

To verify the result of an asynchronous operation, call the get_except function of the Waiter class.

The get_except function returns one of the following values:

- If the operation failed, get_except returns a pointer to an instance of the ExceptionType class. This instance provides information on why the operation failed.

- If the operation succeeded, get_except returns NULL.

EXAMPLE 6–4 Another Task Written as Continuous Prose

12.3.1 Activating Access Control

Access control is set active or inactive during installation. If you want to enforce access control in your application, make sure that access control is active.

To determine whether access control is active, call the get_access_control_switch function of the ACAccessControlRules class.

EXAMPLE 6–4 Another Task Written as Continuous Prose *(Continued)*

To activate access control, call the `set_access_control_switch` function of the `ACAccessControlRules` class. In the call to `set_access_control_switch`, specify the access control switch status as `emAccessControlOn`.

To deactivate access control, call the `set_access_control_switch` function of the `ACAccessControlRules` class, specifying the access control switch status as `emAccessControlOff`.

Writing Procedures

A procedure is usually an ordered set of steps. However, a procedure can include only one step. A procedure can include prerequisites. A procedure can also be preceded by explanatory text or by cross-references to overview or supplementary information.

A procedure can also be followed by one or more examples and pointers to the next procedure or next topic that needs to be addressed.

To write effective procedures, follow these guidelines:

- Write procedures that are easy to follow.
- Place procedures appropriately.
- Use procedure headings appropriately.
- Use one method to describe how to perform steps in a single procedure.

Write Procedures That Are Easy to Follow

To help readers understand and follow procedural content, use these guidelines when writing procedures:

- Try to write no more than 10 steps for each procedure.

  If a procedure is a long, single series of steps, the procedure might be too complex. If a procedure is too long, review the user task analysis to see whether you can divide the task into two or more smaller procedures.

  For online documents, try to write no more than five steps for each procedure. Be sure to read Chapter 4 if you are writing a document for online use.

  Do not break up a long procedure if you cannot logically divide the steps. Do not take users out of a procedure, and then back into the procedure, just to meet the recommended number of steps.

- Do not number single-step procedures.

- Include any prerequisite steps or procedures.

  See "Including Prerequisites" on page 118 for details.

- Provide explanatory text and visual cues.

  Tell readers what is to happen after each step. For example, if a window opens as a result of a step, state that the window opens, and refer to the window by its name.

- Include all required information.

  Readers do not like to frequently flip through pages or go to another document to find required information. In such instances, duplicate the information.

  If procedural content is common to many procedures in a task, include the procedure at the start of the task. Then, in subsequent procedures, cross-reference the common procedure.

- Do not repeat overview information or information that is not related to the task.

  Place overview information in a section or paragraphs before the procedure. Cross-reference any related, detailed supplementary information that supports the procedure.

- After the procedure, add one or more examples if doing so can help readers.

  For information about including examples, see "Providing Examples" on page 118. Then, consider pointing readers to the next procedure or next topic to be addressed.

Place Procedures Appropriately

To place procedures appropriately and consistently in a document structure, follow these guidelines:

- Put one or more procedures inside a section.

  Do not construct a chapter that contains only procedure headings and no section headings.

  Place any explanatory text or overview information that relates to one or more procedures under a section heading. If procedures require such information, the hierarchy contains the following elements:

  1. A section heading
  2. Explanatory text
  3. The procedure heading
  4. The steps
  5. Another procedure heading
  6. The steps

Generally, steps follow a procedure heading. If the procedure requires context, insert the text between the procedure heading and the first step. To introduce the steps, use one of these constructions:

- Full paragraph
- Complete sentence that ends with a period
- Complete sentence that ends with a colon

- Put procedures under a first-level section or a second-level section, not a third-level section.

  Place related procedures at the same level.

  Procedures usually belong higher than a third-level section in a document's hierarchy.

- Do not nest a procedure within another procedure.

  For example, do not put second-level procedure headings under first-level procedure headings. Put second-level procedure headings under second-level section headings.

Use Procedure Headings Appropriately

Procedure headings identify single-step procedures and ordered sets of steps. Any text that includes at least one step is a procedure. When writing procedure headings, follow these guidelines:

- Identify software procedures with procedure headings that start with "To" or "How to."

  To Customize User Files
  How to Customize User Files

  If you know which infinitive phrase your readers are accustomed to seeing, use that phrase. Be sure to use the phrase consistently within the document or documentation set.

Note – Some documentation styles number each heading and begin each heading with a gerund. For example: "3.3 Initializing POST."

- Write succinct yet meaningful procedure headings.

  See "Headings" on page 32 and "Write Meaningful Headings and Subheadings" on page 96 for instructions on writing effective headings.

- Do not place a colon at the end of procedure headings.

- If you provide instructions for more than one way to perform a procedure, indicate the method (in parentheses) in procedure headings, using this wording:

  - To Install the System (Command Line)
  - To Install the System (GUI)
  - To Install the System (Web Browser)

Use One Method in a Single Procedure

If readers can perform a procedure in more than one way, only show one method in a single procedure. For example, do not mix steps that use a command-line interface with steps that use a graphical user interface (GUI) in the same procedure.

Choose one method of presentation, command-line interface or GUI, that best suits the needs of your readers and the organization of the document.

An alternative is to present each method separately. Again, consider the needs of your readers and the organization of the document. Here are some of the more common ways to present each method separately:

- Put command-line procedures in one chapter and GUI procedures in another chapter.

  Ensure that each chapter title identifies the specific method.

- Put related command-line procedures in one section and GUI procedures in another section.

  Ensure that each procedure heading identifies the specific method.

  To Start a Compilation (GUI)
  To Start a Compilation (Command Line)

- Choose the GUI method, showing pertinent screen captures of GUI windows within the procedure.

  Then, at the end of the procedure, include a command-line example that shows the same actions.

  Use screen captures as guideposts only, not as a substitute for steps. Do not overuse screen captures. Provide visual cues only as necessary, and explain what happens after each step. See "Creating Quality Screen Captures" on page 217 and "Protecting Information That Appears in Examples" on page 167 for additional information about using screen captures.

- If only one step has a command associated with it, consider adding a Note with the step that shows the command.

If you provide both GUI and command-line information, provide readers with enough information to choose one method over the other method. For example, explain that GUI procedures offer a simple interface and instant verification. Explain that command-line procedures are often preferred by users who are familiar with using code and want automation in a script.

For guidelines on writing command-line procedures, see "Write Meaningful Steps" on page 130. For guidelines on writing GUI procedures, see Chapter 12.

You can use illustrations to show how to perform hardware procedures. See Chapter 11 for illustration guidelines.

Writing Steps

When writing steps, determine what a user needs to do first, next, and last. Write clearly so that a user understands exactly what to do. To write concise steps, follow these guidelines:

- Number the steps.
- Make each step short and equivalent to one action.
- Write each step as a complete sentence in the imperative mood.
- Write meaningful steps.
- Use branching of steps appropriately.
- Review and refine steps and procedures.

Number the Steps

After you determine the correct order in which to present the steps, follow these guidelines to number the steps:

- If procedures include two or more steps, use numerals to number steps.

  Use letters for sequential substeps.

- Indicate optional steps by including the word "Optional" in parentheses.

  3. (Optional) Reboot the system.

- If users must perform different actions based on the outcome of a step, use a bulleted list to show the alternatives.

  Use letters for substeps.

  1. Determine whether you need to remove the disk drive.

  - If no, go to Step 2.
  - If yes:

    a. Gently pull back on foam piece 2.

    b. Slide the disk drive out of foam piece 2.

    c. Place the drive on the antistatic mat.

  2. Carefully lift the component from the unit.

Note – Do not number the step in a single-step procedure. If you assign a numeral "1" to a single-step procedure, readers might think that one or more steps are missing.

Make Each Step Short and Equivalent to One Action

A user can more easily follow a procedure when each step is short and explains one action. To help a user understand what to do in each step, follow these guidelines:

- Try to use no more than 20 words to write each step.

  Hyphenated terms and multiword product names count as one word.

  Incorrect:

  6. Type the email address of the recipient in the To field of the Compose window, using spaces or commas to separate multiple addresses.

  Correct:

  6. Type the recipient's email address in the To field of the Compose window.

  Use spaces or commas to separate multiple addresses.

- Keep any explanatory text as short as possible.
- Do not bury steps in a paragraph.

  Incorrect:

  Become superuser, stop the NIS server, change your files, and restart the NIS server.

  Correct:

  1. Become superuser.

  2. Stop the NIS server.

  ```
  # /etc/init.d/yp stop
  ```

  3. Make the necessary changes to your files.

  4. Restart the NIS server.

  ```
  # /etc/init.d/yp start
  ```

- Write about only one action in each step.

  Exceptions to this guideline include the following:

  - You conclude a step with "and press Return" because that keystroke is a necessary component of the step.

    However, if all steps in a procedure conclude with "and press Return," do not repeat this instruction at the end of each step. Instead, explain in introductory text to the procedure that users must press the Return key after each step. If the book contains many procedures, explain this use of the Return key in an introductory chapter or the preface.

  - You begin a step with a common instruction such as "Log in as," "Log in to," or "Become superuser," followed by another short instruction.

    However, this combination of steps depends on the audience and the subject matter. Novice users might need this type of instruction, while experienced users would not.

    For novice users, provide this level of detail:

    1. Become superuser.

    ```
    $ su
    Password:
    ```

    2. Reboot the system.

    ```
    # reboot
    ```

  For experienced users, provide general instructions:

  1. Become superuser and reboot the system.

Write Each Step as a Complete Sentence

Verbs do most of the work in instructions. Reserve participles and gerunds for lists. When writing steps, follow these guidelines:

- Write each step as a complete, correctly punctuated sentence.
- Phrase the step as an action rather than a question or statement.

  Incorrect:

  3. Do you have an account on this system?

  What you do next depends on whether you have an account on the system.

  Correct:

  3. Type your password.

  - If you have an account on this system, type your password.
  - If you do not have an account, contact your administrator.

- Ensure that each step contains an active verb in the imperative mood.

  Put the verb at the start of the step unless you are explaining why, how, or where an action takes place. You might clarify a step in order to do one of the following:

  - Qualify the verb.

    Gently lift the I/O board up and out of the unit.

  - Provide information to orient readers.

    In the Add Attachments window, click Add File.

  - State a condition.

    If the card's I/O address conflicts with another device, change the I/O address according to the manufacturer's instructions.

  - Show the desired outcome or reason for the action.

    To secure the board to the unit, tighten both screws.

  - Stress the importance or consequence of an action.

    To shut down the system, type `shutdown`.

- Do not use command names as verbs.

  Incorrect:

  3. `cd` to the new directory.

  Correct:

  3. To change to the new directory, type `cd`.

Write Meaningful Steps

To write complete steps that are effective, do the following:

- Make the task, not the command, the focus of the step.

  Follow the step immediately with command syntax, if applicable.

  Incorrect:

  3. Type `ufsrestore` and press Return.

  Correct:

  3. Verify that you successfully backed up the system.

  ```
  # ufsrestore -t
  ```

- Explain to readers why they are to skip a step or jump to a step.

  5. Determine whether you want the partition table to be the current table.

  - If you want to change the displayed partition table, type n and go to Step 3 on page 9.

  - If you want to use the current partition table, type y when prompted:

    ```
    Okay to make this the current partition table [yes] y
    ```

Use Branching of Steps Appropriately

Use branching if the action to take at a particular step in a procedure differs depending on the user's situation or desired outcome. Follow these guidelines to determine whether a step requires the use of branching:

- Use branching if the procedure is the same for many cases and only differs at one or two steps.

  2. Format the diskette.

  - To format the diskette for a UFS file system, type fdformat and press Return.

  - To format the diskette for an MS-DOS file system, type fdformat -d and press Return.

- If the branching condition applies to the whole procedure, use two different procedures.

  For example, if the procedure has several steps that provide alternatives for HTTP and FTP protocols, create two procedures. Write one procedure that shows how to accomplish the task through HTTP and the other procedure through FTP.

- If a particular condition requires a substitution in most of the steps in the procedure, provide that information in a Note.

  For example, tell readers to use the default directory if their default directory is different from the directory provided in the steps.

  Put the Note at the beginning of the procedure, not in branches of the steps.

- If a user must know certain information to determine which branch to follow, include the process by which the user can find out that information.

  Incorrect:

  3. Ensure that the .html **file is complete.**

  - If the file is complete, post the file on the internal web site.
  - If the file is not complete, see Appendix C.

Correct:

3. Use a text editor to ensure that the `.html` **file is complete.**

- If the file is complete, post the file on the internal web site.
- If the file is not complete, see Appendix C.

Do not use branching in the following instances:

- If a step is optional, do not use branching.

  Incorrect:

  6. Determine whether you want to make this printer the default printer.

  - If no, go to Step 7.
  - If yes, select Default.

  Correct:

  6. (Optional) To make this printer the default printer, select Default.

  If one branch states to proceed to the next step, you might be able to use an optional step, not a branch. However, do not use an optional step if any user needs to complete the step for the procedure to be successful.

- Do not use branching to provide all of the possible actions in a confirmation step at the end of a procedure.

  For example, many graphical user interfaces provide OK, Apply, and Cancel buttons in each dialog box. If you have described the actions of these buttons in a central location, do not repeat this information at the end of every procedure. Assume that the user wants to confirm the settings in the dialog box and just say "Click OK."

Signs of Structural Problems

Use the initial user task analysis to guide your procedure writing. As you write, you might discover that you have to further divide or combine some procedures. This section describes some signs of a possible need for restructuring.

Duplicate Sets of Steps

If two or more procedures begin with the same set of steps, consider creating a separate procedure with the shared steps. Then cross-reference to that procedure in the related procedures.

For example, suppose you have several procedures that are accomplished through a web page deep in the application's hierarchy. To describe how to get to the page requires four steps. You can create a separate procedure such as "To Access the Modify Objects Page." Then, at the beginning of each modification task, Step 1 can say, "If you are not already on the Modify Objects page, see 'To Access the Modify Objects Page' on page 8."

Nearly Identical Procedures

Look for two or more procedures that are alike except for one or two steps that require a different value or choice. Consider combining them into one procedure. Provide information in the steps that require alternative choices.

For example, a word processing application might use the same basic procedure to create generated lists such as tables of contents, lists of tables, lists of examples, and lists of figures. Rather than having separate procedures for each type of generated list, you can provide one procedure that describes how to create generated lists. Then, in the relevant steps you can provide the specific file names related to the type of list the user is creating.

See "Use Branching of Steps Appropriately" on page 131 for details.

Procedures With More Than 10 Steps

As mentioned in "Write Procedures That Are Easy to Follow" on page 123, long procedures are difficult to follow. Look for a logical place to divide the procedure.

You might want to describe the overall procedure, followed by a task map or numbered list that describes the related procedures.

Several Single-Step Procedures

The presence of many single-step procedures might indicate a few different structural problems:

- If many of the procedures describe the same basic action, you might be able to collapse the procedures.

  For example, suppose you have separate single-step procedures for opening different applications from a front panel. You might want to provide one single-step procedure with the heading "To Open an Application From the Front Panel." If necessary, provide a cross-reference from each application.

- If some of the procedures are related logically, you might be able to combine the procedures.

  For example, suppose you must add one line to a system file to set a printer resource and another line to set a scanner resource. You can provide a procedure with the heading "To Add Peripherals to the .Nresource File." The procedure contains the steps that are common to the procedures that are being combined. Then one step includes the different text lines for each peripheral.

- Examine the single-step procedures to ensure that all required steps are provided.

  For example, you might be assuming that the user is at a particular place in the GUI or has already logged in to the system.

CHAPTER 7

Writing for an International Audience

More and more business transactions and communications occur over the World Wide Web, which is an international medium. Writing documentation that can be easily translated into other languages and delivered to audiences in other countries is becoming a mandate for the computer industry. Fortunately, the guidelines that you need to follow when writing for an international audience also apply to good technical writing in general. These guidelines can help you avoid producing documentation that is inadvertently confusing or offensive.

Internationalization involves creating a "generic" document that can be used in many cultures or easily translated into many languages. *Localization* involves converting a document that is specific to a particular language or culture into one that is specific to a different language or culture.

Working closely with translators and localization experts who are based in the countries to which you are exporting is important. See "Internationalization and Localization" on page 323 in Appendix D for books on developing software and preparing documentation for the international market. See "Internationalization and Localization" on page 293 in Appendix A for management issues related to the global market.

This chapter discusses the following topics:

- "General Guidelines for Writing for Translation" on page 136
- "Cultural and Geographic Sensitivity" on page 136
- "Definitions and Word Choice" on page 138
- "Grammar and Word Usage" on page 140
- "Numbers, Symbols, and Punctuation" on page 144
- "Illustrations and Screen Captures" on page 145

General Guidelines for Writing for Translation

Following the basic guidelines for good technical writing can help you avoid producing documentation that is confusing or offensive to translation vendors or to readers from other cultures.

Follow these basic guidelines when you are preparing documentation for an international audience:

- Keep the documentation culturally neutral by avoiding elements that are difficult to translate or hard to read by people whose native language is not American English.

  These elements are explained throughout this chapter. Remember that documentation that is written in English is often distributed worldwide.

- Have your document edited, if possible, before giving it to a translation vendor.

  Many complaints from translation vendors concern basic errors in the English version of a document, such as typographical errors and inconsistent term usage.

- Be aware that text expansion can occur when a document is translated.

  A document can increase in size by up to 25 percent, which can substantially expand the breadth of a hard-copy document. Such expansion can affect the binding, packaging, and shipping constraints.

Cultural and Geographic Sensitivity

More than ever, technical writers need to think globally. Conventions that are standard in one country might be handled differently in other countries. Use the following guidelines when writing for an international audience.

Use Culturally Neutral Examples

- Avoid using examples that are culturally bound, such as names of places, public figures, or holidays that might be unrecognizable to people living in different countries.

  If you do use examples that are culturally bound, use examples that represent a variety of cultures or that are internationally recognized. For example, you could use international cities, such as Paris, New York, Tokyo, London, and Hong Kong.

- Avoid political or religious references.
- Avoid gender-specific references.

Include International Date, Time, and Contact Information

- Be aware that dates are displayed differently in different countries.
  - *Month, day, year* – Used mainly in the United States.
  - *Day, month, year* – Used in Europe.
  - *Year, month, day* – Used in Asia. This format is also used by the International Organization for Standardization (ISO) standard for numeric representation of dates.

  For clarity, write out dates. For example, write "6/28/03" as "June 28, 2003." If abbreviations are necessary, define them and then use them consistently.

- Be aware that times are displayed differently in different countries.

  Time formats that use a 12-hour clock and the *ante meridiem, post meridiem* (a.m. and p.m.) system are not universally understood. Consider using a 24-hour system or describing the time in relation to the time of day. For example, you can write "1:00 p.m." as either "13:00" or "1:00 in the afternoon."

- Ensure that address or telephone information is always complete.

  Include telephone country codes, area codes, and time zones when you provide phone numbers and calling hours in a document that might be distributed internationally. Use "+1-" before the area code for phone and fax numbers within the United States. Be aware that any toll-free telephone numbers that you provide cannot be dialed from most countries outside the United States. Do not forget to specify the time zone if your readers are from more than one time zone.

- Be careful when including information about warranties or technical support.

  Be specific as to which countries honor the warranties or have technical support available, if possible.

Avoid Informal Language and Styles

- Avoid humor.

  What might be funny in one language, whether an illustration or written text, might be obscene in another language. Humor is strictly cultural, and it cannot be translated easily from one language to another language.

- Avoid irony.

  Even native speakers of English have difficulty discerning irony in writing.

- Avoid idioms and metaphors.

  If you use a metaphor to describe an action, provide additional contextual explanation so that the translator does not misunderstand and translate the text incorrectly. If the translator is unfamiliar with the metaphor, the translator might have to guess at the meanings of key terms.

  For example, if you describe a file system hierarchy as a "tree structure," or if you describe a "parent-child" relationship, include an illustration or example. That way the translator understands that you do not mean these terms to be interpreted literally.

Definitions and Word Choice

Follow these guidelines to avoid common pitfalls that make translators and readers uncertain of your intended meaning.

Avoid Jargon and Slang

If a term is not listed in a standard dictionary or a technical source book, do not use it. If a term is specific to your company but is not defined in the text or in the glossary, do not use it. If translators cannot look up an unfamiliar term, they might have to guess at its meaning.

Use Terms Consistently

- Avoid using terms that can have several different meanings.

  For example, the word "system" can refer to an operating system (OS), a combination of OS and hardware, a networking configuration, and so on. If you do use such a term, ensure that you define it and use it consistently in a document. Ensure that you also add it to the glossary.

- Use terms consistently throughout a document.

  Synonymous terms in a document can be troublesome for a translator. The words "show," "display," and "appear" might seem similar enough to use interchangeably. However, a translator might think you used the different words deliberately for different meanings, and a translator might interpret the text incorrectly.

Other inconsistent usage with which translators might have trouble include the following:

- Down, crash
- Menu option, menu item
- Connector, port, plug
- Output, result
- Some, several, many, few
- Platform, architecture, system
- Scroll list, scrolling list, scrollable list
- Executables, executable program, executable code, executable application, executable file

- Be careful about using the word "available" because it can present difficulties to a translator with limited technical knowledge.

  Instead, use definitive words such as "active" or "valid."

- Use uppercase and lowercase letters consistently in like elements throughout a document.

  Using consistent case helps a translator determine the proper interpretation of a term. The use of consistent case is significant for reserved keywords, class names, and variables.

Avoid Abbreviations, Acronyms, and Contractions

- Avoid using abbreviations and acronyms.

  Many languages do not have abbreviations and cannot accommodate them. If you use abbreviations and acronyms in your documentation, define them the first time you use them in text. Provide a list of acronyms and abbreviations at the end of the book as part of the glossary, in an appendix, or in a separate list of abbreviations. When you define the term, give the spelled-out version first, followed by the acronym or abbreviation in parentheses.

  For example, using the initials "DT" for "directory tree," has no Japanese equivalent. Instead, use "directory tree (DT)" initially and "DT" thereafter.

- Avoid using abbreviations and acronyms in the plural form.

- Avoid using contractions such as "can't," " isn't," "don't," and "it's."

  If you do use contractions in your documentation, follow the guidelines under "Contractions" on page 4.

Grammar and Word Usage

If you adhere to English grammar guidelines and use terms correctly in your documentation, you can eliminate much of the ambiguity that slows the translation process.

Follow These Grammar Guidelines

- Ensure that spelling and word usage are correct.

  Use electronic spelling checkers and copy editors to ensure accuracy.

- Do not leave out articles such as "the," "a," and "an."

  Incorrect: Place screwdriver in groove.
  Correct: Place the screwdriver in the groove.

- Include the word "that" when it is used to introduce a restrictive clause.

  See "Differentiate Between Restrictive Clauses and Nonrestrictive Clauses" on page 68.

  Incorrect: Verify your configuration matches what is shown in the example.
  Correct: Verify that your configuration matches what is shown in the example.

- Avoid passive clauses, such as "the program was activated."

  See "Use Active Voice and Passive Voice Appropriately" on page 65.

- Do not put a list in the middle of a sentence.

  See "Introducing Lists" on page 35.

- Check for the correct placement of prepositional phrases.

  Incorrect: Remove the filler panel from the slot with the pliers.
  Correct: Use pliers to remove the filler panel from the slot.

Use Words Precisely

- Be careful about using the same term in multiple grammatical categories, such as verb, noun, and adjective.

  Incorrect: Plug the plug into the wall outlet.
  Correct: Connect the plug into the wall outlet.

Using "plug" as both a verb and a noun is confusing to translators. Translators might have to use a different term in each case. Also, do not use several terms to refer to the same thing.

- Be precise about using the words "when" and "if."

  Use "when" for an inevitable event and "if" for a conditional event.

  > "*When* the prompt is displayed" implies that the prompt will be displayed.
  >
  > "*If* the prompt is displayed" implies that the prompt might or might not be displayed.

- Avoid using the word "may" unless you mean permission, as in "you may apply for an extension if you need one."

  Use the words "might" or "can" in place of the word "may." The word "might" indicates a possibility, and "can" means the power or ability to do something. A translator who must translate the English word "may" in text often chooses whether to translate it as "can" or "might." The original writer is in a better position to know which word is more accurate and should therefore use the correct word.

- Avoid using the words "there" and "it" at the beginning of a sentence if those words take the place of the subject of the sentence and are followed by a linking verb such as "is" or "are."

  This construction delays the subject of the sentence, which can confuse translators.

  > **Incorrect:** There are only a few troubleshooting tickets left.
  > **Correct:** Only a few troubleshooting tickets are left.
  >
  > **Incorrect:** It is a simple path.
  > **Correct:** The path is simple.

- Avoid ambiguous phrases.

  For example, "first-come, first-served" is ambiguous. If possible, rewrite as "in the order received" or "in the order in which they are received."

Use Modifiers and Nouns Carefully

- Be careful with compound modifiers.

  Compound modifiers can be hard to understand and to properly translate. You might need to rewrite the sentence or hyphenate the phrase, for example, "real time-saver," "real-time operation." See "Hyphen" on page 23 for guidelines for hyphenating terms.

- Avoid using general modifiers that might be interpreted in several ways.

  The translation of a term with multiple meanings requires the ability to discern the appropriate equivalent in the target language, based on the context. However, most translators do not have as much technical knowledge as engineers, and they might translate questionable terms incorrectly.

  For example, the following sentence presents a difficult translation:

  > The PlirgSoft GUI is an advanced Motif-based desktop with an easy-to-use interface that provides a consistent look and feel across software platforms.

The phrase "advanced Motif-based desktop" raises questions for a translator such as is it "a desktop that is based on advanced Motif" or is it "an advanced desktop that is based on Motif"? The sentence could be rewritten as follows:

> The PlirgSoft GUI is an advanced desktop system that is based on Motif. This system provides an easy-to-use interface that is consistent across software platforms.

- Do not use noun clusters of more than three nouns.

  Try to clarify noun clusters by using prepositions such as "of" or "for. "

  Incorrect:

  In certain situations, the certificate chain verification process is disabled.

  Correct:

  In certain situations, the verification process for the certificate chain is disabled.

  An exception is a noun string that results when you use a three-word product name as a modifier. A product name that you use as a modifier counts as one word.

- Repeat the modifier in noun phrases that are joined or are linked together.

  Incorrect: You must set up a mail service on a new network or subnet.
  Correct: You must set up a mail service on a new network or new subnet.

- Repeat the main noun in conjoined noun phrases.

  Incorrect: You can access a new or existing network.
  Correct: You can access a new network or an existing network.

Limit the Use of Pronouns

- Avoid vague and uncertain references between a pronoun and its antecedent.

  A pronoun that forces a reader to search for an antecedent can frustrate or mislead the reader, as well as a translator. Ensure that the noun to which the pronoun refers is clear.

- Do not use the following words as pronouns:

All	Either	None	Some
Another	Few	One	Several
Any	Many	Other	
Each	Neither	Own	

When these words are used as pronouns, their antecedent is unclear.

Incorrect:

These macros classify character-coded integer values. Each is a predicate that returns nonzero for true, 0 for false.

Correct:

These macros classify character-coded integer values. Each macro is a predicate that returns nonzero for true, 0 for false.

Incorrect:

Custom layout managers. To provide custom behavior that ensures the best GUI performance, write your own.

Correct:

Custom layout managers. To provide custom behavior that ensures the best GUI performance, write your own custom layout managers.

- Avoid using pronouns, such as "it," "its," "this," "they," "theirs," "that," "these," and "those," especially at the beginning of a sentence.

Use these pronouns only when the noun to which the pronoun refers is clear.

> **Unclear:** This provides the following benefits.
> **Clear:** This support provides the following benefits.

Simplify Sentences

Divide sentences that contain more than two uses of the words "or" or "and."

Incorrect:

The software consists of four daemon processes that coordinate the scheduling, dispatch, and execution of batch jobs and monitor job and machine status, report on the system, and manage communication among the components.

Correct:

The software consists of four daemon processes. These processes perform the following functions:

- Schedule, dispatch, and execute batch jobs
- Monitor job and machine status
- Report system status
- Manage communication among the components

Numbers, Symbols, and Punctuation

Follow these guidelines to minimize confusion about the numbers and symbols in your documentation.

Clarify Measurements and Denominations

Most of the world uses the metric system, although many people in the United States are familiar only with the U.S. equivalents for the metric system. Also, number and currency formats vary worldwide. In many countries, commas and decimal points are used differently. As a courtesy to readers who use different numeric systems, follow these guidelines:

- When providing U.S. measurements, include the metric equivalent in parentheses if it is appropriate for the product you are describing.

  Most standard American English dictionaries contain a U.S.-to-metric conversion chart under the "metric" entry.

- If you use the word "billion" or "trillion," explain the word in a footnote so that the exact value is clear to readers in all countries.

- If you are specifying prices, indicate the currency used.

  For example, write "USD" for United States dollars and "EUR" for the European euro.

Avoid Certain Symbols and Punctuation Marks

- Do not use these symbols:

  - The # symbol to indicate "pound" or "number"
  - A single quote (') to indicate "foot"
  - Double quotes (") to indicate "inch"

  These symbols are not recognized in many countries outside the United States.

- Avoid using symbols such as "/" and "&" in text.

  Many symbols have multiple meanings, and translators might have difficulty deciding which meaning you intended. For example, the "/" symbol can mean "and," "or," "and/or," "with," "divide by," "root," or "path-name divider."

  See "Slash" on page 30 for acceptable uses of the "/" symbol.

Illustrations and Screen Captures

Follow these pointers to maximize the international appeal and comprehension of illustrations and screen captures.

Choose Illustrations to Communicate Internationally

- Use illustrations instead of text whenever possible to convey a complex concept.

  Ensure that the accompanying text complements the message conveyed by the illustration.

- Do not insert an illustration into the middle of a sentence.

  See "Placement in Relation to Sentences" on page 211.

- Remember that not everyone reads from left to right. If necessary, indicate the intended sequence that you want a reader to follow in the illustration, as shown in the following example.

EXAMPLE 7-1 Intended Reading Sequence in an Illustration

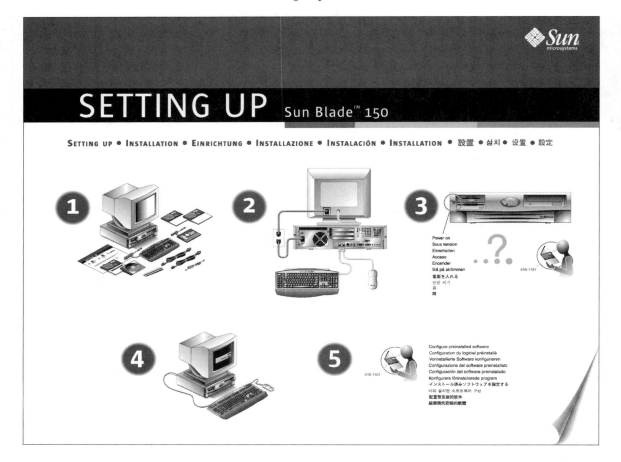

- Use illustrations that are internationally acceptable.

  For example, almost every country has its own type of power connector. Instead of illustrating each type of connector, use generic connectors and receptacles, as in the following illustration.

EXAMPLE 7–2 Illustration of Internationally Generic Connectors and Receptacles

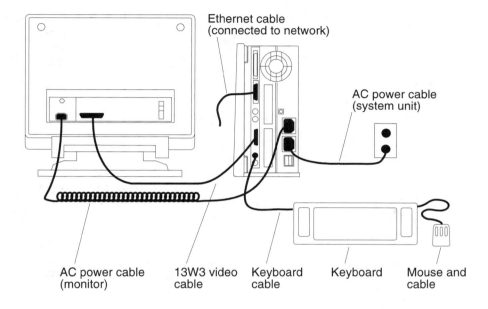

However, when describing various types of connectors and receptacles, illustrate and label the specific type used in each country, as in the following example.

EXAMPLE 7–3 Illustration of Internationally Specific Connectors and Receptacles

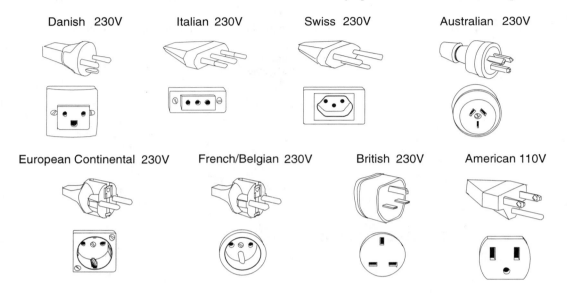

Danish 230V   Italian 230V   Swiss 230V   Australian 230V

European Continental 230V   French/Belgian 230V   British 230V   American 110V

Create Callouts That Are Easy to Translate

A *callout* is a text element that defines a portion of an illustration or provides the reader with additional information about an illustration. When you create callouts in documentation that will be localized, follow these guidelines:

- Keep callouts short.

  Leave ample space, both vertically and horizontally, for callout text in illustrations.

  Translated text might require as much as 25 percent more space than English text.

- Make certain that the callouts correlate with the paragraph text.

  Use callouts instead of text if the concept can best be understood graphically and needs little explanation.

- Format callouts so that you can edit them separately from the illustration.

For more guidelines about creating callouts, see Chapter 11.

Use Charts and Tables

- Use charts and tables to clarify essential information.

  Charts and tables are internationally recognized by readers as containing important material.

- When formatting charts and tables, be aware that text can expand by up to 25 percent during translation.

- Do not insert a table into the middle of a sentence.

  See "Writing Text for Tables" on page 42.

- Do not use sentence fragments for table column headings.

  Incorrect:

If the user asks...	Then you must respond by...
How do I do this?	Showing the user how to perform the task.

  Correct:

User Questions	Answers
How do I do this?	Show the user how to perform the task.

Use International Illustrations, Symbols, and Examples

- Do not use a hand in a symbolic gesture.

  Almost any way that you position a hand can be considered an offensive gesture, depending on the culture, as shown in the following illustration.

EXAMPLE 7–4 Illustration of Possibly Obscene Gestures

- When using code examples or showing screen captures, make sure that the machine names, login names, and system names are not culturally offensive.

  Instead of:

  ```
  heavenly%
  ```

  Use a culturally neutral example:

  ```
  system1%
  ```

- Avoid using road signs in illustrations because they differ from country to country.
- Avoid illustrations that relate to alcohol or alcohol-related material, because those types of illustrations might be offensive.
- Be careful when using everyday objects in examples.

  Be certain that the object exists in most countries. Be aware that the object might be interpreted in various ways in different parts of the world.

  For example, you can use a light bulb to indicate light, but not the concept of an inspiration.

- Avoid using trendy objects, historical references, or film, cartoon, or video characters.
- Avoid using animals, because they might carry symbolic significance.

  For example, some web pages use a dog to indicate a "fetch" function. While this connection might be clear to readers from Western cultures, it might not be understood by readers from other cultures. Dogs are not kept as pets or used for hunting and retrieving in all cultures.

- Do not use color to convey meaning.

  Color communicates different meanings in different cultures. For example, the color green is sometimes used to indicate paper money in the United States. However, the color green does not work in many other countries where money is not green. The color red can signify "stop" or "danger" in the United States. But in China, the color red can indicate happiness, and in France, red can denote aristocracy.

CHAPTER 8

Legal Guidelines

Technical publications professionals need to follow legal guidelines that cover the proper use and marking of trademarks and the protection of intellectual property. Trademarks, copyrighted works, and trade secrets are among a company's most valuable assets. Everyone who is involved in the preparation of materials that use trademarks or who creates materials subject to copyright has a responsibility for securing and protecting the copyrights and trademarks.

This chapter explains how to use and designate corporate trademarks. This chapter also explains how to protect your company's intellectual property and trade secrets. The topics in this chapter include:

- "Copyrights" on page 152
- "Trademarks" on page 155
- "Third-Party Web Site References" on page 162
- "Protection of Proprietary/Confidential Information" on page 165

Note – In this chapter, the term "trademark" refers to a company's master brand and family brands, including associated logos, marks, and other designations. These brands, logos, marks, and other designations are used to identify a company's products and services.

When you see the term "registered trademark" or "service mark," information is specific to that type of trademark.

This chapter sometimes advises you to check with the legal department in your company. If you do not have a legal department, check with counsel specializing in trademark and copyright law. The Kuestler Law Web site at `http://www.kuestlerlaw.com` provides information in this area, plus links to many U.S. and international Web sites relevant to these issues.

Copyrights

This section provides the following information about copyrights:

- General copyright information
- Works that must be copyrighted
- Copyright notice
- Third-party copyrighted information

If you have copyright questions that are not addressed in this section, you might want to consult the Web site of the United States Copyright Office at `http://www.loc.gov/copyright/`.

General Copyright Information

Copyright is a set of distinct rights granted by federal law for most literary, musical, dramatic, and other types of intellectual works, including computer programs. U.S. copyright laws establish a single system of protection for all published and unpublished "original works of authorship fixed in any tangible medium of expression from which they can be perceived, reproduced, or otherwise communicated." With limited exceptions, no one may copy or reproduce, display, prepare derivative works, or distribute copies of copyrighted works to the public by sale, rental, lease, lending, or other transfer of ownership without permission of the copyright owner.

While no universal international copyright protection exists, United States copyrighted works might be protected in foreign countries under various treaties and conventions.

This section discusses these copyright topics:

- Copyright duration
- Copyright registration
- Copyright compared with a trade secret

Copyright Duration

A copyright, unlike a trademark or patent, exists from the time of the creation of a work. For copyright purposes, a work is *created* when the work is fixed in a tangible medium of expression. For example, a chapter that you write becomes protected by copyright law the moment that you save the chapter to a file.

Even though a copyright notice is not required for a copyright to exist, certain legal benefits accrue when the notice appears on the work.

A copyright exists for a finite number of years, generally the lifetime of the author plus 50 years. If the work is done as a work for hire for an employer, the copyright exists for 75 years from the date of publication. After that time, the work becomes part of the public domain.

Copyright Registration

Registering a copyright is not necessary for copyright ownership, but registration takes full advantage of the legal protection afforded copyrighted works.

To register a work, you must submit a copyright registration application to the United States Copyright Office. A copy of the work should be included as deposit. In the case of software, a portion of the source code is included. The material usually consists of the first and last 25 pages, with portions of the material blocked out to protect trade secret information.

The following acts can usually only occur if a copyrighted work is registered:

- Filing an infringement action
- Obtaining statutory damages
- Obtaining attorney's fees
- Enlisting the United States Customs Service to bar the importation of illegal copies of the registered work

A federally registered copyright also gives the registrant various procedural advantages should the registrant want to take action against an infringer.

Copyright Compared With a Trade Secret

Copyright does not protect the ideas and concepts contained in a work, but only the expression of such ideas and concepts. Thus, copyright is not always the best single means of protection for material that contains valuable information that can be exploited.

Confidential business information and information that pertains to potential patent opportunity or application are usually best protected as *trade secrets*.

To safeguard a trade secret, appropriately classify the information. Be sure to include the corresponding proprietary label. Restrict disclosure to third parties. For information about how to protect proprietary and confidential information, see "Protection of Proprietary/Confidential Information" on page 165.

What Should You Copyright?

The following works that are intended for distribution outside your company could benefit from a copyright notice:

- Publications such as books, articles, white papers, and brochures
- Advertising copy and news releases
- Photographs
- Catalogs
- Online documents, including pages on the Web
- Product labels
- Product documentation
- Software applications
- Source code and binary code for software products
- Source documents for which the source is distributed or published

You typically include a copyright notice with any documents or artwork intended for public distribution. If you do not know whether a copyright notice is appropriate for a particular type of work, check with your legal counsel.

Copyright Notice

A work that is suitable for copyright protection should contain a proper copyright notice. A copyright notice consists of the following elements:

- The word "Copyright"

  Do not use (c) or (C) to mean copyright.

  If space is very tight and the text is not being converted into ASCII, you can use the symbol ©.

- The year of first publication of the work

- The name of the owner of the copyright

Your legal department might have a specifically approved copyright statement. The copyright portion of this statement should not be modified (except for the date) without consulting your legal department. The following example is a typical copyright notice.

© 2003 PlirgSoft, Inc., 1854 Hayovel Street, Mountain View, California 94043–1100 U.S.A.

All rights reserved. This product and related documentation are protected by copyright and are distributed under licenses restricting their use, copying, distribution, and decompilation. No part of this product or related documentation may be reproduced in any form by any means without prior written authorization of PlirgSoft, Inc., and its licensors, if any.

Copyright Date for a Revised Document

A previously copyrighted document that is recast, transformed, or adapted is considered a "derivative work" for purposes of copyright. For example, a document is a derivative work if you add a new section, chapter, or appendix.

If a document is a derivative work, change the date in the copyright notice to the date that applies to the created derivative work. Your legal counsel might require the inclusion of the earlier dates in a copyright notice for a derivative work.

A document is not a derivative work if the material contains the following types of changes:

- Fixing of incorrect spelling or style errors
- Changing of the chapter order
- Application of new templates

If a document is not a derivative work, use the original copyright date. Do not change the copyright date or add other dates.

Third-Party Copyrighted Information

If you are using third-party copyrighted material, follow these guidelines:

- If you are paraphrasing information from other publications, use a regular citation, such as a footnote.

  You do not need to obtain permission from the information source.

  "Endnotes, Footnotes, and Bibliographies" on page 49 explains how to cite information from other sources.

- If you are reproducing exact tables or exact graphs or are using several paragraphs verbatim, you *must* obtain permission from the information source.

  Contact your legal counsel for details.

Trademarks

The scope and strength of a company's exclusive rights in its trademarks are weakened when the trademarks are not used properly. This precept applies even when the trademarks are registered. A number of well-known names, such as "escalator," "aspirin," and "cellophane," were once trademarks. Because these names have fallen into common usage, the terms are now generic and can be used by anyone.

For more information in this area, you might want to consult the Web site of the United States Patent and Trademark Office at http://www.uspto.gov/.

Trademark Terms

The following terms are associated with trademarks and are defined as follows:

- **Trademark.** A word, phrase, name, symbol, logo, sound, color, smell, or combination of these elements that are used by a company to identify its particular *brand* of products

  Trademarks fall into two major categories:

  - Trademarks that have been *registered* with the United States Patent and Trademark Office and the trademark offices of other countries
  - Trademarks that are claimed by a company but have *not* been registered

  Both types of trademarks can be protected in the United States and some foreign countries. Registered trademarks, however, are subject to stronger enforcement measures. Registered trademarks might be required in certain countries to prevent other parties from "pirating" a company's trademarks. In some cases, a trademark dispute could disrupt shipments of a company's products.

- **Service mark.** Similar to a trademark except that a service mark is used in connection with the provision of a service

  A service mark usually appears in advertising and collateral material for the service and is used within the same general guidelines as trademarks. See "Proper Use of Trademarks" on page 157 and "Trademarks and Appropriate Nouns" on page 159.

- **Appropriate noun.** A noun that characterizes a product, technology, service, or program offered by a company

  For examples of how to use appropriate nouns, see "Trademarks and Appropriate Nouns" on page 159.

- **Trademark attribution.** A ™ or ℠ or ® symbol that appears after a trademark in text, and an entry in a trademark legend that states what company owns the trademark

- **Trademark legend.** Trademark attributions, without trademark symbols, for all trademarks that are marked in a particular document

- **Trade name.** The name of a company, or its abbreviation, under which the company conducts business

  Do not place a trademark symbol after a trade name. Some trade names, though, are also used as trademarks. For example, Sun is the trade name of a company (Sun Microsystems, Inc.) but Sun™ is also the trademark for that company's line of products. Whether to use the ™ designation depends upon the particular reference being made. Make sure that trade names that are also trademarks are used correctly. Trade names refer to companies, while trademarks distinguish the products and services that companies provide.

Proper Use of Trademarks

To protect trademarks, you must have an understanding of the following topics:

- Trademark symbols
- Trademark symbol placement
- Trademark usage
- Trademarks and appropriate nouns

Trademark Symbols

The guidelines in this section pertain to print documentation. If you work solely on web pages, determine which of the following guidelines are applicable to your work and use the guidelines accordingly.

Follow these guidelines when using trademark symbols:

- Use the appropriate symbol (^{TM} or ^{SM} or $^{®}$).

  If your authoring environment does not include one or more of these symbols, do the following:

  - Type TM or SM or R.
  - Apply the superscript character format.
  - Lower the point size, if necessary and as authoring tools permit.
  - Try to match the point size to the size of any related symbols.

    If your authoring environment does not contain superscript capabilities, enclose the TM, SM, or R in parentheses, for example, "Plirg(TM) workstation."

Trademark Symbol Placement

The guidelines in this section pertain to print documentation. If you work solely on web pages, determine which of the following guidelines are applicable to your work and use the guidelines accordingly.

Follow these guidelines to ensure the correct placement of trademark symbols:

- Most publications use the appropriate symbol to designate a trademark at the first occurrence and most prominent use of the trademark:

  - On book spines and book covers
  - On title pages, in chapter titles and appendix titles, and in headings, depending on your documentation group

    Because documentation groups use various authoring tools and publishing methods, check with your group for guidelines about using trademark symbols in titles and headings.

- In text

   The first occurrence in text can be in the preface, a chapter, an appendix, or similar text element. If a document is lengthy, however, repeat the symbol in any chapter or other text element that contains many occurrences of the trademark.

Note – Do not place a symbol after a trademark in captions, tables, figures, footnotes, or trademark legends.

- On web pages, in the place where readers are most likely to look on the web site

   Use good judgment when adding a symbol at the first occurrence and most prominent use of a trademark. For example, readers might not read a preface or other introductory text where a symbol is likely to first appear. Repeat the symbol in a section that readers are more likely to see.

- If the same trademark appears in a document in two or more product names, only mark the trademark at the first occurrence in text.

   For example, "The Plirg™ 5763 server, the Plirg 5618 server, and the Plirg 5600 server were delivered to the customer today." Even though the Plirg trademark appears three times, only mark the first occurrence of the trademark.

- If a trademark and service mark have the same name and both types of marks appear in the same document, one mark takes precedence.

   Only use the appropriate symbol at the most prominent use and the first occurrence of the trademark *or* service mark in text.

   For example, "Plirg offers the PlirgSoft^{SM} Manager Central service with the PlirgSoft operating environment." In this instance, "PlirgSoft" is used first as a service mark. Thus, you do not have to use the trademark symbol when PlirgSoft is used as a trademark in the same document. However, try to do the following:

   - If the document primarily describes a product, write so that the ™ symbol is prominent and appears first.

   - If the document primarily describes a service, write so that the SM symbol is prominent and appears first.

Trademark Usage

To ensure that trademarks are used correctly, follow these guidelines:

■ Use trademarks as adjectives, not as nouns or verbs.

> **Incorrect:** UNIX® is fun and easy to use.
> **Correct:** The UNIX® operating system is fun and easy to use.

> **Incorrect:** Plirgatize the system.
> **Correct:** Enhance the system for the Plirg™ platform.

For information about the nouns to use with trademarks, see "Trademarks and Appropriate Nouns" on page 159.

■ Do not use trademarks in the possessive or the plural.

Form the possessive or plural from the appropriate noun that the trademark describes.

> **Incorrect:** My dog ate the Macintosh's microphone.
> **Correct:** My dog ate the Macintosh™ system's microphone.

> **Incorrect:** Turn off your Selectric.
> **Correct:** Turn off your Selectric™ typewriter.

■ Do not hyphenate trademarks.

> **Incorrect:** Use the PlirgEd-based application.
> **Correct:** Use the application that is based on the PlirgEd™ technology.

■ Do not change the typeface of trademarks from the typeface of the surrounding text.

■ Do not parenthetically define acronyms and abbreviations that are trademarks.

■ Do not abbreviate trademarks.

■ Do not shorten trademarks.

For example, do not write "Whiz Write" for PlirgSoft™ Whiz Write. Use a trademark in its complete form.

Trademarks and Appropriate Nouns

Trademarks are proper adjectives. As such, they modify nouns. The term "common noun" (sometimes called "generic noun") refers to the noun that a trademark describes. Always link a trademark with an appropriate common noun. Do not capitalize the common noun.

Follow these guidelines when working with appropriate nouns:

- Use appropriate nouns with trademarks.

  The noun does not always have to follow the trademark. However, you must write clearly so that readers know which trademark is used with the particular product, technology, service, or program described by the noun.

  For example, "PlirgSoft recently enhanced these technologies: Whiz Write™, Access Editor™, and PlirgEd™." The noun "technologies" is used with the Whiz Write, Access Editor, and PlirgEd trademarks.

- Do not capitalize appropriate nouns unless the nouns are part of the name of the product or service.

- Define the common noun and use it consistently.

  Repeat the definition after each major heading if you think this repetition would help readers who are retrieving the information online. If the context of the reference is obvious to the reader, you do not need to repeat the common noun's definition too often.

- Do not use nouns such as "developer" or "vision" with trademarks or service marks because these terms are not products or services that your company provides.

  For example, you would not write "PlirgSoft developer," "PlirgSoft software developer," or "developer of PlirgSoft software." These phrases give the impression that a developer is the owner of PlirgSoft software. In this example, PlirgSoft software comes only from Plirg. PlirgSoft is a trademark of Plirg, Inc., not of a software developer.

  However, you *can* create a "defined term" for a trademark and then use the defined term throughout the document. For example, "Developers that write to the PlirgSoft platform ('PlirgSoft developers') use code examples as a main resource." "PlirgSoft developers" is now a defined term that you can use in the document.

- If you use an appropriate noun *in place of* a trademark, choose a noun that does not conflict with related terms in the document.

  Choose the appropriate noun, indicate the full name of the product or service associated with the noun (often, if helpful), and use the noun consistently.

  For example, sometimes the phrase "operating environment" might be a useful replacement for "PlirgSoft operating environment." However, you would not be able to use just "operating environment" when comparing the PlirgSoft operating environment with another operating environment.

The following list provides some examples of frequently used common nouns in the computer industry:

application	interface	screen
architecture	kernel	server
client/server systems	machine	software
distributing computing solution	operating environment	system
environment	operating system	system software
equipment	package	technology
features	peripheral	tool
files	platform	unit
graphical user interface (GUI)	printer	window environment
hardware	program	workstation

Proper Use of Third-Party Trademarks

Treat "third-party trademarks" (trademarks from other companies) with the same respect as trademarks from your company. Use them as proper adjectives with the correct ®, ™, or ᔆᴹ notices, and give them appropriate attribution as trademarks.

Follow these guidelines when using third-party trademarks:

- Mark third-party trademarks with the correct ® or ™ notice on book covers and the first time they appear in text, including chapters, appendixes, and the preface. Most publications do not put trademark symbols in the table of contents, chapter or appendix titles, section heads, tables, or captions.

- Add the third-party attribution to the trademark legend of the legal notice.

- Make an effort to consult product groups or marketing groups, or the third parties themselves, to make sure that third-party trademarks are given appropriate attributions. Corporate Web sites often provide such information. If you cannot obtain the information, mark the third-party product name with a ™ symbol. Include a general attribution similar to the following example in the trademark legend after the specific attributions:

    All other product names mentioned herein are the trademarks of their respective owners.

- Only put trademarks of different companies next to each other if there is a license or agreement between the two parties.

    For example, you would not write "Plirg Ada" unless a licensing agreement existed between Plirg, Inc., and the U.S. Department of Defense.

- Do not parenthetically define existing acronyms or abbreviations that are trademarked terms.

Third-Party Web Site References

A third-party Web site might contain information that you want to reference in a document. To choose and reference an appropriate third-party site involves the following tasks:

- Determining which third-party site to reference
- Determining which third-party URL to use
- Adding a disclaimer and any required third-party wording
- Preventing unapproved references to third-party sites

Note – The guidelines in this section pertain to pointing to third-party sites in printed documentation. If you work solely on web pages, determine which of the following guidelines are applicable to your work and use the guidelines accordingly. Considerations can include your staffing resources and whether to point to nice-to-know information. Also, consider the length of time the material might be available online and whether technical input is required.

This section provides guidelines for referring to third-party Web sites.

Determining Which Third-Party Site to Reference

Sometimes, a third-party Web site might be the best source of information for a topic. If you want to point to a third-party site, first find out if the site prohibits such use.

Often, a third-party site has a Terms of Use page that is available from its home page or legal notice page. The Terms of Use page likely states the third-party's policy for pointing to the site's contents.

- If the site clearly states that you cannot point to its contents, do not point to that site.

- If you are not sure whether you can point to the site's contents, contact your legal counsel.

When you know that you can legally point to a particular third-party site, ask engineering staff or subject matter experts to review the material. The reviewers can determine the value and accuracy of the material and might even be able to provide a better resource.

Allow extra time in your documentation schedule to gather this legal information and technical data.

Determining Which Third-Party URL to Use

After determining which third-party site to use as a source of information, point to a "safe," pertinent, and easily accessible URL:

- Check the third-party Terms of Use page for possible restrictions on pointing to a particular URL.

    - If the third-party terms of use only allow pointing to the home page, then point to the home page.

    - If the third-party terms of use do not prohibit pointing to a page other than the home page, you can point to another page.

        If you seem to be taking a tour of the site to reach the required information, consider using another source.

- Point to need-to-know information, not to information that is nice to know.

    For example, you might point developers to a standards site such as `http://www.ietf.org/rfc`, which provides Request for Comments (RFC) documents. Do not direct users to a general, nice-to-know site, one that discusses computer literacy, for example, or to information that essentially duplicates other content.

- Decide whether users might have difficulty accessing the information or might lose patience waiting for information to be displayed.

    For example, does the site take a long time to load due to large graphics files? Does the site require plug-ins or other software that users might have to download? Has the site crashed on any occasions when you have tried to access it?

- Use text to point to a third-party site.

    For guidelines on referencing a URL, see "Referencing URLs" on page 228.

    Your authoring tool might enable you to use "link text," which is text that you want to appear as the cross-reference. Clicking the link text takes users to the URL that you also specify when creating the link text.

- Link to a third-party site by clicking on a logo or other image *only* if the site's terms of use expressly permit the use of the logo or image.

Adding a Disclaimer and Required Third-Party Wording

Include the following elements in any document that points to third-party sites:

- A disclaimer similar to the following example, which appears as a Note:

Note – Plirg is not responsible for the availability of third-party Web sites mentioned in this document. Plirg does not endorse and is not responsible or liable for any content, advertising, products, or other material on or available from such sites or resources. Plirg will not be responsible or liable for any damage or loss caused or alleged to be caused by or in connection with use of or reliance on any such content, goods, or services that are available on or through any such sites or resources.

- If the third-party site's terms of use mandate the use of special wording, make sure that you add the wording as required.

Preventing Unapproved References to Third-Party Sites

When referring to third-party Web sites, use caution:

- Do not endorse or criticize a book or other content that you reference.

  Be straightforward and neutral. For example, "For information about UNIX commands, see `http://www.unix4fun.com`."

- If pointing to a third-party site is prohibited by third-party freeware being shipped with your product, do not point to the site.

- Do not use any type of framing or inline linking.

  The page that you link to cannot appear in the web browser simultaneously with the page from which you are linking.

- You might not want to point to a competitor's book.

Protection of Proprietary/Confidential Information

Proprietary/Confidential information is defined as any information that when mismanaged, compromised, and ultimately disclosed to unauthorized parties could be detrimental to your company's competitive advantage or could adversely affect your company's operation of business. This information might be technical, financial, business strategic, or operational.

Because this information is not commonly known to others, the information provides your company with a financial advantage in the marketplace. This information has a property value to your company.

Generally, these forms of proprietary and confidential information are safeguarded as trade secrets. A *trade secret* can be any information, technical or nontechnical, that is considered proprietary and confidential. Do not release trade secret information to competitors or the public domain.

This section discusses the types of information that are proprietary and provides guidelines for handling proprietary/confidential information:

- Identifying proprietary/confidential information
- Protecting proprietary/confidential documents
- Protecting electronic communication
- Protecting information that appears in examples

Identifying Proprietary/Confidential Information

The following types of information are proprietary/confidential:

- Drafts of manuals, white papers, and product notes
- Technical data
    - Object code
    - Source code and source documents
    - Flow diagrams
    - Schematics
    - Real host names of computers
    - Public IP addresses
    - Domain names

- Business data
  - Financial results (except publicly published results)
  - Merger and acquisition activity
  - Alliance negotiations
  - Purchasing and bid data
  - Marketing strategies
  - Customer lists and profiles
- Detailed information about new products before public announcement
  - Project code names and descriptions
  - Product features (processing speed, graphics capability)
  - Target dates
  - Pricing
  - Market placement and strategies, and customer information
  - Costs and other financial information
  - Bugs
  - Design data
  - Diagnostic and reliability data
- Email messages and web pages of a proprietary or confidential nature
- Presentation materials, including handouts, transparencies, and slides
- Employee personnel information, such as performance reviews and salary information

Protecting Proprietary/Confidential Documents

Proprietary/Confidential documents must be identified as such through appropriate classification and corresponding labeling. This identification must be in force from the time the documents are created until the documents are released or are securely destroyed.

This section explains the three most commonly used proprietary classifications. If your authoring tool can produce bold type, use bold with these classifications:

- *Company Name* **Proprietary/Confidential: Internal Use Only**

  Use this label for general information, such as job listings that are distributed throughout the company but must remain confidential.

- *Company Name* **Proprietary/Confidential: Need-to-Know**

  Use this label for all prerelease product documentation and information, such as manuals, release notes, white papers, and specifications, which are distributed to product teams. *Remove* the proprietary label before producing the final version of the document *unless* the document remains confidential. For example, do not remove the proprietary label from certain source code documents.

- *Company Name* **Proprietary/Confidential: Registered**

  Use this label for highly sensitive information, where numbered copies are made and carefully controlled.

Most documentation prepared according to these guidelines bear the label *"Company Name* Proprietary/Confidential: Need-to-Know." If you have questions about proprietary labels, contact your legal counsel.

Protecting Electronic Communication

Information that is shared in an electronic format can seem less tangible than a piece of paper. If the information is considered proprietary/confidential, the sensitivity of the information remains the same as a printed document. The information must also be treated the same as a printed document. To protect electronic communication, follow these guidelines:

- Identify proprietary/confidential information in electronic form.

  Use the appropriate label in email, files, and directories.

Note – Do not use email to communicate information that is classified Proprietary/Confidential: Registered.

- Confirm the names on an alias before sending information to a large audience.

  Create smaller aliases for particularly sensitive topics. Do not distribute messages beyond the alias or to addresses outside your company.

- Do not post proprietary/confidential information to external Web sites.

  Information classified as proprietary/confidential should not be placed on or transmitted over the Internet or other public network.

Protecting Information That Appears in Examples

If you create sample text, files, screen captures, illustrations, or any other types of examples in documentation, you should protect certain types of information. This information includes names of computers, or IP addresses, or possibly entire network domains.

Follow these guidelines:

- Do not use real host names of computers at your company in documentation.

  Suppose you create files with real computer names to test the software being documented. If you want to include these files in a document, you must change the real host names to fictitious names. Try to create culturally neutral, easily translated host names, such as `host1`, `newhost`, or `myhost`.

- Do not use public IP addresses in documentation.

  The Internet Assigned Numbers Authority (IANA) has set aside three blocks of the IP address space for use in corporate intranets.

  The IANA's numbering scheme enables a company to use private, "internal" IP addresses inside a firewall. Because these private IP addresses cannot be used by the public, their use in documentation does not conflict with IP addresses used on the Internet.

  The following table shows the *range* of numbers that the IANA has set aside for internal IP addresses. The numeral 255 is the highest number that you can use in respective portions of the IP address. When you use IP addresses as examples in documentation, you should stay within this numbering scheme.

TABLE 8–1 IP Addresses for Use in Documentation

Network Class	Starting Number	Ending Number
A	10.0.0.0	10.255.255.255
B	172.16.0.0	172.31.255.255
C	192.168.0.0	192.168.255.255

  For more information about these standards, specify the RFC number, RFC 1918, at the RFC repository for the Internet Engineering Task Force (IETF) Web site at `http://www.ietf.org/rfc`.

- Do not use real domain names in documentation.

  Instead, use these domain names in examples:

  - `example.com`
  - `example.net`
  - `example.org`

  Any subdomain can be combined with these domain names as appropriate, for example, `janepc.example.com`.

  For details about standard domain names, retrieve RFC 2606 at `http://www.ietf.org/rfc`.

- If a screen capture contains a URL that is not to be made public, change the URL and then take the screen capture.

CHAPTER 9

Types of Technical Documents

Many different types of technical documents exist. These documents can range from a single-chapter manual, such as a white paper or simple installation guide, to a highly technical user's guide or training manual. Documents can also be part of a documentation set that contains several documents.

This chapter discusses the following topics:

What Is a Documentation Set?

A *documentation set* includes one or more types of documents that a customer receives with a product. A typical documentation set might include the following:

- Manuals
- Textual pieces of a CD-ROM package
- Online help
- Release notes
- Other related documents, such as white papers

If you work at a large company, you might create or update a specific document, such as a user's guide or reference manual. In smaller documentation groups, a writer might work on all parts of the documentation set, including planning documents.

The following sections describe the parts of a documentation set.

Documentation Plans

Publications groups often use planning documents to describe the contents and packaging of documentation sets and the individual documents within these sets. You can also use planning documents to describe individual documents.

Your involvement in the creation of planning documents depends on the scope of the project and your position within the writing team.

Documentation Set Plan

The *documentation set plan* describes the overall characteristics of a proposed documentation set. You might think of a documentation set plan as a publications architecture document, similar to an engineering specification.

For large documentation sets, the publications manager or project lead often designs the documentation set plan with input from individual contributors. For smaller sets, individual contributors might provide documentation set plans.

Documentation Set Plan Template

Use a documentation set plan template when you create a new set of manuals. The plan template might include the following:

- Structure of the set
- Audience description
- Document content plan, for each document in the set
- Documentation schedule
- Reviewer list
- Roles and responsibilities of publications members and product team members
- Issues, including decisions that have not been made or known problems
- Dependencies that must be met for the project to be successful
- Localization plans
- Related documentation efforts
- Competitive analysis
- Publications quality assurance plan
- Media formats, such as print and online
- Format of the set, including bindings, cover type, and other items
- Packaging plans

Documentation Set Revision Plan Template

Use a documentation set revision plan template when you update one or more manuals that are part of a set or when you add or delete one or more manuals from a set. The plan template might include the following:

- Structure and delivery, including differences from the previous set
- Documentation schedule
- Reviewer list

Document Plan

A *document plan* describes the characteristics of a *specific manual*. The document plan might include a content outline, production considerations, and an explanation about how an individual document will be implemented. Typically, the writer or project lead creates the document plan.

Document Plan Template

Use a document plan template when you create a new, standalone manual that will *not* be part of a documentation set. The document plan template might include the following:

- Content outline
- Audience description
- Manual schedule
- Reviewer list
- Roles and responsibilities of publications members and product team members
- Issues, including decisions that have not been made or known problems
- Dependencies that must be met for the manual to be effective
- Manuals that will be referenced from this document
- Localization plans
- Publications quality assurance plan
- Media formats, such as print and online
- Format of the manual, including size, cover type, and similar details
- Packaging plans
- Related documents
- Competitive analysis

Document Revision Plan Template

Use a document revision plan template when you revise an existing standalone manual that is not part of a documentation set. The document revision plan template might include the following:

- Content outline
- Manual schedule
- Reviewer list
- Related documentation
- Structure and delivery of the revised manual

Abstracts

An *abstract* conveys to potential readers what is in a book so that they can make an informed decision about whether to read the book. When writing an abstract, reduce text to a few sentences and to no more than two paragraphs. Use the appropriate trademark symbols where necessary.

Structure of Manuals

Typical technical manuals might consist of either a single chapter or multiple chapters.

Manuals With a Single Chapter

Manuals with a single chapter are usually small and narrowly focused on a single subject. Examples of manuals with a single chapter include the following:

- Simple installation manuals
- Release notes
- Product notes
- White papers

Note – Release notes require special consideration. See "Release Notes and Product Notes" on page 183 for more information.

The following table lists the components of a typical single-chapter manual. The components are listed in the order in which they usually appear within the manual. The *optional* components depend on the individual book. For example, you probably do not need a table of contents if the document has only one or two pages. Likewise, an index is unnecessary for a document of fewer than 20 pages. Manuals with a single chapter usually require title pages and legal notice pages.

TABLE 9–1 Possible Components of Manuals With a Single Chapter

Part of the Manual	Requirement
Title page	Required.
Legal notice	Required.
Table of contents	Optional.
List of figures	Optional. Helpful if many numbered figures are used.
List of tables	Optional. Helpful if many numbered tables are used.
List of examples	Optional. Helpful if many captioned examples are used.
Chapter	Required.
Index	Recommended if the chapter has more than 20 pages.

Manuals With Multiple Chapters

Manuals with multiple chapters are the most common types of technical manuals. These manuals usually require a title page as well as front and back matter.

In addition to being divided into chapters, some manuals are further divided into parts. A part contains one or more chapters. Manuals can be divided into parts for various reasons. One example is a single manual that is both a user's guide and a reference manual.

If a manual is divided into parts, the manual must have at least two parts. The parts must also be identified by a part divider page. See "Part Dividers" on page 177.

The following table lists the components of typical manuals with multiple chapters. The components are listed in the order in which they appear within a manual. *Optional* means that the component of the manual might be required in certain writing situations.

TABLE 9–2 Possible Components of Manuals With Multiple Chapters

Part of the Manual	Requirement
Title page	Required.
Legal notice	Required.
Table of contents	Required.
List of figures	Optional. Helpful if many numbered figures are used.
List of tables	Optional. Helpful if many numbered tables are used.
List of examples	Optional. Helpful if many captioned examples are used.
Preface	Required.
Part I	Optional. Use a Roman numeral.
Chapter table of contents	Optional.
Chapters	Required.
Part II	Required if a Part I is used.
Parts III and higher	Optional.
Appendixes	Optional.
Glossary	Optional.
Bibliography	Optional.
Index	Recommended for manuals that are longer than 20 pages.

Descriptions of the Manual Parts

This section describes the general editorial formats of the parts of a typical manual. The parts are listed in the order in which they usually appear within a manual.

Title Page

Most manuals have a title page, which contains the manual title, current address block, and release date. Your company's specific information might also include elements such as the corporate telephone number and document revision information.

Legal Notice

The legal notice contains various copyright and trademark statements.

Table of Contents

The table of contents can list the first-level headings, second-level headings, and third-level headings in a manual. Headings can be numbered or unnumbered, depending on the style determined for your document.

A manual should have a table of contents if the manual has more than one chapter. The table of contents usually begins on a right page in a printed manual.

List of Figures

The list of figures lists all numbered figures in the manual. Consider including the list of figures if the manual has more than one numbered figure and more than one chapter. The list of figures usually begins on a right page in a printed manual.

List of Tables

The list of tables lists all numbered tables in the manual. Consider including the list of tables if the manual has more than one numbered table and more than one chapter. The list of tables usually begins on a right page in a printed manual.

List of Examples

The list of examples lists all numbered code examples and other types of examples in the manual. Consider including the list of examples if the manual has more than one numbered example and more than one chapter. The list of examples usually begins on a right page in a printed manual.

Preface

The preface describes the purpose and scope of the manual and includes an overview of the parts of the manual. The preface usually begins on a right page in a printed manual.

Depending on the purpose and complexity of the manual, the preface might contain all or some of the sections listed here. The preface might also contain sections specific to a documentation set.

First, explain the purpose of the manual in one or two sentences. Identify the level of technical sophistication that the reader must possess to use the manual effectively. Next, include sections similar to the following if the additional information is relevant to the book:

- **Who Should Use This Book.** Describe the audience or class of reader for whom the manual is intended. The audience description might include the following information:

  - Required knowledge, such as a specific programming language

  - Required experience or familiarity with the software or hardware platform

  - Definition of the type of user or functional responsibility, such as applications programer, system administrator, or field engineer

  - Terms that relate to the tasks the user might perform

- **Before You Read This Book.** If this manual requires that the user read other documents before effectively using this manual, list those other documents.

- **How This Book Is Organized.** Briefly describe the contents of the manual. Consider using a live cross-reference to list each chapter and appendix.

- **Related Books.** List titles of internal documents that are related to the manual. Also list third-party books, and their authors and publishers, that are mentioned in the text or that readers might find useful.

- **Accessing Documentation Online.** Inform readers how to view documents online if your company provides this service.

- **Typographic Conventions.** List and explain special symbols, characters, or typography that are used in the manual.

Chapters

The three general types of chapter page numbering and heading styles are:

- **Single.** Single chapters are not numbered. There is no chapter number, first-level headings are not numbered, and the page numbers run sequentially starting from 1. This format is used only in manuals with one chapter. See "Manuals With a Single Chapter" on page 172.

- **Multiple, unnumbered.** The chapters are numbered, but the headings are not. Pages are numbered sequentially, starting from 1, or pages can be numbered sequentially within each chapter, starting from 1-1.

- **Multiple, numbered.** The chapters are numbered, the first-level headings through the third-level headings are numbered, starting from 1.1. Pages are numbered sequentially within each chapter, starting from 1-1.

The type of page numbering style that you use is optional and depends on various factors such as personal preference, history of the manual, or the manual's subject matter. All chapters begin on a right page in a printed manual.

Part Dividers

Part dividers are used only in manuals that need to be divided into parts. See "Manuals With Multiple Chapters" on page 173. Part dividers are numbered with Roman numerals, for example, Part I, Part II, Part III, and so on, and include a title. The part dividers can have a cross-reference listing of the chapters that are included in the part. You might also include text and illustrations, either on the front or on both the front and back of the part dividers.

Part dividers begin on a right page in a printed manual. Part dividers do not have a page number in a printed manual. For more information, see "Part Dividers" on page 56.

Appendixes

Appendixes provide supplementary information to the main body of the manual. Appendixes appear at the end of the manual. Appropriate material for appendixes includes the following:

- Long programming code examples
- Long lists, charts, and tables
- Summary information, such as a list of a program's function keys
- Technical specifications

Do not use an appendix as a repository for "odds and ends" that do not benefit the reader's grasp of the subject.

Appendixes can use numbered or unnumbered section headings, depending on the chapter style of the manual. For example, you would use numbered section headings in appendixes for manuals that use numbered section headings in chapters.

Each appendix is designated by a letter, for example, Appendix A, Appendix B, and so on. Each appendix begins on a right page in a printed manual.

Glossary

A glossary is an alphabetical list of defined terms, phrases, abbreviations, and acronyms. The glossary defines terms that might not be clear to the reader.

The glossary is included within a manual in the following location:

- At the end of the manual, following the last appendix
- At the end of the manual, following the last chapter if the manual contains no appendix
- Before a bibliography or index

The glossary begins on a right page in a printed manual.

Your publications department might have developed a glossary with more specific definitions for terms that are specific to your product area. For more information about glossaries, see Chapter 13.

Bibliography

A bibliography is a list of the sources to which you refer in your manual. Bibliographies follow a specific format for each kind of resource that is cited. A bibliography begins on a right page in a printed manual. For more information, see "Writing Bibliographies" on page 51.

Index

An index is recommended for a manual of more than 20 pages. Indexes begin on a right page in a printed manual. For more information about indexing and index formats, see Chapter 14.

Types of Hardware Manuals

This section briefly describes some of the types of manuals that are typically written for a hardware product. Some of the different types of hardware manuals include the following:

- Installation
- System overview
- User's guide
- Service
- Configuration
- Specification
- Site planning
- Troubleshooting
- Getting started

Installation Guides

In general, there are two types of installation guides:

- System installation guides for workstations, servers, and external expansion systems
- Internal installation guides for field-replaceable units (FRUs) inside systems

  The FRUs could include subsystems (mass storage systems and switches), individual devices (drives), components (CPU modules and memory modules), and chassis units (fan trays).

System Overview Guides

System overview guides are designed for users who are responsible for setting up and administering large server systems. These guides cover technical features and functions of the system.

User's Guides

User's guides are written for users who are responsible for setting up and administering systems. User's guides usually contain instructions for installation, configuration, and setup, as well as information about administration and troubleshooting.

Service Manuals

Service manuals are typically prepared for platforms and storage systems rather than for a single board or a single device.

Many large companies have internal service organizations that use the service manuals to maintain their equipment. Therefore, the readers of service manuals might be experienced service technicians who work on a given company's equipment only occasionally. When writing a service manual, you cannot make any assumptions about the reader's knowledge of your company's computers.

Configuration Guides

Configuration guides are typically written for families of products. These manuals tell the user how to fit the pieces together and how to add certain devices to the system configuration. This type of manual might also be used by Marketing to assist customers in meeting their installation requirements.

Types of Software Manuals

This section briefly describes some of the types of manuals that you might write for a software product. Software documentation typically includes the following types of manuals:

- Installation
- Programmer's guide
- System administration
- User's guide
- Reference

Installation Guides

Software installation guides explain how to install and configure the software on the user's system. When writing the manual, you must assume that the reader has already assembled the hardware and is awaiting instructions for installing the software.

Programmer's Guides

Software programmer's guides vary in scope, depending on whether you are discussing the programming features of the operating environment, a language compiler application, or an application programming interface (API). Typical operating system programmer's guides might range from an application packaging developer's guide, which is written for a general audience of applications developers, to a book about writing device drivers, which is directed to highly specialized system programmers.

Programmer's guides explain how to write programs that take advantage of the features of the particular product. Compilers and language-development tools have their own documentation sets that are specifically geared toward programmers who use the tools.

System Administration Guides

System administration guides tell readers how to set up, maintain, and troubleshoot software activities on their computers, and, by extension, networks of their computers. The reader might be anyone from a novice to an experienced network manager.

User's Guides

User's guides tell readers how to use the features of a software product. The guide's complexity depends on how sophisticated readers must be to use the product. You might write the user's guide for your product as a tutorial.

Reference Guides

Reference guides give very specific details about a software product, such as syntax statements for programming languages or explanations of each feature of a graphics software package. Usually, the subjects are arranged in alphabetical order.

Other Product Documents

Though manuals form the bulk of typical technical documentation, you might also find yourself writing other types of documents. Some of these documents could be considered manuals, but their uniqueness demands special consideration.

These documents include the following:

- White papers
- Online help
- CD text
- Release notes and product notes
- Demos
- Road maps

White Papers

White papers are optional documents that are usually used to publicize a new product or a new feature before official documentation is available. Your involvement ensures that all product information is consistent with the product documentation, uses the standard documentation format, and meets company editorial guidelines.

When working on a white paper, you might interact with Product Marketing, Engineering, or other consulting groups regarding schedules, customer requirements, and other issues.

Online Help

Online help is information that a computer displays to assist users in doing tasks. You might be required to write help text in addition to conventional manuals. Most products require you to use compatible help viewers and authoring tools.

CD Text

Many software products are supplied on CD-ROM media. The textual pieces of the CD-ROM package are often considered part of the documentation set. These pieces are the following:

- CD faceplate text
- Text insert

CD Faceplate Text

The CD faceplate text appears on the disc faceplate and typically includes the following information:

- Product title
- Hardware platform supported
- Operating system and other software compatibility
- Applicable legal notice and third-party trademarks
- File system format

File system format refers to the file system structure of the software on the disc. An example is MS-DOS format.

CD Text Insert

The CD text insert is a glossy paper brochure that forms the cover text for the CD-ROM package. The CD text insert typically consists of a title page, legal notice, and textual information.

Information that you supply on the title page template typically includes the product title and hardware and software platforms supported. The legal notice provides the applicable trademarks and third-party trademarks for the product, consistent with the legal notice for the documentation set.

The content and length of the textual information for the brochure can vary. The textual information typically includes a brief description of the product and might also include instructions for mounting the CD.

Release Notes and Product Notes

Release notes for software products and product notes for hardware products are the final documents that are written before a product ships. The purpose of these notes is to inform the customer about any major problems with hardware, software, or documentation that were discovered after the manuals were printed. Release notes also contain other late-breaking information and additional information needed at installation.

Release notes might be printed material in product boxes or in ASCII or HTML on the product CD. Release notes might also become part of a product's online documentation set if one exists.

Typically, release notes go to production for a "quick print" one to two weeks before the product is shipped. Release notes and product notes should be as short and succinct as possible.

Release notes might include the following sections:

- Title page
- Legal notice
- Table of Contents
- Preface
- Installation Bugs
- Runtime Bugs
- New Features
- End-of-Support Statements
- Driver Updates
- Patches and CERT Advisories
- Documentation Issues

Product notes might include the following sections:

- Title page
- Legal notice
- Table of Contents
- Preface
- Getting Help
- Compatibility
- Known Problems With the Hardware
- Known Problems With the Software
- Documentation Issues
- Bugs Fixed Since the Last Release

Demos

The purpose of some demos is to provide customers with an opportunity to test that the software has been installed properly. Other demos enable a customer to see and try new features.

Demos are usually produced by engineers who write the code for the feature being demonstrated. You might be asked to review the demo, or to write one or more of the following documents:

- README file
- Instructions for loading and running the demo
- An explanation of what the demo is intended to illustrate

Training Documents

Training documents are yet another type of technical documentation. Training documents vary widely in format, style, and delivery method, depending on how they are used. For example, a training document that an instructor uses in front of a classroom is different from a training document that a student accesses over the Web for self-paced learning.

Typical training documents include the following:

- Training materials for use in instructor-led courses that are delivered in classrooms

  These materials might include a student guide, an instructor guide, which consists of the student guide plus additional notes, overheads, workbooks, and study guides.

- Training materials that are delivered on a CD that uses proprietary software
- Training that is delivered over the Web and that uses multimedia capabilities

Student Guides and Instructor Guides

Student guides and instructor guides are used in instructor-led training. This type of training typically takes place in a classroom with a group of students. The general editorial format of a student guide resembles the format of a hardware or software manual, except that the information is organized according to modules and learning objectives rather than by chapters.

Student guides might include the following components:

- Title page
- Legal notice
- Table of Contents
- Preface
- Modules
- Labs
- Exercises
- Appendixes
- Index

Instructor guides closely resemble student guides, except that the instructor guides contain additional directions and notes for the classroom instructor.

Other Training Documents

Other documents that are used for training purposes might include the following components:

- Study guides
- Student workbooks
- Lab manuals
- Certification exams
- Video or audio presentations
- Technology-based training (TBT) delivered on CD
- Classes accessed on the Web
- Consulting materials, such as skills assessments or white papers

CHAPTER 10

Working With an Editor

Writing computer documentation involves converting raw information from engineers and marketing professionals into a useful, well-written document. The final document often is a result of efforts from the entire publications team, including writer, editor, designer, illustrator, and production coordinator. However, the content of the document is most closely developed through the work of writer and editor.

This chapter discusses the following topics:

Technical Editor's Role

An editor helps a writer focus on content and effective presentation and provides another set of eyes to check all the details. The partnership of writer and editor produces easy-to-use, high-quality, effective documents.

Any editor is concerned with use of language, flow, tone, grammar, punctuation, capitalization, spelling, sentence structure, consistency, and so forth. However, a *technical editor* is also concerned with technical content, compatibility of the technical depth with the reader's background, and effective communication of technical information. Other areas of concern include consistent use of technical terms and symbols, and careful coordination of text and artwork. By marking text and suggesting an alternative, an editor indicates to a writer that the original might be, for example, misleading, awkward, imprecise, confusing, or incomplete.

Editor's Role in Producing Online Documents

Editors can help the writers of online documents with the following tasks:

- Identify the document's readers and purpose.

  An editor can help a writer use this information to decide which documents to optimize for online, which documents to optimize for print, and how to establish priorities for conversion projects.

- Define online document structure and the links that are under the writer's control.

  Writers have control over links that are embedded in the text and links that are in jump lists. However, writers typically do not have control over standard navigational aids such as Back, Forward, and Home, which are predefined in design templates.

- Ensure that the document accommodates scanning and nonsequential access by readers.

  An editor can help ensure that text complies with online writing style guidelines. See Chapter 4.

- Assist with a visual inspection of the online document.

  The visual inspection checks for inconsistencies and formatting problems that result from document conversion.

- Verify that all links are contextually appropriate.

  An editor can review the link wording and surrounding text to ensure that sufficient context minimizes reader disorientation.

- Verify that links are appropriately placed within the document to avoid overlinking or underlinking.

- Assist with usability testing.

  Usability testing can determine whether document navigation follows pathways that readers are likely to follow.

Types of Editing

A document could undergo more than one editorial review, each for a different purpose. The type of edit that a document receives usually depends on where the document is in the product cycle. For example, a *developmental edit* of a document occurs early in the cycle, around the pre-alpha test or alpha period when there might be more time to address issues such as organization and structure. A *copy edit* is best during the beta review, when the manual is more complete and stable. And finally, *proofreading* is the last review a document receives.

Developmental Editing

Developmental editing is hard to define because its functions depend on the documentation set or book under consideration. Think of developmental editing as a document production phase that assesses the document's overall focus and direction. This edit is the phase when a documentation set or a book is restructured, chapters or sections are reorganized, and major rewriting is done. The issues that the editor raises during a developmental edit can affect the character of subsequent sections or chapters of a document. This effectiveness is increased if the edit is done on a sample chapter or an early draft of a manual. Some global copy editing issues can be raised at this time as well, especially when these issues provide the writer with examples of style or word usage.

Developmental Editing Checklist

Structure and Organization

- Audience definition, purpose of document, and how to use the book are clear.
- Information is appropriately presented for the audience.
- Concepts flow logically.
- Superfluous or redundant material is eliminated.
- Headings are useful, descriptive, and specific.
- Information is easy to find.
- Information is task oriented where appropriate.
- Reference and conceptual information are eliminated from task descriptions.
- Distinctions between parts and chapters are clear.
- Page numbering scheme is appropriate for the type of book.

Writing

- Reader context is established and reinforced.
- Tone is appropriate for the reader and to the focus of the book.
- Critical information is covered clearly.
- Task-oriented writing is clear. User actions and system actions are distinct.
- Assumptions are clearly supported.
- Writing and layout are optimized for online presentation.

Style

- Terms are used consistently and appropriately.
- Terms are defined and used in context correctly.
- Terms and abbreviations avoid jargon and follow guidelines for localization.
- Documentation set conventions are established and followed.

Formatting and Layout

- Document conforms to house publications standards.
- Standard templates and formats are used.

Illustrations

- Illustrations appear where needed.
- Artwork is integrated within the text.
- Tables, figures, and illustrations are used effectively and appropriately.
- Illustrations follow artwork and localization guidelines.

New Elements

- New graphics or presentation techniques are identified and used effectively.
- Innovations meet house design and usability standards.

Copy Editing

The editor does minimal rewriting, if any, during a copy edit. Issues regarding structure and organization are addressed throughout the developmental edit. At the copy editing stage, the editor does two kinds of review: *mechanical editing* and *editing for house style.* Mechanical editing addresses issues such as punctuation, capitalization, subject-verb agreement, and so forth. Editing for house style involves interpreting and applying your company's style guidelines. The editor also reads for correct usage of fonts, tags, or other markup, and for structural elements such as tables, illustrations, lists, and procedures. The best time for a copy edit, also called a *line edit,* is before or during the beta review.

Copy Editing Checklist

Readability

- Sentences are clear, direct, and concise.
- Repetition is used effectively.
- Parallel structure is used effectively.

Style

- Headings, lists, and sentences have parallel construction.
- Headings follow hierarchy guidelines.
- Voice and tone are consistent.

Transitions

- Text is easy to follow.
- Information is complete and appropriately placed.
- Transitions between parts, chapters, and sections are clear.
- Transitions are effective online and in hard copy.
- Cross-references are correct, worthwhile, and sufficient.

Grammar

- Sentences are complete.
- Subjects and verbs agree, and pronouns and antecedents agree.
- Verb tense is consistent.
- Modifiers are used appropriately.
- Word choice and sentence structure follow guidelines for localization.
- Long sentences are divided for readability and localization.

Punctuation, Capitalization, and Spelling

- Punctuation follows editorial and documentation set guidelines.
- Capitalization follows editorial and documentation set guidelines.
- Spelling follows editorial and documentation set guidelines.

Mechanics

- Typeface conventions are followed in all document elements.
- Product names are used correctly and consistently.
- Trademarks are used correctly and include appropriate attributions.

- New terms are defined and appear in a glossary if there is one.
- Abbreviations and acronyms follow editorial and localization guidelines.
- Numbers and symbols follow editorial and localization guidelines.
- Cross-references are punctuated correctly and refer to the intended target.
- Numbered lists and steps are used appropriately and are numbered correctly.
- Figures, tables, and examples are referred to in preceding text.
- Table continuations are noted correctly.
- Notes, Cautions, and Tips are used correctly.
- Footnotes are used correctly.
- Running headers, footers, and page numbers are correct.

Formatting and Layout

- Document conforms to house style standards.
- Standard templates and formats are used.
- Page breaks and line breaks are effective.
- Page numbering scheme is appropriate for the type of book.

Illustrations

- Illustrations are consistent and sized appropriately throughout the book.
- Illustrations follow artwork and localization guidelines.
- Figure callouts are capitalized correctly and are in the correct font.

Proofreading

Proofreading is the last step that writers and editors can take to ensure further quality. Proofreading involves one final scan of the document for errors that might have been overlooked in previous reviews. The writer also might have introduced errors when incorporating new technical material or editorial comments. The proofreader's primary responsibility is to make sure that typographical errors, incorrect font usage, and formatting mistakes have not crept into the document.

Proofreading Checklist

Front Matter

- Title page shows correct title, company name and address.
- Legal notice is current and trademarks, including third-party ones, are listed.
- Table of contents includes correct headings and page number references, and is formatted correctly.

- Figures, tables, and examples are listed in the front matter.
- The preface uses the correct template and contains correct chapter numbers, descriptions, and any required product-specific information.

Back Matter

- Appendixes are in the correct order.
- Templates and formats are used correctly in appendixes and glossaries.
- Glossary is correctly presented.
- Bibliography is correctly presented.
- Index is formatted correctly and contains no errors.

Grammar

- Sentences are complete.
- Subjects and verbs agree, and pronouns and antecedents agree.
- Verb tense is consistent.
- Modifiers are used appropriately.

Punctuation, Capitalization, and Spelling

- Punctuation follows editorial and documentation set guidelines.
- Capitalization follows editorial and documentation set guidelines.
- Spelling follows editorial and documentation set guidelines.

Mechanics

- Typeface conventions are followed in all document elements.
- Product names are used correctly and consistently.
- Trademarks are used and attributed correctly.
- New terms are italicized and defined, and appear in a glossary if there is one.
- Abbreviations and acronyms follow editorial and localization guidelines.
- Numbers and symbols follow editorial and localization guidelines.
- Cross-references are punctuated correctly and refer to the intended target.
- Numbered lists and steps are used appropriately and are numbered correctly.
- Figures, tables, and examples are numbered correctly.
- Table continuations are noted correctly.
- Footnotes are used correctly.
- Page headers, footers, and numbers are correct.
- Change bars do not appear.

Formatting and Layout

- Document conforms to house publications standards.
- Standard templates and formats are used.

Illustrations

- Figure callouts are capitalized correctly and are in the correct font.
- Artwork is aligned correctly on the pages.

Edit Schedules

Writers need to allocate time for editing when creating a documentation plan. The nature of the document and the schedule determine how much editing is possible.

Consider these points:

- You can involve the editor as early as the research stage.

  The editor can help you with research on how similar products are handled and who the audience is.

- The editor can help you prepare your documentation plan.

  Consult the editor if you want advice on overall organization. Go over your editing needs with the editor and include editing cycles in the schedule.

- The alpha review is a good time for a full developmental edit.

  Beta review is usually too late to make the kinds of changes that might come out of a developmental edit.

- A copy edit at the beta review can clean up grammar, spelling, and conformance to your company's style standards.

- Proofreading before the final release provides one last check for formatting issues and typographical errors.

If you are writing a white paper or other nonstandard document, plan to allow time for developmental edits and copy edits.

Document Submission

Before submitting a document for editing, complete these tasks:

- Run your document through a spelling checker.
- Check cross-references.
- Include illustrations or indicate placement of illustrations.

Include a Request for Editing form with the document you submit. This form supplies information such as your name and phone extension, the stage of the document (alpha, beta, final release), and the name of the set to which the document belongs. See "Request for Editing Form" on page 305 in Appendix B for a sample form.

Editing Marks

Your editor will be glad to explain any editing marks that were used in the edit. You can find an online guide to editing marks at the University of Colorado at Boulder Web site. For an explanation of standard proofreaders' marks, see *The Chicago Manual of Style, Fourteenth Edition*, or *Merriam-Webster Collegiate Dictionary*, which is available online at http://www.m-w.com.

Edit Style Sheet

Maintaining a *style sheet* can help you keep track of special spellings, terminology, punctuation, capitalization, and other document-specific words or formats.

A style sheet is where you and the editor can log the decisions made about product names, numbers, abbreviations and acronyms, hyphenation, and capitalization. If the document that you are writing or editing is part of a set, using a style sheet helps maintain consistency among the various books.

When you create a style sheet, remember to pass it on to others who might benefit from it. These people might include writers of related documents, editors, illustrators, and production specialists.

A sample style sheet form follows.

Editorial Style Sheet

Document title: Project:

Writer: Editor:

Date:

A B C	D E F	G H I

J K L	M N O	P Q R

S T U	V W X	Y Z Numbers

Cover capitalization, spelling, hyphenation.

(n) noun	(v) verb	(a) adj preceding noun
(pa) predicate adjective	(col) collective noun	(s) singular
(pl) plural	(TM) trademark	(R) registered trademark

Abbreviations

Trademarked Terms

Special Font Conventions

Miscellaneous Notes

CHAPTER 11

Working With Illustrations

A good illustration transmits dense and complex information at a glance. It also helps a reader retain more information. Combining text and images focuses attention and helps a reader filter data quickly for specific information. As documentation moves online, you might find yourself in the role of a screenwriter or director as you blend text, still images, video, audio, and animation in online multimedia documents.

A high level of image quality is essential to visual communication in any medium. From the printed page, to paint on canvas, to dots on a computer screen, similar rules apply. Even though the elements of good visual art can sometimes defy simple explanation, most people can say they know quality when they see it. In basic terms, the human eye should be able to scan a quality image without backtracking to retrace a path or disengaging to refocus. Quality images also contain balanced elements, consistent line weights, and a discernible flow.

Images of poor quality are usually easy to identify, even though beauty is sometimes in the eye of the beholder. In general, images of poor quality contain unbalanced proportions, jarring colors, jagged or crossed lines, or illegible or blurry elements. If the images in your document appear substandard, contact your illustrator or production specialist immediately for assistance.

This chapter discusses the following topics:

Working With an Illustrator

If your document contains visual elements, include an illustrator on your team. Illustrators are experts in visual communication and have access to specialized graphics tools and graphics repositories.

Involving an illustrator means that any work that is created can be shared with other writers. The work might also be added to an image library or catalog and be made to adhere to approved graphics standards.

The illustrator can do the following:

- Review your documentation plans and devise a visual strategy.
- Collaborate with you as the document changes throughout its life cycle.
- Resolve file format, platform, and tools issues.
- Maintain a consistent look and feel throughout the document.
- Reuse illustrations in other documents while maintaining quality.

Illustration Standards and Processes

Writers who have illustration skills and tools can still work with an illustrator for several reasons:

- Time spent on complex drawings can compromise deadlines.

  Illustrators can usually handle difficult or complex drawings more efficiently and effectively.

- Artwork created by illustrators can be archived and shared with others.
- Visual consistency is enhanced when all work is done by illustrators who are equipped with the same tools and templates.
- Maintaining open relationships and communication with illustrators speeds up the production process and improves quality.

When to Contact an Illustrator

Involve illustrators at the outset of a documentation project in the following instances:

- When you are unable to locate existing illustrations to meet your needs
- When existing illustrations must be modified
- When composite illustrations combining text layers and backgrounds must be created

- When you have concerns about the quality of illustrations in your document
- When you have a concept or a rough sketch that needs professional execution

Submitting an Illustration Request

When requesting help with illustrations, remember to include information that the illustrator needs to know:

- Number of documents in your project and their identification numbers
- Estimated number of illustrations
- Marked hard copies or changes to existing illustrations
- Original source files for illustrations to be modified
- Hand-drawn sketches or concept diagrams
- Estimated production dates or deadlines

See "Artwork Request Form" on page 306 in Appendix B for a sample form.

Illustration Formats, Styles, and Types

This section describes the basics of the formats, styles, and types of illustration.

- *Formats* establish how files are recognized and handled by the computer and the printer.
- *Styles* are broad categories of illustration, such as 2–D, 3–D, and photographic.
- *Types* include data processes, line drawings, concept drawings, screen captures, cartoons, icons, and glyphs.

Illustration Formats

Understanding graphics formats can help you choose the best approach for your project. Two main file types are used in illustrations: vector and raster.

Vector Graphics

Vector-based images contain mathematical image data based on x,y coordinates. Vector graphics can therefore be scaled to any size without quality loss and with a lower relative file size. Vector graphics are ideal for print use because they can be output to printers at any resolution setting. The most common vector-based file type extension is Encapsulated PostScript (.eps). Vector-based images are used for line art and composite images with typography.

Raster Images

Raster images are also known as *bit-mapped* images or *paint* files. Raster images contain a grid of colored pixels that are fixed in place. Unlike vector graphics, raster images cannot be easily scaled without distortion. Raster images are most useful for screen captures, digital photography, and web graphics. Common file extensions are `.tif`, `.gif`, and `.jpg`. Contact your illustrator or production specialist for help understanding and choosing the best file format for your project.

For guidelines on rasterized screen captures, see "Creating Quality Screen Captures" on page 217.

Illustration Styles

Four common styles of illustration are used in computer documents:

- *Isometric drawings* are a type of perspective drawing often used in engineering manuals. The mathematical structure puts all lines at angles of 30, 60, or 90 degrees.

- *3–D drawings* are online images designed to be viewed from all angles. Typically, you can rotate, bisect, and scale these images.

- *2–D drawings* are the most common style of illustration. They might be drawn in perspective, depending upon the subject matter.

- *Photographs*, *video stills*, and *animation* are styles that are appropriate for online use.

Illustration Types

Illustrations can be broken down into these main types:

- *Hardware line drawings* are common in technical manuals. Examples include black-and-white line drawings of disk drives, drawings of "exploded" SCSI ports, and drawings of people installing SIMMs. Line drawings can be shown in 3–D, 2–D, isometric, and other styles.

- *Clip art* is "generic" art that you can use as-is or in combination with other graphics. The subject matter is fairly nonspecific. For example, the art would be a picture of a monitor rather than an illustration of a specific, identifiable monitor.

- *Icons* and *glyphs* are visual cues that represent an object (such as hardware or an application window), a process (such as an application), or a structure (such as a network).

Icons are interactive and are used online. These small, mnemonic graphic images serve as visual placeholders for a larger object or process.

EXAMPLE 11–1 Icon

Glyphs are noninteractive symbols that convey easily recognized information, often without the use of text. Examples of glyphs include the lightning bolt set inside a triangle to represent Cautions, and the broken wine glass found on the sides of cartons indicating that the contents are fragile.

EXAMPLE 11–2 Glyph

- *Graphs* and *charts* depict a process or a flow of information. What that information is and how it relates to other types of information is up to the writer. Examples include marketing graphs showing profits by years, flowcharts of a process, roadmaps of a procedure, and charts depicting the course of a project.
- *Screen captures*, sometimes called *screen shots*, are "snapshots" of screen images that make very effective graphics. Use them as you would any other illustration.
- *Cartoons* lend an air of informality to your document. While often used humorously, cartoons can also be sketches of activities or situations. Humor is a tricky technique in a global market. See "Illustrations and Screen Captures" on page 145 in Chapter 7 for more information.

Examples of Illustrations

This section illustrates the types of illustrations commonly used in technical documentation.

Diagrams

Diagrams encompass a wide range of illustration uses, from simple flowcharts and presentation aids to complex architectural diagrams.

EXAMPLE 11–3 Diagram

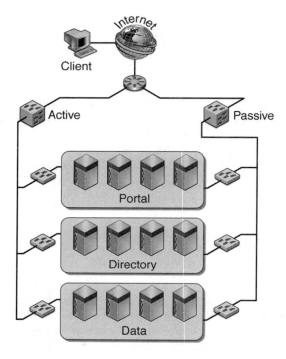

Online Graphics

Online graphics include drawings, icons, and navigational buttons. Online graphics are usually raster images that are highly compressed and optimized for web delivery. If online graphics must be altered, locate the original source files and submit the files to the technical illustrator on your team.

EXAMPLE 11–4 Online Graphics

Line Art

Line art illustrations of hardware are usually based on engineering diagrams or computer-aided design (CAD) drawings. When possible, try to locate the original vector-based source file and use it in your document. The vector format preserves quality and also provides the most versatile image editing options.

EXAMPLE 11–5 Line Art

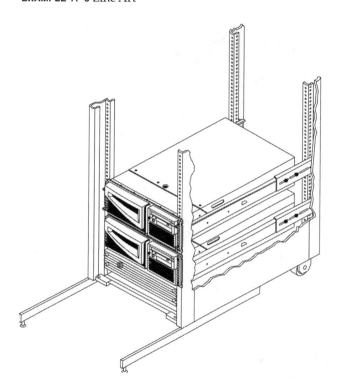

Screen Captures

A screen capture is always created as a raster image. Screen captures represent an exact snapshot of the dots that are displayed on a computer monitor. Once created, screen captures cannot be easily resized without distortion. A technical illustrator can advise you on the proper way to scale and crop screen captures, if necessary.

See "Creating Quality Screen Captures" on page 217 for more information.

EXAMPLE 11–6 Screen Capture

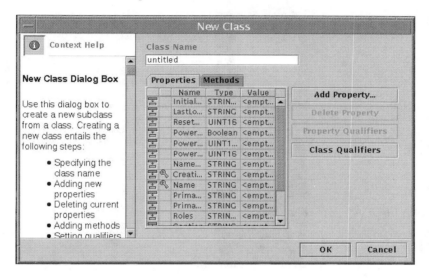

Composites

A composite illustration is a vector graphic or raster image with text labels or callouts placed on top. Localization considerations dictate that the background images must exist on a layer separate from the layer displaying the superimposed text labels.

EXAMPLE 11–7 Composite Illustration

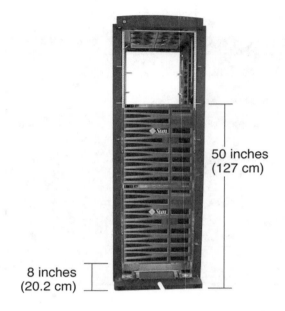

50 inches
(127 cm)

8 inches
(20.2 cm)

Photographs

Photographs can be captured in raster format from a digital camera or scanned from a photo print. File sizes can be large, depending on the resolution, size, and number of colors used. The technical illustrator on your team can edit and manipulate photographs.

EXAMPLE 11–8 Photograph

2–D Animations

You do not have to reserve animation for films or online documents. You can use animation effectively in print. The following example shows an animation that illustrates how to unpack a shipping carton.

EXAMPLE 11–9 2–D Animation

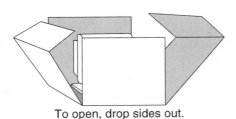

To open, drop sides out.

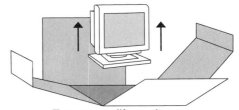

To remove, lift monitor up.

Web Animations

Web animations can be created as vector graphics or raster images. The file format and tools that illustrators use to create animations often depend on the web browser capability of the end user. Animations can impact download times, so they must be well designed and used sparingly. An illustrator's help is critical to the design of effective and compact animations.

EXAMPLE 11–10 Animation

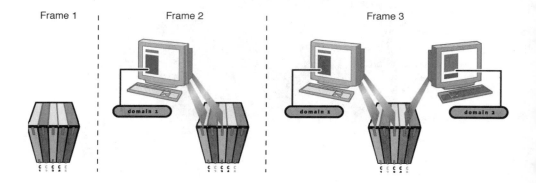

Placing Illustrations

Your illustrations must appear to belong in your document. You can achieve this effect in print and on the web by using consistent placement, spacing, and alignment.

Some publishing tools handle spacing automatically, but others do not. This section contains guidelines for spacing your illustrations and for aligning illustrations with the other elements in your document.

Placement in Relation to Sentences

Do not insert an illustration between the beginning of a sentence and the end of the sentence.

Incorrect:

This diagram

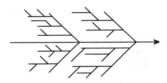

is commonly called a fishbone or Ishikawa diagram.

Correct:

The following diagram is commonly called a fishbone or Ishikawa diagram.

Spacing in Print

The following table contains guidelines for how much spacing to allow between an illustration and printed text above and below it.

TABLE 11–1 Illustration Spacing Guidelines

Element	Minimum Distance	Maximum Distance
Text above	0.25 inch (0.64 cm)	0.75 inch (1.9 cm)
Text below	0.25 inch (0.64 cm)	0.75 inch (1.9 cm)

Alignment in Print

Align illustrations and callouts flush-left to the margin of the text column in most instances. If the drawing is wider than the text column, align the drawing flush-left to the page margin. Example 11–3 shows an illustration that is flush-left to the margin of the text column. Example 11–10 shows an illustration that is flush-left to the page margin.

Online Alignment and Spacing

When placing illustrations in online documents, apply the following guidelines:

- Follow a consistent spacing and alignment method on all of your web pages to create a consistent look and feel.
- Follow any preexisting guidelines for your project that might already be documented by previous webmasters or content creators in your group.
- Know the minimum sizing and performance limitations of your audience's web browser.

  Keep your design within those parameters.

Writing Captions for Illustrations

Captions help set the context of the illustrations within the document. Captions also uniquely identify each illustration for cross-referencing. This section contains guidelines for writing unique captions.

When to Use Captions

Use captions consistently when doing so can help your reader. For example, sometimes an illustration of a menu does not need a caption, whereas a conceptual illustration does require a caption. Use captions in the following instances:

- When you want to cross-reference the illustrations
- When you want to generate a list of figures

Guidelines for Writing Captions

Follow these guidelines when writing captions:

- Use the same capitalization style for figure captions as you use for section headings.
- Do not start a figure caption with an article. For example, write "File Menu," not "The File Menu."
- Limit the figure caption text to one line.
- Introduce the context of the illustration to the reader in the text preceding the illustration.
- Ensure that the figure captions are numbered sequentially throughout the document if your authoring tool does not number figure captions automatically.

Writing Callouts for Illustrations

Callouts help connect illustrations to the surrounding text. This section contains guidelines for integrating callouts and illustrations. When creating callouts, also follow these guidelines:

- Use the minimum number of callouts necessary.
- Use the shortest and fewest words possible.
- Move lengthy callouts to a note or legend outside the drawing.
- Capitalize the first word in a callout.

  Capitalize proper nouns, abbreviations and acronyms as you do in text. Also capitalize prepositions of four or more letters. All other words are lowercase.

Similar to text, callouts must be translated when a document is localized. See Chapter 7 for more information about making sure that your callouts can be easily translated.

Callout Style

The following table contains style specifications for callouts.

TABLE 11–2 Callout Specifications

Specification	Description
Typeface	Helvetica
Type weight	Regular (not bold)
Alignment	Left or right
	Exception: In flowcharts, callouts are centered.
Numbering	Clockwise, beginning at the one o'clock position

Placement of Callouts

Arrange callouts consistently throughout a document. Place callouts far enough apart to be read clearly. Space callouts evenly so that the illustration does not look cluttered and is not difficult to read.

The following examples show callouts with appropriate spacing.

EXAMPLE 11–11 Callout Spacing

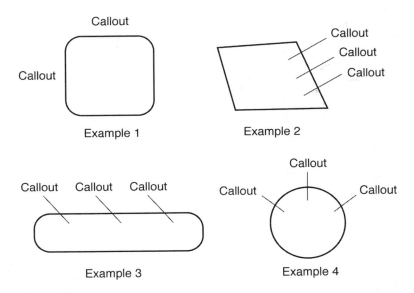

The following figure shows numbered callouts in a legend, with line art.

EXAMPLE 11–12 Numbered Callouts in Line Art

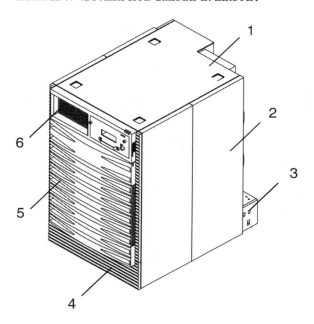

1 Callout   4 Callout

2 Callout   5 Very long callout

3 Callout   6 Callout

The following figure shows callout placement in a flow diagram.

EXAMPLE 11–13 Callouts in a Flow Diagram

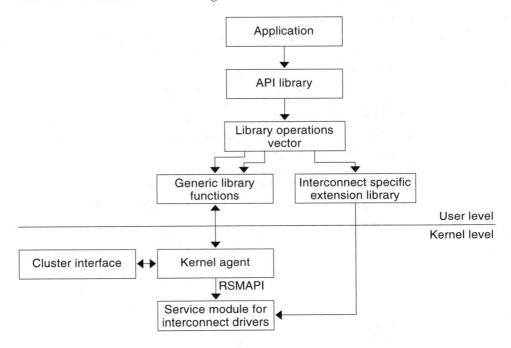

Creating Quality Screen Captures

Including screen captures in your documents is an effective way to help communicate graphical user interface (GUI) operations.

Guidelines for Creating Screen Captures

When creating screen captures, follow these guidelines:

- Check your capture settings.

  Screen capture tools often default to 72 dots per inch (dpi) when capturing images. Make sure that you capture your images at an acceptable size and resolution for your target document.

  Note that the dpi of printed raster images affects physical size. For example, a 72-dpi capture shrinks 50 percent when printed at 144 dpi. Print standards often require 300 dpi or higher, while 72 dpi is sufficient for online viewing.

- When creating screen captures for print, use a printer-friendly color palette or use a greyscale desktop color scheme.

- Save your screen capture in a high-quality format, such as .tif (for print) or .gif (for the web).

- Do not resize your screen capture by dragging or stretching its boundaries.

  This method causes image distortion.

Using Screen Captures as Guideposts Only

When including screen captures in online documents, place them at chosen points to serve as guideposts in navigation. These guideposts can help readers remain properly oriented and confirm that the document is proceeding as expected.

Including too many screen captures can be redundant. Avoid using screen captures in the following instances:

- When forms and dialog boxes are designed consistently across the GUI

- When GUI forms are self-explanatory and require no further explanation

- When data entry fields are labeled clearly and consistently

- When the GUI provides adequate feedback when used incorrectly

  For example, when users enter invalid data, feedback is generated.

Ensure that screen captures in online documents are not mistaken for actual software interfaces. Even sophisticated readers can confuse the two. For guidance on cropping, highlighting with color, and other strategies to make the distinction more obvious, contact your illustrator or production expert.

Creating Leader Lines

A *leader* is a line that points from a callout to a specific part of an illustration. This section contains instructions for creating leader lines and guidelines for using leader lines in illustrations.

Leader Style

The following table contains recommended specifications for leader lines.

TABLE 11–3 Leader Line Specifications

Specification	Description
Line weight	0.4 point
Length	Minimum length: 0.25 inch (0.64 cm)
	Maximum length: as short as possible
Angle	Consistent in drawing when possible
	Never perpendicular or parallel to text
	Not blended with illustration unless necessary

Additional Guidelines

When creating leader lines, follow these guidelines:

- Arrange callouts so that leader lines cross as few illustration lines as possible.
- Arrange leader lines so that the lines never cross.
- Terminate the leader line on the element.
- Begin the leader line at the corner closest to the callout.

Simplifying Online Illustrations

Complicated illustrations that work effectively in print work less well online because of screen readability problems. What is legible in print might not display clearly online.

To keep illustrations simple and to facilitate online reading, apply the following guidelines:

- Increase line weights and text size.

  Fine lines and small text are difficult to read online.

- Use fewer details online.

  Due to low resolution on some monitors, details that are effective in printed illustrations might be unreadable online.

- Reduce the size of large illustrations and crop them tightly.

- Limit the number of illustrations per page.

- Try to use tables instead of illustrations.

  When deciding whether to use an illustration, ask yourself: Would a table convey the information better? If a table and an illustration offer equal benefit, use a table. A table is simpler to create and maintain than an illustration.

CHAPTER 12

Writing About Graphical User Interfaces

A *graphical user interface* (GUI) provides the user with a visual way of interacting with a computer and its applications. The main purpose of a GUI is to make the activities that are involved in doing a task simple and quick. Common GUIs require a person to use a mouse or some other pointing and selecting device. GUIs are typically built around *windows* and *menus*, which provide a simple means of manipulating files and directories.

The term "graphical user interface" also includes web browsers.

This chapter discusses the following topics:

- "Using GUI Terminology" on page 221
- "Writing About Windows, Dialog Boxes, and Menus" on page 225
- "Writing About the Web" on page 228

Using GUI Terminology

Most computer users today are familiar with GUIs. However, you might still need to explain to novice computer users the basic concepts of the GUI and how to work in it.

Once you have established how to work in a GUI, write about the task the user wants to accomplish. You need not describe the detailed steps required to initiate the task. For example, a user rarely chooses menu items or clicks buttons with the goal of displaying other menus or dialog boxes. Rather, users want to accomplish a task that is activated by the menu item or button.

Writing About GUIs

When writing about GUIs, follow these guidelines:

- In the preface, define terms that you use throughout your document, such as "point," "click," "double-click," "select," or "choose."

  You also might provide an illustration of a typical window to clarify terms.

- Provide only the essential details or information that the user needs to know to accomplish the task.

- Distinguish windows, dialog boxes, and menus with their proper names. Avoid repeated use of the same name when the meaning is clear.

  For example, say you have told the user to choose Print from the File menu and the Print window is displayed. You do not need to keep saying "in the Print window" if that is the window in which you want the user to work.

- Document field names and menu option names as they appear in the GUI.

  You may add initial capital letters even if the word is not capitalized in the interface *only* to increase the readability of running text.

  > **Incorrect:** Select Prompt for credentials for every server for maximum security.
  > **Correct:** Select Prompt for Credentials for Every Server for maximum security.

- Do not use special text formatting such as an alternative font or bold type for GUI element names such as menu names, menu options, or field names. In documents with a large number of GUI procedures, such text formatting can be distracting and confusing for the reader.

- Do not include a colon or ellipsis points associated with a field name or menu option when mentioning the item in running text.

- Mention certain technical GUI distinctions only when necessary.

  For example, mention that a menu is a *pop-up menu* or a message is a *status message* only if that information is germane to the task at hand. This usage might be appropriate if you have multiple types of menus with similar names, for example.

Writing About Mouse Actions

When writing about a mouse, follow these guidelines:

- The plural for "mouse" is "mouse devices."

- The buttons on the mouse are referred to as *mouse buttons* to avoid confusion with control or command buttons in application windows.

    Click mouse button 3 in an empty part of the workspace.
    Click the right mouse button and drag across the object.

- The indicator that shows where the mouse action occurs is called the *pointer* or *cursor*.

    Keep the user's attention focused on the screen by writing about the pointer, not the mouse.

    Incorrect: Drag the mouse so that the cursor is on a corner of the object.
    Correct: Place the cursor on a corner of the object.

Using Common GUI Verbs

When writing about GUIs, reserve certain verbs for specific activities. The following table lists common usages. The terminology of your GUI might require alternatives.

TABLE 12–1 GUI Verbs

Verb	Action	Example
Choose	To open a menu or initiate a command.	Choose New from the File menu.
		Save your file, then choose Print.
Click	To press and release a mouse button without moving the pointer.	Click the left mouse button.
		Click the OK button.
Close	To close a window. Synonym for "dismiss."	Close the Add Users window.
Copy	To place a duplicate of the selection on the clipboard.	Copy the first figure in Appendix B.
Cut	To remove the selection from the current location and place it on the clipboard.	Cut the second entry in the list.
Dismiss	To close a window.	Dismiss the Add Users window.
Double-click	To click a mouse button twice quickly without moving the pointer.	Double-click the File Manager icon to open the program.

TABLE 12–1 GUI Verbs *(Continued)*

Verb	Action	Example
Drag	To move the pointer or an object by sliding the mouse with one or more buttons pressed.	Drag the pointer to draw a text box. Drag the icon to the upper left corner of the screen.
Highlight	Use "highlight" as the noun or adjective describing the appearance of selected text or an active button. Use "select" or "emphasize" as the verb form.	The selected text is highlighted. You can display the highlight in color.
Move	To move the pointer on the workspace by sliding the mouse with no buttons pressed.	Move the pointer outside the Mail window.
Open	To start or activate an application, or to access a document, file, or folder. To open an application window or web browser window.	Open FrameMaker. Open the Samples document. Open the Add Accounts window.
Paste	To place the clipboard contents at the insertion point.	Paste the figure into Chapter 3.
Point	To move the pointer to a specific location on the screen by moving the mouse with no buttons pressed. After the user is familiar with mouse techniques, you do not have to use this term. You can simply write "Click the Trash icon."	Point to the Trash icon and click to select it.
Press	To push a mouse button down and hold it down. Do not say "press and hold down," since the action of pressing includes holding down the button.	Press mouse button 3 on the File button.
Release	To let up on a mouse button to initiate an action.	Release mouse button 3 when the Print submenu appears.
Select	To highlight an entire window or data in a window, or to pick something from a list. To describe picking something from a menu, use "choose." Use "select" as the verb and "highlight" as the noun.	Select the Compose window. Select the second sentence. Select the file name in the list.
Size	To enlarge or reduce the size of a window.	Size the Text Editor window so that you can display more characters per line.

Writing About Windows, Dialog Boxes, and Menus

A graphical user interface includes the basic elements in which the application displays text and the user interacts with the application: windows, window controls, dialog boxes, and menus.

For examples of how to write procedures for GUI applications, see Chapter 6.

Window Elements

A *window* is the primary, rectangular area in which application elements are displayed.

The elements in a window vary from application to application. The names of window elements appear in the document's default font. The following table describes some common window elements.

TABLE 12–2 Window Elements

Element	Description
Background	Bordered rectangle in which the application displays its data or the user enters data
Control area	Region where controls, such as buttons or settings, are displayed
Footer	Region in which the application displays status and error messages, or state and mode information
Header or title bar	Region in which the application displays a title as a long-term message
Icon	Pictorial representation of a base window
Pop-up window or secondary window	Window that provides related or secondary information

Window Controls

Controls in windows enable the user to perform actions. The names of controls appear in the document's default font. For controls such as sliders, radio buttons, and check boxes, name the control type only when you need to distinguish it specifically. Some common window controls are described in the following table.

TABLE 12–3 Common Window Controls

Control	Description	Example
Button	Small area within the main window on which the user clicks to execute commands (command button), display pop-up windows (window button), or display menus (menu button).	Click the OK button.
Check box (some interfaces use "checkbox")	A yes or no, or on or off, control. When a setting is selected, a visual indicator appears in the square check box.	Select the No Markers check box.
Gauge	A read-only control, usually at the bottom of a window, that shows the percentage of use or the portion of an action that has been completed.	The gauge in the status bar shows the progress of the document composition.
Radio button	A yes or no, or on or off, control. Usually, only one radio button in a group can be selected.	Select the Add User option.
Resize corner	Control that enables the user to size the window without changing the scale of the contents.	Drag the resize corner to change the size of the window.
Scrollbar	Control that moves the view of the data that is displayed in the window.	Scroll to the top of your document.
Slider	Control that is used to set a value within a range and to give a visual indication of the setting.	Drag the slider to the desired saturation value.
Text field	Input area for text. If the field name includes a trailing colon, do not include the colon when referring to the field in running text. Text field names do not generally appear in an alternate font. Use monospace font for any specific text that you are instructing the user to type into a field.	Type your company name in the Organization field.

Dialog Boxes

A *dialog box* is a pop-up window in which the user provides information or issues commands. (In some GUI applications, a dialog box is called a *secondary window*.) Keep in mind that a user does not select menu items or buttons "to display the dialog box" but to do a task through the dialog box.

Incorrect:

1. **Choose Add Users from the Actions menu to display the Add Users dialog box.**

Correct:

1. **Choose Add Users from the Actions menu.**

   The Add Users dialog box appears.

Menus

A *menu* or a *submenu* is a list of application options.

If you are writing for novice users who might be unfamiliar with GUIs, use step-by-step instructions when you first write about choosing items or settings from a menu.

Menu option names appear in the document's default font and do not receive any special typographic styling. Also, even if a menu option includes ellipsis points in the GUI, do not include the ellipsis points when mentioning the option in text.

Here is an example of detailed steps that use menu options.

To paste text:

1. **Press mouse button 1 on the Edit button in the menu bar.**

   The Edit menu is displayed.

2. **Drag the pointer to the Paste item and release the mouse button.**

   The contents of the clipboard are placed at the insertion point.

After you have explained how menus work, streamline the process by saying "Choose Paste from the Edit menu" or "From the Edit menu, choose Paste."

Alternatively, you can use an arrow symbol to show the menu selection. For example, "Choose Edit $\Rightarrow$ Paste."

Writing About the Web

The World Wide Web is a relatively recent medium. No solid consensus has been reached on industry-standard terminology for browsers or navigation. This section provides some guidelines for usage.

Web Terminology

Use the following terminology when writing about the web:

- Use "web browser" rather than "web browser window" or "browser" when referring generally to web browsers or to the main or first web browser window.
- You "start" a web browser and "open" additional web browser windows or web pages.

  Start Netscape Navigator™.
  Open the Display Users page.

- Use the verbs "navigate" or "browse" when referring generally to moving through a web page rather than "explore" or "surf."
- Assume that URL is pronounced "you-are-ell" and use the appropriate related article ("a URL").
- Use a capital "w" when discussing items on the World Wide Web that are accessible through the Internet.

  Additional product information might be available at the company's Web site.
  Do not include proprietary information on the public Web site.

- Use a lowercase "w" when discussing general web references or an intranet site.

  A web browser reads HTML pages.
  The design of your web site should help readers find what they need.
  The hr.central web site contains useful employee information.

Referencing URLs

Use monospace font for URLs.

For information about legal requirements for linking to a third-party Web site, see "Third-Party Web Site References" on page 162. For guidance on writing links, see Chapter 5. For information about referring to online articles or journals, see "Citing Electronic Sources" on page 52.

When introducing URLs, both internal and external, follow these guidelines:

- Make references to URLs as simple and direct as possible.

  Readers no longer need to be told to type a URL. For example, you do not need to write detailed instructions such as "Point your web browser at the following URL."

  Incorrect:

  You can find further information by typing the following URL: `http://www.plirg.com`.

  Correct:

  Further information is available at `http://www.plirg.com`.

  Incorrect:

  Open the following URL in your web browser: `http://www.plirg.com`.

  Correct:

  Go to `http://www.plirg.com`.

- Precede a URL with "at" or "to" when a preposition is needed.

  Incorrect:

  Check for updates on `http://www.plirg.com`.

  Correct:

  Check for updates at `http://www.plirg.com`.

  Correct:

  To check for updates, go to `http://www.plirg.com`.

- Provide explanatory text about the web site before giving the URL.

  A URL is acceptable at the end of a sentence. Readers no longer confuse end punctuation with spelled-out URLs.

  Incorrect:

  Go to `http://www.plirg.com` for resources for developers and service providers.

  Correct:

  For resources for developers and service providers, go to `http://www.plirg.com`.

  Correct:

  PlirgSoft offers resources for developers and service providers at `http://www.plirg.com`.

When placing URLs in text, use the following guidelines:

- If the URL is long, place the URL on its own line and introduce it with a colon.
- If the URL is short, weave it into the sentence.
- If your document provides two or more URLs in the same paragraph, place them in a bulleted list.

If you need to refer to an extremely long URL, use one of the following techniques:

- Provide the base URL and an indication of what links to click to get to the specific page.

  Awkward:

  For more legal information, see:
  `http://plirglegal.north/Legal_Ops/plirglegalweb/`
  `legal_orgchart.html`.

  Clearer:

  Click Organization Chart on the main Legal web site at
  `http://plirglegal.north`.

- Substitute text for the URL in print and use the same text online as a link.

CHAPTER 13

Glossary Guidelines

This chapter explains how to create a glossary for a technical manual. Most technical manuals increasingly introduce a number of new terms. A glossary improves the usability of a technical manual by simplifying a reader's search for definitions for these new terms. Before you create a glossary, consider its use and organization.

This chapter discusses the following topics:

Glossary Content

The terms that you select for a glossary must be important to the subject, with simple and concise definitions that are appropriate for the context. A glossary can contain some background definitions that are not defined within your book if these definitions enhance understanding of the subject. An example is units of measure.

A glossary can also include terms that have another meaning apart from technology. Examples are "front porch" and "portal." You might also include terms that are unique to the book.

Some terms are not considered appropriate for a glossary. These terms include the following:

- Commands from a programming language or from an operating system
- Window menu selections
- Terms that a reader can find in a standard dictionary or an industry glossary

Finding Definitions

For terms that are specific to your particular product, try to obtain definitions from your technical subject matter expert, usually an engineer. For standard industry terms, first check a standard dictionary. If the term is not in this dictionary, check the third-party reference books that are listed in Appendix B.

Online glossaries are usually easy to access. You might find the definition that you need without much difficulty.

Note – If you need to borrow definitions from another source, ensure that you rewrite the definitions so that you are not guilty of plagiarism. To inspire originality, define a term as if you were creating a definition for someone who is unfamiliar with the term or technology.

Ensure that your glossary is verified in a technical review, along with your main text.

Creating New Terms

If you need to create an entirely new term for a name in a new product, follow these guidelines:

- Ensure that the new term can be pronounced as you intend.

  If you have any doubts, use a different term. An example is "invalid," which can be pronounced two ways with two different meanings.

- Ensure that the new term cannot be read as obscene and that the term's meaning cannot be mistaken.

- Ensure that a translator can adequately translate the new term.

Formatting a Glossary

Glossary page formats differ from book to book. You can see these differences especially in Internet glossaries, which use a variety of publishing software for their online presence. All glossaries do have some common characteristics:

- All terms are arranged alphabetically.
- Each term begins on a separate line.
- Each term is followed by its definition or expansion.

Some glossaries capitalize the first letter of each important word in an entry. Other glossaries capitalize only proper nouns in terms. Examples in this chapter follow the correct capitalization of the term as used in the book. Terms often follow the capitalization that is recognized by a standards organization, such as ANSI, IEEE, or ISO. The typeface, margins, and indents are determined by the templates and the publishing software that you use to create the glossary.

Terms for an International Audience

If your document or documentation set has a glossary, ensure that the language of definitions in the text is consistent with that glossary. If you are working with a translation or localization group, provide a glossary and a style sheet for your document.

When you are writing glossary definitions, remember the concerns of translators and nonnative speakers. This audience sometimes struggles to understand a new term in English in the process of rewording the term in another language. Therefore, be as complete as possible when you write a glossary entry. Try to include the following items:

- Grammatical use in a sentence, when a distinction is important

  For example, is the term a plural noun that is more commonly used in English as a singular noun?

- Source, location, and usage of the term

  For example, where is the term used: in software, a graphical user interface, help files, hardware, marketing material, web navigation, or legal documents?

- Sample sentence that shows the term's usage (optional)

In many instances, the term is so widely used that the particulars do not need to be carefully defined. But the value of the glossary increases as you add details for the international audience. For more information about internationalization, see Chapter 7.

When to Include a Glossary

If you are documenting new technology, a glossary is almost mandatory. An audience that is unfamiliar with the topic can probably benefit from a major set of definitions.

To decide whether you need a glossary for your book, consider your content. If your content describes a new product with many new vocabulary words that you define within the text, include a glossary.

Alternatively, if the scope of your content does not extend to new material, you might not need a glossary. If you do not need to define many terms as you write, your audience might be familiar with the terminology.

If your book is a legacy book that has never had a glossary, add a glossary if you have time. The inclusion of a glossary especially applies to books that are undergoing major revisions. If you define many new terms within the text, you need to create a book glossary.

Writing Good Glossary Entries

Ideally, you define each new term at least three times:

1. At its first usage in text

   Give a brief but concise definition of the term.

2. At its first usage in a subsequent chapter if the book is hard copy only

   Here, a short, summary definition suffices.

3. In the glossary

   Users expect a complete definition in the glossary.

The best time to write a glossary entry is when you first introduce an unfamiliar term in your text.

Introducing Glossary Entries in Text

When you write text, you frequently need to introduce terms to your audience. Define new terms and technical terms that are not listed in a standard dictionary the first time that those terms occur in text. Italicize terms when you first define them. Also, include these terms in a glossary. For example:

> Several configuration files are included with your package. A *configuration* file is a text-readable file that is used to set up or configure a part of the system.

The use of italic indicates that an entry for the word "configuration" appears in the glossary.

Tip – Some authoring environments for online presentation enable you to link a definition directly to the italicized term.

---

configuration (1) (n.) The way that you have set up your computer.

(2) (n.) The combination of hardware components that compose a computer system: CPU, monitor, keyboard, and peripheral devices.

(3) (n.) The software settings that enable various hardware components of a computer system to communicate.

Wording a Glossary Entry

Glossary style usually presents the glossary term in a simple, singular noun form. The part of speech that you use for the term demands that you use the same part of speech as a keyword in the definition. An example follows.

concatenate (v.) To string together two or more sequences, such as files, into one longer sequence.

node (n.) An addressable point on a network. Each node in a network has a different name. A node can connect a computing system, a terminal, or various other peripheral devices to the network.

Wording the Definition

The definition, which immediately follows the term, does not restate the term. The restatement might be assumed, along with the unwritten words "is a" or "is," if the article is included. An example follows.

debugger   (n.) A program that locates operational errors in another program. The debugger usually enables the developer to examine the malfunctioning portion of the program for bad data and to check operational conditions. See also debug.

decryption   (n.) The process of converting encrypted data to plain text. See also encryption.

Ensure that the definition agrees in number with the term. The definition does not need to be a complete sentence.

Defining Multiword Terms

Defining a term that consists of multiple words, usually one or more modifiers and a noun, is similar to defining a single word. An example follows.

shell procedure   (n.) An executable file that is not a compiled program. A shell procedure calls a shell to read and execute commands that are contained in a file. This procedure enables you to store a sequence of commands in a file for reuse. Also called a shell program or command file.

Defining Parts of Speech

Of all glossary users, translators and nonnative speakers can benefit the most from knowing the part of speech for a term. However, all users can improve their understanding of a term by knowing how to use that term in a sentence. The following list shows the abbreviations for parts of speech.

adj.   Adjective

adv.   Adverb

n.   Noun

v.   Verb

The following example shows two parts of speech:

format   (1) (n.) The structure of data that is to be processed, recorded, or displayed.

            (2) (v.) To put data into a structure or to divide a disk into sectors for receiving data.

Creating Multiple Definitions

When a term requires more than one definition, use a numeral that is surrounded by a set of parentheses and no other punctuation. Append a space to this text. Start a new paragraph for each definition, as the following example shows.

luminance   (1) (n.) The generic flux from a light-emitting or light-reflecting surface. The subjective response to luminance is brightness.

(2) (n.) The specific ratio of color primaries that provides a match for the white point in a specified color space.

(3) (n.) The portion of a composite signal that carries brightness information.

Defining Acronyms and Abbreviations

Acronyms and abbreviations are alphabetized letter-by-letter, as described in "Alphabetizing a Glossary" on page 238. Occasionally, you need only give an expansion of the term. At other times, you need to provide a definition as well.

Because most users are familiar with just the acronym or abbreviation, spell out the meaning and give the definition immediately after the acronym or abbreviation. You can double-post the abbreviation and the expansion. The following examples show entries with abbreviations and expansions.

SIP   (single inline package) (n.) The packaging of an electronic component with all leads protruding from one side only.

SMPTE   (n.) Society of Motion Picture and Television Engineers.

SNMP   (Simple Network Management Protocol) (n.) The preferred network management protocol for TCP/IP-based internets.

When you use multiple definitions for an acronym or abbreviation, use a numbering system, as the following example shows.

BSD   (1. Berkeley Software Distribution) (n.) UNIX versions that were developed at the University of California, Berkeley. These versions have names such as BSD 2.7 and BSD 4.2.

(2. block schematic diagram) (n.) A circuit board flowchart.

Note – If an acronym or abbreviation that is expanded in your book chapter contains initial capital letters, ensure that you repeat the capitalization in the glossary.

Using "See" and "See Also" References

When you refer to another term, use the word "See" to direct the reader to use another word. Do not define the term when you use "See."

solid model   (n.) See surface model.

Use "See also" after you have defined a term to direct the reader to other terms with similar meanings. If you are referring to an acronym or abbreviation, use the short form. The following examples show two ways to use "See also."

composite drive   (n.) A single logical drive that is composed of more than one physical drive. See also disk array, RAID.

`crontab` **file**   (n.) A file that lists commands which are to be executed at specified times on specified dates. See also `cron`.

Alphabetizing a Glossary

The writer is responsible for arranging a glossary alphabetically. Most publishing software does not automatically alphabetize a glossary. Most glossaries are alphabetized by the letter-by-letter method. This method does not observe spaces between words. An example follows.

> typefaces
> type form
> typescript
> type size

Creating Online Links

For online use, your glossary definition can contain multiple online links. These links reduce the number of "See also" citations. In the example that follows, a set of underscores indicates online links. These links are not displayed as sets of underscores in online text.

namespace table   (n.) The place where all _namespace_ information is stored, for use by the _classing engine_ as well as a _namespace manager_. Each namespace table consists of entries (rows) and each entry consists of a set of named attributes.

For more information about online writing style, see Chapter 4.

Indexing Glossary Terms

Do not index the glossary. Because the glossary is arranged alphabetically or searched by keyword, a reader can find any definition quickly, with no need for index entries.

However, a reader might look for a glossary term in the index to determine how the term is used in the main text of the document. Consequently, some terms that are in the glossary might also appear in the index. These index entries should cite only pages that are in the main text.

CHAPTER 14

Indexing

An index is often a reader's primary information retrieval device. When readers search for a particular topic and find it referenced in an index, they are assured that the topic is covered in the document and their search has ended. When readers do not find a topic in an index, they might decide that the topic is not covered in that document and they might look elsewhere.

This chapter discusses the following topics:

What Is an Index?

According to *The Chicago Manual of Style*:

> A good index records every pertinent statement made within the body of the text. The subject matter and purpose of the book determine which statements are pertinent and which peripheral. An index should be considerably more than an expanded, alphabetical table of contents. It should also be something other than a concordance of words and phrases.[1]

---

1   *The Chicago Manual of Style,* 14th ed. Chicago: University of Chicago Press, 1993, p. 703.

Style and Format

The following figure shows two examples of the indented indexing style. One example shows the index format for unnumbered chapters, the other example is for numbered chapters. The only differences between the two examples are the format of the page numbers and the use of "to" as a separator for page ranges in the book with numbered chapters.

EXAMPLE 14–1 Index Formats

Unnumbered chapter format example:

A

application architecture, 12
application gateway, **211**, 345–351
automounter facility
 See also mounting
 overview, 49
 setup, 51
  remote mounting, 52
  specifying subdirectories, 51

B

backing up
 file systems, 58
  dump command, 89–92
  dump strategies, 81

Numbered chapter format example:

A

application architecture, 1-2
application gateway, **4-18**, 5-76 to 5-81
automounter facility
 See also mounting
 overview, 2-12
 setup, 2-15
  remote mounting, 2-16
  specifying subdirectories, 2-14

B

backing up
 file systems, 3-1
  dump command, 3-34 to 3-37
  dump strategies, 3-26

Nested Entries

Many technical documents use up to three levels of nested entries: *primary* entry, *secondary* entry, and *tertiary* entry. Each entry level is indented from the previous level. These three levels appear as follows:

primary entry
 secondary entry
  tertiary entry

The primary entry is the principal subdivision of an index. A simple primary entry includes the entry and a page number. A primary entry covering two or more page numbers is usually divided into secondary entries. Each secondary entry must bear a logical relationship to the primary entry. A secondary entry covering several page numbers can be further divided into tertiary entries. Each tertiary entry must bear a logical relationship to the secondary entry.

In an indented style, each secondary entry and each tertiary entry begins a new indented line unless there is only one secondary entry. If an entry runs over the width of the column, it is indented in flush-and-hang style. That is, the first line is set flush and the rest of the entry is indented below it.

> Least-Recently-Used (LRU) Ring functional
> > description, 3-17
> > elements of, 3-24

Page Number Style

A comma and a space are inserted between the entry and the first page number. Subsequent page numbers are separated with a comma and a space. Page numbers appear in ascending order.

Do not include a page reference in the primary entry if it has two or more secondary entries.

> functional description
> > input block, 2-3 to 2-32
> > introduction, 2-1
> > output block, 2-33

Major Page References

In certain cases, you might want to identify a particular page as the main source of information for a given topic, especially if the topic cites two or more pages. You can identify the main page by marking the page number in bold.

> application gateway, 211, **345–351**
> :
> dragging operations, 13, **37**, 114

Page Ranges

In a page range spanning several pages of a numbered chapter, separate first and last page numbers with a space, the word "to," and another space. For example:

> screen adjustments, 1-6 to 1-12

In a consecutively numbered page range, use an en dash to separate page numbers. For example:

    screen adjustments, 6–12

Special Typography

The index is subject to many of the same typographic style conventions found in the text of the document itself. For example, if file names and commands appear in monospace font in your book, then they appear that way in the index.

    core file, 16
    rlogin command, 166

"See" and "See Also" References

"See" and "See also" cross-references require special consideration. For more information, see "How to Use "See" and "See Also" References" on page 256.

Capitalization

Do not capitalize any word in an index entry unless the word is a proper noun, an acronym, or an abbreviation that is supposed to be capitalized. Use standard rules for capitalization.

    subwindow button, 37
    SunView accelerator, 34

Punctuation

If an entry is followed immediately by page references, insert a comma between the entry and the first page reference and between subsequent page references.

    scrolling, 12, 16, 27

If you invert an adjective and a noun or noun phrase in an entry, separate them with a comma.

    controls, window, 21

Use no punctuation between a primary entry without page numbers and subsequent secondary entries.

    selection
        adjusting, 6
        extending, 59

Creating an Index

A document needs an index if it has 20 or more pages. This rule applies to any type of document, from a user's guide to a technical reference manual.

Indexing is an iterative process. Your first pass at an index is merely the foundation on which to build your final index. The first pass will be full of similar primary entries that you need to divide into secondary entries. When you first develop your index, you might introduce spelling errors and have incomplete page ranges in individual entries. Such errors can be corrected during the editing phase. See "Refining and Checking an Index" on page 263 for possible solutions.

Time Required to Create an Index

Generally allow one full day for indexing for every 25 pages of text. A 100-page document might take four full days to index. An experienced indexer might require less time; a first-time indexer might require more time. Certain types of documents are much more difficult to index than others. Those documents require even more time than given in this guideline.

Note – If your index is prepared by a professional indexer using dedicated indexing software, approximately 50 to 60 pages of technical material can be indexed per day.

Deciding Which Parts of a Document to Index

The first decision you need to make when starting to create an index is to determine which of the following parts of a document to index:

- **Front matter.** Do not index the title page, copyright page, table of contents, and lists of figures, tables, and examples.
- **Preface.** Index the preface if it contains information about the subjects within the document and not just why the document was written. Topics you might index in a preface include prerequisite knowledge, other applicable documents, or document conventions.
- **Chapters.** Use the main body of the document as the source for most of the index entries.
- **Tables and figures.** Index topics within tables and figures if they are of particular importance to the discussion. Do not index items within tables that merely reproduce information already contained in the text. Including index references to the subjects of the tables and figures themselves is often helpful to a reader.

- **Footnotes.** Index footnotes if they expand on the information in the text. Do not index footnotes that merely document statements in the text.

- **Appendixes.** Index appendixes if they contain pertinent material omitted from the main body of the document. Do not index appendixes if they merely reproduce information already contained in the main body. A quick reference in an appendix, for example, is usually not indexed. Nor is a questionnaire. Worksheets in an appendix are indexed unless they merely repeat the main text.

- **Back matter.** Do not index terms in a glossary if they are explained elsewhere in the document. Do not index a bibliography or a reader comment form.

Selecting Topics to Index

When you take on the task of creating an index, you must first decide what the pertinent statements or topics are. A topic can be a single word, a phrase, or even a concept. A topic has no minimum or maximum size.

As you analyze a topic, decide whether the topic contains information a reader might expect to find in the index. If it does, create one or more index entries.

To determine whether a topic requires an index entry, analyze the topic for the following attributes:

- **Describes how to perform a task.** Tasks are the key subjects in certain types of documents, such as installation manuals.

- **Contains a definition of a term, acronym, or abbreviation.** Definitions are frequently the key to a reader's understanding of the document. An effective index makes it easy for a reader to find the definition or, similarly, an acronym or abbreviation. However, do not identify in an index definitions, acronyms, and abbreviations by glossary page numbers, but rather by text page numbers. See "Create Index Entries for Acronyms and Abbreviations" on page 252.

- **States a restriction, such as a Caution.** Awareness of the restriction might help a reader avoid costly mistakes.

- **Explains a concept or an idea.** This type of topic is most helpful to a reader. However, creating index entries that describe a concept or an idea is fairly difficult. The difficulty is in describing the whole concept in a few words.

Do Not Index Superfluous Entries

Frequently, superfluous entries are in an index because the person creating the index refers to every occurrence of selected words or phrases in the document. The index is not a concordance, but rather an information retrieval device.

For example, assume that the following sentence appeared in the text being indexed:

Separate chapters of this manual discuss the use of disk and tape storage devices.

In this example, the sentence provides no information about disk or tape storage. Therefore, a reader would gain nothing from these index entries:

disk storage, 37
⋮
tape storage, 37

Include entries in an index only if they refer a reader directly to useful information.

Avoid Entries That Are Too General

Do not use entries so general that they apply to a global level of information. Such an entry is too broad to inform a reader of the entry's corresponding content in the text.

For example, do not include entries such as "File Manager, creating files in" in a book about File Manager; or "features, of Netscape Navigator" in a book about this application. The only entries under the name of the application you are documenting address its use, for example, entries such as "installing" or "quitting" the application.

Include Common Industry Terminology

Terms for common procedures and commands might differ, depending on the technology or company. If you know of a common synonym for a process or command, include an entry to direct a reader to the term used in your book, as shown in these examples:

abort, *See* cancel
delete, *See* cut
search, *See* find

Avoid Using Headings as Index Entries

Using headings as the basis for index entries results in an index that is hard for the reader to scan.

Incorrect	Correct
running the QuickView utility, 42	direct virtual memory access (DVMA), using, 87
using direct virtual memory access (DVMA), 87	hidden file, definition, 28
	QuickView utility, running, 42
What is a hidden file?, 28	

Consider Including "Commands" as a Primary Entry

An editor can help you decide whether including "commands" as an index entry is useful. If you decide to include "commands" as a primary entry, follow it with subentries for each command appearing in the book.

```
commands
    aset
    chmod
```

Describing a Topic

Once you have determined that a topic merits an index entry, find one or more ways to describe it to a reader. The descriptions that you create become the subjects of the index entries. To describe a topic, follow these guidelines:

- Anticipate a reader's needs.
- Select the proper words for the subjects.
- Arrange the words for emphasis.
- Create multiple entries (double-post).
- Group the entries.

Anticipate a Reader's Needs

When a reader uses an index, it is usually to answer one of the following questions:

- Where can I find information about a certain task, term, or topic?
- Does the information described by an index entry tell me what something is, how it works, or how to use it?
- Which pages can I ignore because they contain information I already know?

By anticipating a reader's needs as you describe topics for your index, you can create an index that helps a reader find information quickly and easily.

Include Only Terms a Reader Is Likely to Look Up

When creating an entry, ask yourself whether you would be likely as a reader to look in the index for that entry.

Questionable entries include the following:

- Entries starting with terms such as "how" or "why"
- Entries starting with irrelevant terms

- Commands or widgets used only in sample programs or examples

  For example, in a book in which an exercise involves creating the buttons "Hello!" and "Adios!," do not include "Hello!" and "Adios!" as index entries.

- Titles of books in a "Recommended Reading" section
- Entries that use the same phrasing as section headings

Select Proper Words for Subjects

The words that you select are an abstract of the topic. Choose words that are as descriptive as possible. Using words from the text as subjects of index entries might satisfy readers who know the terminology used in the document. For other readers, provide subjects or cross-references worded so that they can find the desired information without specific prior knowledge.

Use Gerunds

Use a gerund, not an infinitive or a plain verb, as the main subject of an index entry when appropriate. For example, use "initializing" rather than "to initialize" or "initialize."

Identify the Entry Type

Identify each entry for a computing term by including the type of entry after its name. For example, this type might be a command, file, function, or attribute:

```
apropos command
  width attribute
```

Arrange Words for Emphasis

Typically, make the most important word the first word of the subject. The choice of most important word depends on what you want to stress or what is most important to a reader. For example, if the words you choose to describe a topic are "pixwin background color," the primary entries might be as follows:

```
background color, pixwin
color, pixwin background
pixwin background color
```

Use Plural for Main Entries

In general, index the plural forms of nouns.

> clients
> ⋮
> servers

The exceptions to this rule are nouns that are only singular or nouns that are only used in the singular in the context being documented. Another exception is proper nouns such as the names of applications.

> `get` command
> ⋮
> Tmark database

Assign the Proper Font to the Entry

Keep in mind that certain terms require different fonts if you refer to the terms in different contexts. You also need to include a word such as "command," "file," or "directory" after such terms to further clarify the entry.

> `quit` command
> quit, in contrast to exit

Group Entries

Grouping entries means combining entries that have common first words into primary entries and secondary entries.

Ungrouped Entries	Grouped Entries	
SBus, introduction	SBus	*Primary entry*
SBus block diagram	block diagram introduction	*Secondary entries*
SBus specifications	specifications	

When selecting a subject to be followed by secondary entries, be careful to group subjects properly. Do not merely select a word or phrase for a subject because it is common to several entries.

For example, assume that the following subjects appeared in your document:

> igneous rock
> metamorphic rock
> rock music

To isolate "rock" and create three secondary entries is incorrect. If you analyze the use of "rock" in each entry, you can see that it is used in two different ways.

Incorrect	Correct

rock
    igneous
    metamorphic
    music
	rocks
	    igneous
	    metamorphic
	rock music

Create Index Entries for Cautions, Notes, and Tips

You want readers to be able to locate the various restrictions or ease-of-use features in your document, including the following:

- Sets of rules
- Value limits (maximums and minimums)
- Incompatibilities between features and options
- Caution notices
- Ease-of-use Notes or Tips

Most of the topics that qualify as restrictions are not stated as such in the text. You must analyze the text to find the restrictions to index. Write index entries so that the subject describes the nature of the restriction.

You can also index those Notes or Tips that provide ease-of-use information or features.

Make sure to enable readers who are familiar with the document organization to ignore the entry if they already know the restriction or feature.

Incorrect	Correct
symbolic names, restriction	symbolic names, maximum length of
Window menu shortcut	Window menu shortcut, F9 key

In many documents, certain restrictions are identified specifically because of their importance. For example, assume that the following Caution notice appears in your document:

Caution – Never turn the system unit on or off while a diskette is in the disk drive. You might damage the diskette.

Index this restriction flagged with the word "Caution." The entry might be as follows:

    turning system on or off, Caution notice

Create Index Entries for Acronyms and Abbreviations

Include an acronym or abbreviation in your index if it is unique to your document or documentation set and if it is not likely to be found in common usage. Many acronyms and abbreviations need not be included in an index. For example, the abbreviations for most units of measure, such as Btu, in., or lb, are not good candidates for indexing.

Alphabetize acronyms and abbreviations as words, rather than as the spelled-out version of the acronym or abbreviation. When you include an acronym or abbreviation in an index, follow it with the word or words from which it was formed. Place those words within parentheses.

    CCP (console command processor), 1-5

Double-post the entry by adding an entry for the words that form the acronym or abbreviation, followed by the acronym or abbreviation in parentheses.

    console command processor (CCP), 1-5

Double-Posting Entries

Double-posting means identifying a topic in two different places in an index. For example, a topic that appears as "address switch" and "switch, address" is double-posted in the index. A topic that appears in three places is triple-posted, and so on.

Entry	Double-Posted or Triple-Posted Entries
power indicator	power indicator indicator, power

Entry	Double-Posted or Triple-Posted Entries
C shell command interpreter	C shell command interpreter command interpreter, C shell interpreter, C shell command

Be careful of over-indexing with double-posting. Certain entries do not deserve double-posting. For instance, the following example might be acceptable in a document that refers to only a few commands.

Entry	Double-Posted Entries
grep command	grep command command, grep

However, for a manual with many commands, the entries under "command" might grow too numerous. In this case, rather than creating a primary entry of "command" with many secondary entries, index the commands under the command name and do not double-post the entries. Instead, include a cross-reference.

Entries	Double-Posted Entries
cat command grep command history command ⋮	commands, *See* specific command names

Double-posting increases the number of index entries available to a reader, which broadens the scope of the index. The knowledgeable reader is not forced to scan the index for a general entry when seeking a specific topic.

Double-posting has a dramatic effect on usability. It is an essential technique for creating a high-quality index. Try to double-post entries for all key concepts and important terminology.

Keep in mind, however, that double-posting an index can affect your schedule. Because an extensively double-posted index provides a denser, more comprehensive view of a document's topics, be sure to include enough time in your schedule for double-posting your index.

Creating "See" and "See Also" References

You cross-reference index entries by creating "See" and "See also" references.

When to Use "See" and "See Also" References

- Use a "See" reference when you have so many secondary entries that repeating them is unreasonable.

  > configuration, *See* measurement configuration
  > ⋮
  > measurement configuration
  >   applying storage thresholds
  >   calculating line speeds
  >   defining data fields
  >   defining entities

- Use a "See" reference to send readers from a broad category to a more specific category.

  The next example is valid only if there are several secondary entries under "display thresholds," "exception thresholds," and "storage thresholds." Otherwise, you would double-post.

  > thresholds, *See* display thresholds; exception thresholds; storage thresholds

- Use a "See" reference to direct a reader from a term not used in the document to a term that is used as an index entry.

  > cars, *See* automobiles

- Consider using a "See also" reference to direct a reader to related information at another index entry.

  Depending on how your index is structured, you might also use a "See also" cross-reference from a specific category to a general one.

  > dBASE, 37
  >   *See also* database applications

- Use a "See also" reference to avoid fourth-level entries.

  > performance database
  >   *See also* update, performance database
  >   backing up data in
  >   deleting
  >   updating
  > ⋮
  > update, performance database
  >   automatic
  >   displaying status
  >   manual
  >   starting
  >   stopping

- Clarify index entries for some noun modifiers, such as "data" and "file," that are ubiquitous.

  If you have several long and complicated entries that start with the same word, readers might not look far enough to find a given topic. In this case, use a "See also" reference to help a reader.

  > data
  >> *See also* data files; data records
  >> collecting
  >> deleting

- Never use a "See" reference with an entry that includes a page number.

  Never include a page number in a "See also" reference.

Incorrect	Correct
structured files, 7-3 *See* files, structured structured files, 7-3 *See also* chaotic files, 8-4	structured files, *See* files, structured structured files, 7-3 *See also* chaotic files

- Make sure that a "See" or "See also" reference repeats the exact wording of the entry to which it refers.

Incorrect	Correct
database, *See* PDB ⋮ performance database (PDB)	database, *See* performance database (PDB) ⋮ performance database (PDB)

- Do not use unnecessary "See" references.

  If you can reasonably double-post an entry, do so. Readers have every right to be upset if you send them elsewhere in an index just for one or two page numbers.

Incorrect	Correct
command objects, *See* objects ⋮ objects, 5-2, 5-8	command objects, 5-2, 5-8 ⋮ objects, 5-2, 5-8

In particular, do not send readers from a specific entry to a general entry, under which they must then search for the specific entry. However, be careful that you include general information under the specific entry as well. In the following example, "changing report attributes" must be under the entries for specific reports because a reader might not look at the general entry.

Incorrect	Correct
forecast reports, *See* reporting	forecast reports, 3-67
⋮	changing report attributes, 3-122
reporting	⋮
automatic, 2-33, 3-174	reporting
changing report attributes, 3-122	automatic, 2-33, 3-174
forecast reports, 3-67	changing report attributes, 3-122
predefined reports, 3-71	forecast reports, 3-67
	predefined reports, 3-71

- Do not use a "See also" reference to send a reader to a duplicate (double-posted) entry in an index.

  Incorrect:

  entry-sequenced files, 7-3
      See also files, entry-sequenced
  ⋮
  files, entry-sequenced, 7-3

How to Use "See" and "See Also" References

Here are basic formatting and punctuation rules for "See" and "See also" references:

- Italicize the words "See" and "See also."

  base window, 45
      See also pane

- Never include page numbers with "See" and "See also" references.

  Use those references to direct a reader to another index entry.

  floppy, *See* diskette

- Place the "See" reference on the same line as the index entry, separated with a comma.

  search, *See* find

- Place the "See also" reference at the beginning of the entry.

  Place the "See also" reference on a line by itself, and indent the reference from the line above.

  aggregation scheme, 16
      See also summarization, data

- Use a semicolon to separate multiple "See" and "See also" references.

  local area network, 24
      See also Ethernet; standards, networking; wide area network

- For secondary entries, use "See" and "See also" references as follows.

Incorrect	Correct
files	files
comparing, 30	comparing, 30
deleting, 24	deleting, 24
initialization, 121	editing, *See* vi editor
renaming, 141	initialization, 121
files, editing, *See* vi editor	printing, 35
files, printing, 35	*See also* PostScript documents
See also PostScript documents	renaming, 141

Avoiding Indexing Problems

This section explains some established rules for indexing. If you disregard them, you might confuse or annoy readers. You might also appear incompetent to any reader who is knowledgeable about indexing.

Use a Single-Level Entry for a Single Topic

If you can use the primary entry alone, do so. A primary term with only one secondary term must be on a single text line. If you feel that the primary entry alone is misleading, rewrite it.

Incorrect	Correct
optimization routines	optimization routines, 38
use of, 38	
	or
	optimization routines, use of, 38

Use an Adjective With a Noun as a Primary Entry

Use adjectives with related nouns to provide enough information for a reader.

Incorrect	Correct
implicit	implicit commands
logoff command, 6-4	logoff, 6-4
open command, 6-1	open, 6-1
wait command, 6-6	wait, 6-6

This rule applies to noun modifiers, that is, nouns that are being used as adjectives. This rule eliminates awkward, confusing constructions in which the primary entry is a noun relative to some secondary entries and an adjective relative to others.

Incorrect	Correct

data
    collecting, 81
    files, 90
    purging, 62
    records, 47
    ⋮
wait
    command, 29
    parameter, 33
	data
	    collecting, 81
	    purging, 62
	data files, 90
	data records, 47
	    ⋮
	wait command, 29
	wait parameter, 33

Avoid a Primary Entry That Is Too General

Generally, if a primary entry is followed by half a page or so of secondary entries, either the primary entry is too broad or you are over-indexing. For example, in a printer manual, the primary entry "printer" is too broad to be indexed as a term.

If you feel that it is necessary or helpful, use "commands" plus a "See" reference to send a reader to alternate methods of locating a given command.

Incorrect	Correct

commands
    alias, 14
    at, 19
    batch, 23
    ⋮
    ypmatch, 132
    ypwhich, 134
    zcat, 135
	(no entry at all, if most of the document describes commands)
	
	or
	
	commands, *See* individual commands by name
	
	or
	
	commands, summary of, 18

Do Not Over-Index

For manuals that have a repetitive structure, do not provide so many entries that they get in a reader's way. For example, in a reference manual containing many commands or utilities, you might be tempted to index the subheadings under each command. This often results in over-indexing, as shown in the following tables.

Incorrect	Correct

ast command
    attributes, 42
    syntax, 33
    examples, 36
ast_process command
    attributes, 49
    syntax, 53
    examples, 56
ast_subvolume command
    attributes, 50
    syntax, 54
    examples, 57
	ast command, 33, 36, 42
	ast_process command, 49, 53, 56
	ast_subvolume command, 50, 54, 57

Over-indexing also occurs if you create several secondary entries under a primary entry when all entries are on the same page.

Incorrect	Correct

input devices
    buttons, 167
    dials, 167
    digitizer, 167
    scanner, 167
	input devices, 167

Do not provide two adjacent entries that are very similar. However, always double-post acronyms and abbreviations even if it is possible that the entries might be adjacent in the index. The test: If you omit an entry, can a reader still find the right place in the document?

Incorrect	Correct
`delete_file` command, 41 deleting a file, 41	`delete_file` command, 41

Do Not Under-Index

Some kinds of under-indexing are very obvious because they do not provide enough specific information to be useful.

Incorrect	Correct

reports, 31–39, 77	reports
	    exporting, 77
	    generating, 34
	    preformatting, 33
	    specifying format, 36–39
	    types of, 31–33

Other types of under-indexing are not obvious, except to a reader. It is especially important to index *concepts*, not just the terms that appear in the document.

Incorrect	Correct
`archive` command, 77	`archive` command, 77 backing up data to tape, 77 tape backups, 77

Alphabetize by Keyword in Subentries

Alphabetize subentries by keyword, not by beginning articles, conjunctions, or prepositions. Reword subentries so that the keyword or key term, rather than an irrelevant introductory word, appears at the beginning of the subentry. If the subentry requires an article, conjunction, or preposition to flow correctly, try to include these additional words at the end of the subentry rather than at the beginning.

Incorrect	Correct
accounting	accounting
software for, 11	command summary, 38
summary of commands, 38	software for, 11
table of terms, 14–17	terms, table of, 14–17
addressing	addressing
issues for virtual networks, 34	naming conventions, 52
naming conventions, 52	virtual network issues, 34
backing store	backing store
and accumulation buffer, 10	accumulation buffer and, 10
and double buffering, 12	architecture, 5
and Z buffer, 40	device pipeline support, 22
architecture, 5	and double buffering, 12
device pipeline support, 22	overview, 1
overview, 1	and Z buffer, 40

Alphabetize by First Letter After a Symbol

For path, file, or variable entries that begin with a symbol, alphabetize these entries by the first letter of the first word following the symbol.

Incorrect	Correct
Symbols	**C**

`_config`
`/etc/uucp/Limits`
`.info`
`$PATH`
	`cancel` command
	`_config`
	Create menu

E	**E**
error reporting external files	error reporting `/etc/uucp/Limits` external files
	I
	ID numbers `.info`
	P
	`$PATH` primary numbers

Refining and Checking an Index

While creating the first draft of an index, you probably concentrated on the individual entries and their secondary entries. While editing the index, you are concerned with the index as a whole.

Editing an index might require that you create or delete entries, combine or split entries, and regroup or reword entries. In a sense, editing an index is not very different from editing the document. Namely, you verify that all necessary material is included, that it is in the intended order, and that it is error free.

Remember that you are reading an index in an abnormal way, that is, you are reading it from start to finish. Normally, readers search directly for the word or phrase they hope to find. Because you are reading an index this way, you might think that many entries are not necessary or are redundant. For some entries, this might be true, but to delete many entries on that basis alone is risky. Unless your analysis of the topic was incorrect when you created the entry, you probably had a specific reason for adding the entry.

The following sections review common problem areas in indexing.

Spelling

Many publishing systems do not check the spelling in the embedded index entries when the spelling checker is run on the body of the document. For this reason, always carefully proofread and run the spelling checker on index entries to catch spelling and typographical errors.

Differences in Wording

Check the subjects to determine whether slight variations in wording are intentional or whether you should use only one wording. If there are valid subjects that differ only slightly in wording, examine them to be sure that readers can recognize the difference. You might have to reword the subjects to make the differences apparent.

After creating the index, you might discover that you have used inconsistent terminology in the document. A consistency check and any necessary corrections are well worth the time it takes to standardize terminology.

For example, "AdminTool" might also appear as "Admin Tool"; "Administration Tool"; and "setting up, configuring." You also must standardize usage for terms such as "home directory" and "root directory," and "superuser" and "root user."

Misused Singular Forms and Plural Forms

Check the entries for the misuse of singular forms and plural forms. Usually, only one form of a subject is justified. If you find more than one, combine secondary entries under one subject. Using both forms of a subject, such as "data set" and "data sets," can cause errors. Several other entries and their subsequent secondary entries might intervene between the singular and plural forms of a subject. Spare readers the trouble of checking the index for both forms.

Incorrect	Correct
data set	data sets
input	address
output	area
data set address	format of
data set area	input
data sets	output
format of	table of
table of	

Effective Double-Posting

Check that all meaningful variations of a subject's wording appear in an index. See "Group Entries" on page 250.

Number of Page References for Entries

Include no more than two to four page references per index entry. If an entry has more than two to four page references, see if you can create secondary and tertiary entries to reduce the number of page references.

Incorrect	Correct
block diagram, 21, 28, 33, 37, 45	block diagram
	attribute generator, 33
	frame buffer, 37
	front-end processor, 28
	SBus adapter, 21
	system unit, 45

Proper Topic Cross-References

Check that the page references for each occurrence of a topic are the same and that they appear in each place. In the example, a reader looking up "operator messages" would not be aware of all the other places where information exists. Create secondary entries under "operator messages" and give readers the same information they would have found had they looked up "messages."

Incorrect	Correct

messages
    from operator, 2-34
    to operator, 2-15, 3-7
    to programmer, 5-12
    ⋮
 	
operator messages, 2-34, 3-7
    ⋮
	messages
	    from operator, 2-34
	    to operator, 2-15, 3-7
	    to programmer, 5-12
	    ⋮
	
	operator messages
	    from operator, 2-34
	    to operator, 2-15, 3-7
	    to programmer, 5-12

"See" and "See Also" References

Check that each "See" reference refers to an entry with secondary entries. Read "Creating "See" and "See Also" References" on page 253.

Bad Page and Column Breaks

One form of a bad page break results when a primary entry with multiple secondary entries and perhaps tertiary entries breaks in the middle at the foot of the last column on a right page. The first column on the following page begins with an indented secondary or tertiary entry. Bad page breaks cause problems for a reader, who must look back to the previous page to find the primary entry.

Correct bad page breaks by repeating the primary entry above the carried-over secondary entry followed by the word "continued" in italic and surrounded by parentheses.

graphical user interface
    menus
        Edit, 8
        File, 10
        Format, 12
        general navigation, 3

graphical user interface
    menus (*continued*)
        Graphics, 16
        Special, 20
        Table, 21
        View, 22

Avoid having a single primary entry at the beginning of an alphabetic section at the bottom of a column. Force the alphabetic character to the top of the next column, carrying the single primary entry along with it.

Likewise, do not leave a single line at the end of an alphabetic section at the top of a column. Force a column break one or two lines before the widowed line.

Secondary Entries

When refining your index, examine secondary entries carefully in the following problem areas.

Levels of Secondary Entries

Check the levels of secondary entries so that proper indentation shows the relationship of one entry to the preceding one. See "Nested Entries" on page 242.

Redundant Secondary Entries

Check main entries that are followed by secondary entries having the same page reference.

In many cases, you can eliminate the secondary entries because a reader can find all the information on one page. Redundant secondary entries often occur when items in a table are indexed. See "Do Not Over-Index" on page 259.

Incorrect	Correct

data sets
    format of, 2-7
    table of, 2-7
	data sets, 2-7

Possible Primary Entries in Secondary Entries

Check whether a secondary entry can also appear as a primary entry. If it can, verify that it exists as such or create the primary entry and insert it in the proper place.

Possible Rearrangement

Check whether secondary entries can be rearranged to stress a certain point. In this example, all three secondary entries can be in the same form. The form depends on what you want to stress.

Incorrect	Correct

window system
    colors, changing, 8-11
    icon, moving, 4-22
    saving properties, 8-15
	window system
	    colors, changing, 8-11
	    icon, moving, 4-22
	    properties, saving, 8-15

Appropriately Combined Secondary Entries

Review an index to make sure that you have combined relevant entries.

Incorrect	Correct

DeskSet
    selection protocol, 2-4
DeskSet atoms, 4-8
DeskSet drag-and-drop atoms, 4-4
DeskSet drag and drop handshaking, 4-2
DeskSet integration
    why do it, 1-2
	DeskSet
	    atoms, 4-8
	    drag and drop
	        atoms, 4-4
	        handshaking, 4-2
	    integration, 1-2
	    selection protocol, 2-4

Secondary Entries Under More Than One Topic

Check for secondary entries that can be arranged under one topic rather than several. Such division of secondary entries is usually the result of misused "See also" references.

Incorrect	Correct

find function
    See also search function
    examples, 8-22
    use of, 8-15
    variables, 8-18
       ⋮
search function
    dialog box, 8-9
    and replace function, 8-21
	find function
	    dialog box, 8-9
	    examples, 8-22
	    and replace function, 8-21
	    use of, 8-15
	    variables, 8-18
	       ⋮
	search function, *See* find function

Secondary Entries When Using a Combined Term Separately

Check for and move a secondary entry if you included the combined term as a separate entry.

In the next example, the entries starting with "database" under the "classing engine" main entry belong under the "classing engine database" main entry.

Incorrect	Correct

classing engine
    adding a new file type, 6-6
    attributes, 6-4
    database, accessing, 6-7
    database, converting, 6-8
    database, reading, 6-8
    interactive modification, 6-5
    mapping function, 6-3
classing engine database
    location of, 6-7
    network, 6-9
	classing engine
	    adding a new file type, 6-6
	    attributes, 6-4
	    interactive modification, 6-5
	    mapping function, 6-3
	classing engine database
	    accessing, 6-7
	    converting, 6-8
	    location of, 6-7
	    network, 6-9
	    reading, 6-8

Secondary Entries Under Various Forms of One Topic

Check that the number of secondary entries under various forms of the same topic are all the same. In the example, "attention key" appears after the "terminal, communications" entry so that readers are aware of the information regardless of how they look it up.

Incorrect	Correct

communications terminal
    attention key, 4-16
    polling character, 4-11
    READY indicator, 4-10
    ⋮
 	
terminal, communications
    polling character, 4-11
    READY indicator, 4-10
	communications terminal
	    attention key, 4-16
	    polling character, 4-11
	    READY indicator, 4-10
	    ⋮
	
	terminal, communications
	    attention key, 4-16
	    polling character, 4-11
	    READY indicator, 4-10

Checking the Size of the Index

After you have edited the index, compare the size of the index with the size of the document. Although the index size is not an indication of its quality, an index that is too small for the size of the document is suspicious and might indicate serious omissions.

A minimum length for an index is one page of index entries for every 20 pages of text, or about one index entry for every 100 words of text. This can be considered a "5 percent" index. For dense technical material, however, this guideline is too low. For a dense technical manual, try to provide one page of index entries for every 10 pages of text, which can be considered a "10 percent" index.

If you check the length of your index by page count rather than by word count, do not count text pages that contain any of the following if they occupy more than about two-thirds of a page:

- Flow diagrams
- Figures
- Code examples
- Front matter (title page, table of contents, and so on)
- Blank space longer than three-quarters of a page
- Glossary or bibliography

If the index falls below the guidelines, check that all topics in the document are entered in the index.

Global Index

The type of index most writers work with is the "back of the book" variety. A *global index* combines the back-of-the-book indexes from all the books in a set. A global index is a valuable information retrieval device for a reader who is not familiar with all the books in a set. A global index provides a single place where readers can find the information they seek without having to look through several individual indexes.

Formatting a Global Index

In a global index, merely referring a reader to page numbers is insufficient. Because a global index combines the indexes from several books in a set, a reader also needs to know the book in the set to which the reference applies. For this reason, a global index requires a special page numbering style. One method is to use a four-letter abbreviation for an entry's book title, with a running footer that provides a legend on each index page for the abbreviations. If such a footer is not possible or desirable, put a legend for abbreviations at the beginning of the index.

Editing a Global Index

Because of its size and complexity, a global index is by far the most difficult type of index to create properly. You cannot just combine the indexes from several books and assume that, if the previous back-of-the-book indexes were correct, a global index will also be correct.

When combining indexes to make a global index, the indexer must edit the global index for most of the indexing mistakes described under "Refining and Checking an Index" on page 263. Specifically, the indexer must check for the following:

- Consistent page numbering style
- Levels of secondary entries
- Differences in wording
- Misuse of singular and plural forms
- Meaningful variations (double-posting) of a subject's wording
- Possible rearrangement of secondary entries
- Bad page and column breaks

Many of these mistakes might be in a global index even though they might not be in the original indexes. These mistakes happen when common terms in different indexes are combined, slightly different terminology is used in different books, and different indexing choices have been applied in each book.

There are two ways to fix the problems that result from creating a global index:

- Edit the index entries in the original text and re-create the index.
- Edit the global index and leave the index entries as they are in the original text.

Online Index

If your writing tool supports an online index, consider including one to help readers scan the content of your document and quickly find what they need.

Multiple page numbers translate into many links next to an entry in an online index. So while in print you can collapse repetitive entries, for online indexes elaborate them as much as possible to help the readers find the correct entry quickly.

Incorrect	Correct

`ast` command, 33, 42
`ast_process` command, 44, 49
`ast_subvolume` command, 51, 55
	`ast` command
	    attributes, 42
	    syntax, 33
	`ast_process` command
	    attributes, 49
	    syntax, 44
	`ast_subvolume` command
	    attributes, 55
	    syntax, 51

An online index simplifies and expedites a reader's search for specific information much more than a search engine. A search engine alone can be inadequate for finding information quickly, especially if the tool searches a large database of documents.

For instance, a search engine scans text looking for occurrences of the word or phrase typed in the search box. Then, it lists every document that contains any mention of the word or phrase. A reader can lose a considerable amount of time sifting through these documents before finding the desired information. Also, a search engine cannot provide a topic analysis or overview of the document.

In addition to following the guidelines for a good print index, a good online index makes full use of hypertext by linking index entries to the relevant text in your document.

Developing a Publications Department

As a member of a publications department, your charter is to develop, write, edit, validate, and publish documentation that supports the information needs of your customers.

This appendix provides guidance to help you meet the goals of that charter by giving you information on aspects of publications departments ranging from staffing concerns to technical review procedures. It is primarily intended for companies undergoing rapid growth in their documentation requirements. While most publications-related issues are covered, this appendix does not deal with general management issues such as hiring or personnel reviews.

Topics discussed include:

- "Establishment of a Publications Department" on page 274
- "Scheduling" on page 282
- "Documentation Process" on page 284
- "Internationalization and Localization" on page 293
- "Online Documentation Considerations" on page 294
- "Final Print Production" on page 296
- "Post-Production Considerations" on page 300

For a list of books that cover the topic of management issues in more detail than can be provided in this appendix, see the section "Project Management" in Appendix D, "Recommended Reading."

Note – This appendix explains how the publications department fits into a software computer company's organization as an example, so you might have to modify some of the recommended processes and procedures to match your own situation.

Establishment of a Publications Department

The documentation presence in a company usually begins with a few people producing written material to accompany products. Publications departments can range from a single permanent publications manager working solely with outside contractors to a department featuring several writing, illustration, and production groups. Table A–1 describes the maturity levels of documentation organizations and their goals at each level.[1]

Use this table to see where your department fits on the continuum. When analyzing your organization, judge its performance as a whole over a long period of time. Although your organization might exhibit some features of a particular level, one instance does not define your organization as having achieved that level of maturity.

TABLE A–1 Process Maturity Levels of Documentation Organizations

Level	Description	Publications Project Management	Transition to the Next Level
Level 0: Oblivious	Unaware of the need for professionally produced publications. Publications are produced by anyone who is available and has time.	None	Staffing with professional technical communicators
Level 1: Ad hoc	Technical communicators act independently to produce publications with little or no coordination. They may be assigned to different technical managers.	None	Development of a style guide
Level 2: Rudimentary	The beginning pieces of a process are going into place. Some coordination occurs among the technical communicators to assure consistency, but enforcement is not strong.	None to very little	Introduction of some project planning

---

1 From *Managing Your Documentation Projects* by JoAnn Hackos. Copyright © 1994 by Wiley Publishing, Inc. All rights reserve Reproduced here by permission of the publisher.

Level	Description	Publications Project Management	Transition to the Next Level
Level 3: Organized and repeatable	A sound development process is in place and being refined. People are being trained in the process. Project management is in the beginning stages, with senior technical communicators learning the rudiments of estimating and tracking.	Introduction of project management	Strong implementation of project planning
Level 4: Managed and sustainable	Strong project management is in place to ensure that the publications-development process works. Estimating and tracking of projects are thorough, and controls are in place to keep projects within budgets and schedules. Innovation gains importance within the strong existing structure.	Strong commitment to project management	Beginning of the implementation of more effective processes
Level 5: Optimizing	Everyone on the teams is engaged in monitoring and controlling projects. As a result, effective self-managed teams are becoming the norm. Innovations in the development process are regularly investigated and the teams have a strong commitment to continuous process improvement.	Strong commitment to project management and institution of self-managed teams	Strong and sustainable commitment to continuous process improvement

Establishing the Value of the Department

If you want to expand your department, the first step is usually to convince management of its value. However, measuring the "value added" of accurate, comprehensive documentation written by professional technical communicators is not easy. Your focus is on added ease-of-use for the user, in the product interface as well as the documentation. However, that is often not as important an argument to management as actual costs saved.

This section provides some ways in which you can show how good documentation adds value and offers some metrics from other studies that you can use.[2]

---

2 The material in this section is based on information from Janice C. Redish, "Adding Value as a Professional Technical Communicator," *Technical Communication* 42:1 (1995), pp. 26–39. Used with permission.

Accounting for Value Added

Traditional accounting practices often make showing the benefits of improving quality very difficult. For example, many accounting systems still track costs by department rather than project. If customer support costs go down, the customer support group looks good. The documentation group does not get any credit for reducing support costs, even if good documentation contributed substantially to the reduction.

Many accounting systems are still based on a manufacturing model rather than a labor-intensive service model. For example, a documentation group that is measured only on pages per day appears to cost more if their higher-quality documents have fewer pages. Value that the documentation group is adding through activities other than writing and production (such as interface evaluation) or the greater benefits of shorter documents might not be reflected in the accounting reports.

Tracking Avoided Costs and Costs Saved

When considering the value added by a professional publications staff and good documentation, costs avoided are as significant as costs saved. For example, say a company gets 100,000 support calls a year at a cost of $30 a call. If better documentation reduces the call volume by 10 percent (either the number of calls or a shorter duration of call), the technical communicators save the company $300,000 a year.

Another aspect you can point out is the cost per problem at different points in the product development cycle. Problems found in the writing/editing cycle are much less expensive to fix than problems found once the product is in the field.

Measures that show *increased benefits* resulting from good documentation include:

- More sales
- Increased productivity
- A higher percentage of forms or response cards returned
- Forms or response cards returned more quickly
- More users' problems identified early in the process

Measures that show *reduced costs* resulting from good documentation include:

- Fewer support calls, which results in lower support costs
- Less need for training, which results in lower training costs
- Fewer requests for maintenance, which results in lower maintenance costs
- Less time needed for translation, which results in lower translation costs
- Less effort (time, lines of code, rework) when technical communicators are involved early in the development process than when they are not

- Lower costs for writing, paper, printing, and so on because technical communicators showed developers that they did not need all the documentation that they were planning
- Fewer errors in specifications written by technical communicators than in specifications written by engineers

When trying to find ways to illustrate *value added* by good documentation, consider the following techniques:

- Estimating avoidable costs from historical data, for example, costs of writing and sending updates and bulletins about problems and solutions, support costs, and costs to the customer's company.
- Comparing two documents or two situations in which one document used the services of publications personnel and the other document did not. For example, you might submit a previous version of a document that has been revised, or interview users who have access to the documentation and those users who do not have access.

Establishing Expertise

Companies, especially those with fledgling publications groups, often regard documentation as merely writing down what the product does. You should also try to establish a role as the user advocate. You can offer your expertise during the project development stage in areas such as interface evaluation, menu item and error message wording, usability, and so on. If you encounter resistance to early writer involvement, point out that problems like inconsistent interface features take much less time, and therefore less money, to correct at early stages in product development than if the writers are not involved until the actual writing cycle begins.

Funding the Publications Department

Once you've convinced management that your department should be expanded, you might be asked to help determine how your publications department is funded.

Some possibilities for funding are as follows:

- Funding by the division to which the publications department reports regardless of who receives the documentation services. For example, a publications department might report to and be funded by the marketing division even though the department is developing documentation for the engineering group.
- Funding for department personnel from the budget of the project they are documenting. The publications manager identifies the staffing level required for a given project and the positions are funded by the project's budget.
- Funding for centralized services such as editing, illustration, and production by the division to which the publications department reports, with individual writers funded by the project they are documenting.

Obviously, each scenario has advantages and disadvantages. For example, if you are a writer reporting directly to an engineering project manager, you will probably have a closer relationship with the engineers on the project than if you are a member of a separate publications department. At the same time, your concerns as a publications-oriented team member might not be taken as seriously in an engineering group as they would if you reported to a publications manager.

Determining the Roles of the Publications Team

When you have permission to expand your staff, consider the roles your staff members need to fill. The following sections describe the roles of various publications personnel. Smaller departments or projects might need to combine these functions.

Manager

- Supervises all personnel matters: recruiting, hiring, training, supervising, and evaluating
- Plans and schedules projects, and might oversee them
- Acquires and allocates resources: monetary, personnel, equipment, outside resources
- Works with project initiation, design, and planning teams

Writing Team Leader

- Coordinates and maintains the documentation plan (see "Writing a Documentation Plan" on page 284 for more details)
- Coordinates and tracks schedules
- Assigns writing tasks to individual writers and consults with them to set priorities
- Makes sure technical or hardware problems encountered by writers are resolved
- Represents the writing team at project team meetings or other department meetings relating to the project
- Holds weekly meetings of the writing team and issues weekly status reports
- Coordinates multiple technical reviews
- Serves as the liaison with the production staff

Writer

- Determines scope and contents of assigned books with input from the project writing team and relevant departments such as marketing and usability testing
- Writes the documentation plan if there is no writing team leader (see "Writing a Documentation Plan" on page 284 for more details)
- Gathers and verifies source data, which includes attending engineering and product design meetings
- Disseminates project information to the rest of the documentation team
- Writes the documentation according to the audience and technical content defined in the documentation plan
- Develops or works with an illustrator to create illustrations
- Incorporates editorial and technical review comments
- Arranges for validity and usability testing

Editor

- Directs and guides the writers to write clearly and consistently, with the user in mind at all times
- Provides editorial support at all levels: developmental editing, copy editing, and proofreading (see "Types of Editing" in Chapter 10, "Working With an Editor")
- Ensures that grammar, syntax, and spelling are correct in all documents
- In projects with more than one writer, brings the different styles of the various writers into a consistent whole to achieve a single voice
- Maintains the project style sheet
- Keeps all writers on a project informed of stylistic decisions, title changes, and so on
- Ensures correct use of copyright and trademark information
- Checks that all figures and tables (from chapter to chapter and book to book) are consistent in style and quality, are in the right position, and, if appropriate, are numbered correctly

Graphic Designer

- Develops the overall look and design of the documentation product
- Determines how typography, use of color, and general layout of the information are handled
- Designs graphic elements, such as icons and glyphs, that assist a reader

- Possibly produces graphics for the software interface or online documentation
- Helps redesign the documentation format for a company, a set of documents, or a single document
- Designs packaging and manual covers

Illustrator

- Works closely with the writer to create drawings for information products
- Participates in the project documentation team and understands the material, especially on large projects
- Works with the graphics designer on projects that require numerous illustrations

Deciding on Contract or Permanent Staff

Once you have determined who is paying for the publications staff and defined their tasks, you can start hiring staff. One of the primary decisions in this area is whether to hire permanent staff or to use contractors. Small companies might choose to hire a documentation manager who supervises a staff of contractors. Larger companies might have a mixed staff of contractors and permanent writers, or they might hire contractors for peak loads or short-term projects only.

Advantages of Using Contractors

- **Expertise**. Full-time contractors can offer a high level of experience and professionalism. These qualities are especially important if your publications department is young and your processes are not fully in place.
- **Flexibility**. In slow times, you do not need to maintain a full staff.
- **Opportunity to evaluate prospective employees in real work conditions**. More and more companies are using contractors with an option to convert them to permanent staff. This practice enables you to see whether the employee is productive and works well in your environment.
- **Cost**. The cost per hour of contractors is necessarily higher than permanent staff. However, you save on paying for health benefits and vacation, and sometimes the office space and equipment costs, of a permanent position. Also, experienced contractors can often produce documentation quickly.

Disadvantages of Using Contractors

- **Learning curve**. Contractors are usually unfamiliar with your product, your processes, and the employees of your company, whether in your own department or in other departments from which they need to gain information.

  Not only must you allow time for the contractor to "get up to speed," but the knowledge gained also departs with the contractor rather than benefiting the company.

  Also, for editors especially, lack of familiarity with your in-house style and the lack of an established relationship with in-house writers can be difficult factors to overcome.

- **Accessibility**. If contractors are working off site, they are not available for spur-of-the-moment meetings or decision making.

- **Communication**. The adage "out of sight, out of mind" is unfortunately often true when you mix permanent staff and contractors. For example, sometimes tacit agreements on style or processes are made in casual hallway conversations that the contractor misses and that the on-site personnel forget to pass on.

Considerations When Hiring Contractors

After deciding to hire a contractor, make sure that you consider the following factors:

- **On-site time commitment**. Establish a clear understanding of how much time the contractor is expected to be on site, for meetings or other necessary commitments.

- **Tax regulations**. Make sure that you comply with the regulations of federal, state, and local tax agencies. Some payment agreements and on-site time considerations might affect whether tax agencies will consider contractors as permanent employees.

- **Non-disclosure agreement**. You should have the contractor sign a standard agreement that protects your company's proprietary information.

- **Compatible software delivery mechanism**. Make sure that the contractor has compatible software and hardware and can deliver easily into your current system.

- **Delivery of material**. Materials such as updated schedules and project style sheets must be delivered to the contractor. Material to be received from the contractor includes drafts or schedule updates. You should have an easy and efficient method of delivery.

Considerations When Hiring Permanent Staff

If your company has a personnel office, hiring procedures are probably already established. However, if your hiring is less formal, you might need to consider the following tasks:

- Developing job descriptions
- Determining grade or salary levels for levels of writers, editors, or illustrators
- Evaluating the level of seniority needed for a position (for example, could you use entry-level applicants or college interns?)
- Establishing the interviewing team (for example, should developers on the project be included?)
- Conducting orientation and training

Scheduling

One of the more difficult tasks facing any publications department is developing accurate and realistic schedules and modifying them while the project is underway. This section provides some basic information about schedule estimates and contingencies, but it is by no means exhaustive. For a list of books that deal specifically with managing documentation projects, see the section "Project Management" in Appendix D, "Recommended Reading."

Estimating Task Times

The following table shows a rough formula for calculating the hours needed for documentation tasks.[3] Keep in mind that these are *estimates only* and that they might vary depending upon the nature of the documentation. For example, very technical documentation is usually more time-consuming to write and edit than is overview information. Outside factors such as poor source material or limited availability of subject matter experts can also affect schedules.

---

3 L. Fredrickson and J. Lasecke, "Planning for Factors that Affect Project Cost" *Proceedings of the 41st International Technical Communication Conference* (Arlington, VA: Society for Technical Communication, 1994), pp. 357–359.

TABLE A–2 Productivity Formulas

Activity	Formula for Calculating Hours
Writing new text	3–5 hours per page
Revising existing text	1–3 hours per page
Editing	6–8 pages per hour
Indexing	5 pages per hour
Production preparation	5 percent of all other activities
Project management	10–15 percent of all other activities

You might want to consider setting up a system to track the amount of time your staff members spend on each project. You can use this data to more accurately predict the amount of time needed for future projects.

Developing a Project Schedule

When developing the schedule, tie your deliverables to project milestones rather than to calendar dates. Estimate the time before or after a milestone at which you expect to deliver the component (for example, "The first draft of the documentation will be completed two weeks after the alpha version of the software is delivered to Product Test"). That way, you can more easily adjust your documentation schedule to match the progress of the project. Be realistic in your own assessment of actual progress in other departments, such as product development and testing.

The following table shows a typical publications project schedule.

TABLE A–3 Sample Publications Schedule

Milestone	Date Information
Engineering specification	Date from engineering
Documentation plan	Start and end dates
Alpha software delivery	Due date
First draft	Due date
Technical review	Start and end dates
Developmental edit	Same start and end dates as technical review
Usability test of draft	Same start and end dates as technical review
Index development	Same start and end dates as technical review

TABLE A–3 Sample Publications Schedule   *(Continued)*

Milestone	Date Information
User interface freeze	Date from engineering
Illustrations complete	Due date
Feature/function freeze	Date from engineering
Second draft	Due date
Copy edit	Start and end dates
Validity testing	Same start and end dates as copy edit
Final draft	Due date
Proofread	Start and end dates
Final draft to production (hard-copy and online versions)	Due date

Be sure to keep track of changes in delivery dates, and let other departments involved in the project know if a date is going to slip. Setting expectations up front is the best way to establish credibility and to call attention to late deliverables on which your own deliverables depend.

Documentation Process

This section walks you through the process of planning documentation, writing it, and getting it reviewed.

Writing a Documentation Plan

The documentation plan informs the rest of the product team about your plans for the product documentation. The plan should be reviewed by representatives of all departments involved with the product. Keep the plan up to date throughout the project, with major changes being announced when necessary.

The documentation plan is based on input from various departments. The following table provides some ideas of the type of information you might get from other departments.

TABLE A–4 Documentation Plan Input From Other Departments

Department Name	Relevant Information
Marketing	Product definition, product name, customer profile, feature and function product requirements
Development	Feature and function schedule, user interface concerns, error message data, names of experts on subject matter
Legal	Trademarks, product names
Customer Support	Customer profile, previous product troubleshooting logs, ways to obtain technical support, names of experts on subject matter
Manufacturing and Operations	Part numbers, product packaging, production schedules, shipping lead time

The following table lists the components of a typical documentation plan. It is a sample only, and not all sections are relevant to all product types or publications departments.

TABLE A–5 Documentation Plan Sample Topics

Topic	Content
Product information	Product name and version, brief description of the product's intended use.
Documentation resource requirements	Personnel, equipment.
Revision information	Differences from the documentation of previous versions of the product if any.
Documentation objectives	Overall objectives of the documentation set or of each book.
Documentation overview	Full list of documentation deliverables and the format in which they will be delivered.
Documentation descriptions	Brief description of the chapters and appendixes in each book, with the estimated page counts. If the books in the documentation set are large, each book might require a separate documentation plan.
Documentation schedule	Publications schedule milestones and other milestones from the project schedule that affect the documentation. Publications milestones might include draft delivery dates, technical review dates, and the final document delivery date to production.
Technical review	List of technical reviewers and the projected review schedule.

TABLE A–5 Documentation Plan Sample Topics   *(Continued)*

Topic	Content
Test plan	Plans and dates for validity testing, usability testing, and, if relevant, media testing.
Edit plan	Editing schedule and book priorities.
Localization plan	Languages into which the document will be translated, required resources, and schedule.
Documentation design	Format of the documentation components, including book sizes, online media, and other design details.
Production plan	Printing and packaging specifications.
Issues	Any projected issues that might affect documentation, such as suspected schedule slips, engineering uncertainties, or known project design difficulties.
Critical dependencies	Items needed from other groups, including the due date and the impact if the information is not provided or is late. These dependencies might include the following items: ■ Prototype delivered ■ Subject matter experts designated ■ Technical product specification received ■ User interface frozen ■ Features and functions frozen ■ Alpha version of working software available ■ Installation specifications completed ■ Beta software released to testing ■ Technical review sign-off meeting held ■ Development frozen ■ Final list of error messages, causes, and remedies received ■ Product name confirmed

Coordinating With Product Development

Documentation concerns especially affect product development at two points in the schedule: during technical review and at the end of the project.

- **Technical review**. Your subject matter experts *must* dedicate time to complete a thorough and expert review of your documentation. Unfortunately, technical reviews usually occur when the development staff is busy with last-minute engineering and bug fixes. Management support is often crucial in making sure that the development staff take the time to review the documentation thoroughly. Documentation must be considered an important part of the product by all departments for technical review to be treated with the attention it requires.

- **Code freeze**. The other development concern arises at the end of the product cycle, when you need to freeze your screen illustrations and descriptions of the product but the development staff is still fixing bugs. Make sure that the developers, and management, realize that the documentation requires production lead time. They also need to realize that changes to the product after the documentation has gone to production are difficult, if not impossible, to incorporate and will cost more.

Writing Process

This section deals with the writing of the documentation and with the hand-offs the writer must deliver. The following figure shows a sample process.

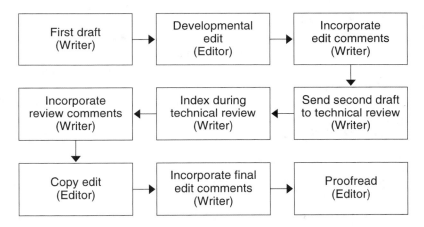

First Draft

The first draft focuses on where information goes and how it should be presented. When writing the first draft, the writer should focus on these tasks:

- Determine organization. Fill out outlines from the documentation plan, making adjustments when necessary. Work with other writers and the editor to define the interrelationships among the manuals.

- Ascertain places where technical information is missing or incomplete, and alert engineers and the other writers.

- Develop thematically unified examples (a scenario) if needed.

- Identify terminology issues, and raise them for discussion and resolution.

- Develop an approach to the audience defined in the documentation plan, and develop the voice appropriate for that audience.

- Develop ideas for art and screen illustrations, and compile a preliminary list of figures.

Second Draft

The second draft should be as complete as the state of the software and the specifications permit. It should be fully illustrated. The writing should be polished.

In the writing of the second draft, the writer should focus on these tasks:

- Incorporate edits and comments from reviewers of the first draft.
- Revise for clarity and consistency of voice and terminology.
- Fill in the technical gaps from the first draft as information becomes available.
- Make sure that all terminology and usage decisions made since the first draft are reflected.
- Compile a list of index entries, and begin to develop main entries, subentries, and cross-references.
- Arrange for a validity test (or perform each procedure yourself) for all chapters to ensure technical accuracy and completeness.
- Complete assembly of screen illustrations, and incorporate other types of illustrations.

Editing Process

An ideal editorial cycle includes:

- **Developmental edit** – A review of structure and organization at the first-draft stage
- **Copy edit** – A review of readability and style at the second-draft stage
- **Proofreading** – A final review prior to production

As your company's publications needs become greater and your publications staff begins dealing with more projects, you will probably want to develop a company style guide. This guide should cover editorial and writing guidelines specific to your publications style and your product line. Besides using *Read Me First!* as a model, you might want to examine some of the books mentioned in Appendix D.

For more information on working with an editor and for checklists describing the different levels of edit, see Chapter 10, "Working With an Editor."

Illustration and Graphics Design

If your illustration and design needs are minimal, someone on your team, such as a writer or publications manager, might be able to handle graphics design and illustration coordination. However, as your needs increase, you should consider adding a production coordinator to your staff. This person can coordinate with outside vendors, contract for illustration and graphics design help, or hire permanent staff in this area when necessary.

Illustration Concerns

Processes for dealing with illustrations vary depending on the type of illustrations, the availability of compatible screen capture software, your staffing (in-house or contractors), and your budget.

If screen capture software is available for the operating system you are running, the writer is usually responsible for capturing the screen illustrations. The writer is the one most familiar with what the screen should illustrate and with the software being documented and so can more efficiently set up the screen appropriately. However, you might want to send these illustrations to an illustrator to be "cleaned up" for the best final reproduction quality.

Concept illustrations, on the other hand, usually benefit from having an illustrator render them. Not all writers are gifted artistically, and the time spent producing art is time *not* spent writing. Illustrators are also more familiar with the "language" of illustrations and can usually produce a more professional concept illustration.

The writer, illustrator, and editor should meet periodically to discuss rough sketches and specifications for illustrations.

A preliminary list of illustrations required for the project is produced by all the writers. (For a sample illustration request form and art tracking form, see Appendix B.) The writers periodically review the illustrations for their specific books with the illustrator until both are satisfied with the final art.

Note – If your documentation consists in large part of updating existing documentation for a standard set of products, consider archiving generic illustrations of your product or its basic concepts for use in future documentation.

Graphics Design Process

The graphics design for your documentation set might already be established or might be standard for each book or online component. However, you might need a graphics design plan if you are adding new types of components to your documentation set or if you have a new product line for which you want a different look. The following figure illustrates the graphic design process.

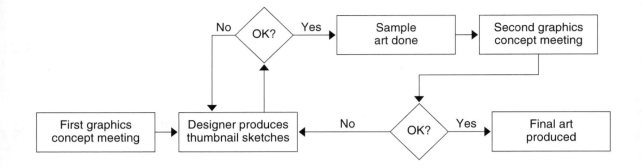

- **First graphics concept meeting**. The writers, editor, and graphics designer should hold an initial meeting to identify and discuss product concepts that could best be conveyed through graphics, page layout, and other documentation design issues. The result of this meeting is a graphics design direction for the project. A graphics designer can often also help in designing online tutorials or other online documentation.

- **Second graphics concept meeting**. A second graphics concept meeting is held to approve the final graphics design. If rework is necessary, the graphics designer either produces another sample for another review or executes the art with the final changes incorporated.

Technical Review

This section explains some of the issues related to the publications team and the reviewers during a technical review process. Remember, thorough technical review is an important contribution to the accuracy and usefulness of your documentation. Unfortunately, this concept is sometimes difficult to convey to other groups. This section provides information on how to promote and conduct a technical review.

Make sure that you provide details about the technical review, including its schedule, in your documentation plan or during planning meetings. Emphasize the importance of having accurate documentation that is thoroughly reviewed and tested. Point out the advantages to the whole company in saved support costs, a good reputation, and favorable industry reviews.

Make sure that the relevant departments allow time for their personnel to review the documentation and that they know the seriousness of the review. For successful completion of a documentation project, the reviewers must be available to conduct reviews and to attend review meetings at the time specified in the documentation plan or the review cover letter. (See the sample review cover letter in Appendix B.)

Once reviewer comments have been returned and evaluated, hold a review meeting. This meeting should help ensure the accuracy of the documentation, resolve conflicts between reviewers, and collect final comments. See "Review Meeting" on page 292.

At the conclusion of the technical review and the review meeting, designated reviewers from each department should "sign off" that the documentation, with the agreed-on changes, meets with their department's approval.

Comment Acceptance

Comments regarding technical *errors* in the documentation should be incorporated.

Comments regarding technical *completeness* should be accepted or rejected depending on the scope and intent of the documentation as specified in the documentation plan or as interpreted by the writer, writing team leader, or manager.

Comments regarding the *purpose and scope* of the manual, including the intended audience, should be accepted or rejected based on the related material in the documentation plan.

Comments on *editorial style, organization,* or *cosmetic changes* should be accepted or rejected based on style and design guidelines.

Participants in the Technical Review

Participants in the technical review process should ideally already be members of the project team. However, even those outside the project team, such as customer support personnel and testers, might be able to provide valuable feedback.

Departments you might want to have represented, and their review responsibilities, are listed here. You might want to provide this information, modified for your own situation, as part of the documentation plan.

Product Development

- The documentation accurately describes the technical aspects of the product.
- The text, examples, and illustrations are technically correct.
- All technical information specified in the documentation plan is included.

Product Test

- The documentation accurately describes the technical aspects of the product.

- The text, examples, and illustrations are technically correct.

- All technical information specified in the documentation plan is included.

- The procedures in all written and online documentation have been performed to ensure technical accuracy and completeness.

Marketing

- The documentation describes the product as it is specified in any marketing requirements document.
- The documentation is appropriate for the target audience.
- Proprietary information or information deemed inappropriate for publication outside the company is not included in the documentation.

Customer Support

- The documentation accurately describes the technical aspects of the product.
- The procedures in all written and online documentation have been performed to ensure technical accuracy and completeness.
- The documentation is appropriate for the target audience.
- The documentation includes information about how to obtain technical support.

Usability Testing

- The documentation is appropriate for the target audience.
- The documentation facilitates users' successful completion of tasks that the product supports.
- The instructional objectives of any tutorial material are met.

Publications Department

- The documentation conforms to current department and corporate standards and guidelines.
- The documentation is written in accordance with the documentation plan.
- The documentation is easy to read, well organized, and easy to use.
- The documentation is composed correctly: Tables and figures are clear and easy to read, there are no typographical errors, misspellings, and so on.

Legal

- The documentation properly uses all trademark and copyright conventions.
- All product names in the documentation are accurate and used correctly.

Review Meeting

The review meeting is chaired by the documentation manager or a designated representative. The sign-off reviewers designated in the documentation plan should attend the review meeting. Sign-off reviewers attending the review meeting are responsible for consolidating comments from their area into one copy and for resolving conflicting comments from different reviewers in their area before submission.

The writer or writing team leader should prepare an agenda of comment items. In an ideal situation in which comments have been collected online before the meeting, you can distribute reports that list those comments that have been accepted without discussion, those comments that have been rejected, and those comments that are unresolved. Otherwise, mark on the review copies those comments that are unresolved or rejected.

The agenda for the meeting should include rejected comments that reviewers still want to have considered and unresolved comments.

The chairperson leads a discussion of each item on the agenda. Once the items have been resolved, the sign-off sheet should be distributed for representative signatures.

Often, engineers and others think that their comments regarding organization or writing style should receive as much weight as their comments on technical matters. Keep in mind, and make sure they keep in mind, that *you* are the expert on publications, just as *they* are the experts on coding or testing.

Internationalization and Localization

If your company does a portion of its business internationally, you might need to localize or internationalize your documentation. *Internationalization* involves creating a "generic" document that can be easily translated into or used in many languages or cultures, converting any language-specific or culture-specific references into generic ones. *Localization* involves converting a document that is specific to a language or culture into one that is specific to a different language or culture. See Chapter 7, "Writing for an International Audience," for more specific details.

Some companies simply translate their documentation into specific languages. Other companies fully internationalize or localize the product and documentation. Although large companies generally have a dedicated department to handle this process, others depend on the publications department.

Internationalization and localization is a large and complicated area that requires some expertise. Decisions about the process that affect publications include the following factors:

- How soon the localized versions need to be ready after the native-language product is finished. This schedule is often determined by marketing and sales concerns rather than publications resources.

- How changes to the documentation within the product release and in subsequent releases are tracked and passed on to the translators.

- How long the translation cycle takes, including review and revisions.

- How to handle exchanging documents between different formats, both hardware and software.
- How the document is delivered.

For smaller documents, you might want to have all languages in one document. For larger documents, you probably will want separate documents for each language. This decision must also take into account your company's manufacturing, product kitting, inventory methods, and the number of copies to be printed for each locale.

Online Documentation Considerations

Producing documentation for online presentation involves different concerns than the considerations for printed paper documentation. This section briefly discusses some issues you need to take into account, but it is by no means comprehensive. See Appendix D for books that deal with this subject in depth.

Many companies are turning to online presentation of their documentation to provide customers with easier access to product documentation, to save on printing and production costs, and to provide searchable linked information. If your company is considering such a move, research presentation and usability issues thoroughly.

See Chapter 4, "Online Writing Style," for detailed information about considerations for online presentation. The sections below contain summary information intended for publications departments new to online documentation.

Writing Issues

Because printed text has existed for hundreds of years, writers and readers instinctively know how to use it. Online text, however, is new and constantly changing. People writing and using online text do not have the combined knowledge that comes from generations of experimentation and example.

- **Writing style**. To design online information, writers must change from the familiar writing style used for printed text to an unfamiliar, sometimes undefined, style used for online presentation. Writers also often have a hard time going back and forth between the two writing styles.
- **Scheduling**. Time must be built into the schedule to allow writers and editors to develop their online writing style, and to transition between the printed and online formats.
- **Platform-specific versions**. Some information providers use a "write once, publish twice" scheme that presents the same documentation online and in print. To most effectively take advantage of the benefits of online publishing, however, writers should write text specifically for that medium.

Content Issues

The following list presents some content issues related to online presentation.

- **Access**. You need to determine how the user will find and retrieve information and what navigation aids you will provide.

- **Text format**. First, you must decide whether to duplicate information in both online and print formats, or whether you will provide some information only online and some only in print. If you choose the latter strategy, you need to decide the appropriate format for each type of information.

  One typical strategy is to provide task information or brief explanatory information online, and more in-depth information or background information in print.

- **Graphics**. If you decide to provide graphics in your online documentation, you must decide what format they will be in, how they will be included, and whether they will be linked.

- **Hyperlinks**. Some decisions to be made about hyperlinks include which information should be linked and whether links should be accessed only through text or also through graphics. You might also decide to limit the number of links you want in a given body of information. See Chapter 5, "Constructing Links," for more detailed information.

- **Page design**. Type size, page size, and page layout work differently online than in print. You must decide whether to optimize your design for online or print presentation or whether to use two separate designs.

Management Issues

The following list presents some management issues related to online presentation.

- **Scheduling**. Designing and planning online documentation is usually more time-consuming than print presentation because of the possibility of linked information and the ramifications of online display.

- **Authoring tools**. Online documentation usually requires a different set of authoring tools than your standard word processing or desktop publishing software. These tools sometimes involve separate products for authoring and for online viewing.

- **Outside resources**. Support from other departments is usually required to a greater extent for online documentation than for print documentation. For example, you need to work more closely with graphic designers, product testers, and the software integration team. When planning your online documentation strategy, make sure that the various groups have agreed to provide these resources.

- **Delivery mechanism**. Will your online documentation be part of the interface (as is usually the case with online help, for example) or the product code? Your deadlines and testing procedures will be affected by this decision.

- **Integration**. How will your documentation be connected to the product? You need to find out how the user will access the online information and how it will be installed and set up.

- **Testing**. Testing online documentation involves both the content of the documentation and the delivery media. Links that the user can click to go rapidly to cross-referenced information, for example, are one of the benefits of many online delivery products. Each link must be tested to make sure that it goes to the appropriate location. If the documentation is being delivered as part of the product, the online documentation must work correctly with the product code. Finally, the medium itself must be tested to make sure that it works on all supported platforms.

- **Legal**. Presenting information online usually means a change in how copyright and trademark issues are handled. Consult with counsel.

- **Production**. If your online documentation will be produced on CD-ROM media, you must determine whether it will be included with the product software or on a separate disc. This can also affect your packaging.

- **ASCII text**. Often, last-minute product changes or additions are documented in a brief online file in ASCII text. Consider drafting some formats for this type of presentation.

Final Print Production

Activities associated with the final production of hard-copy documentation are:

- Printing
- Binding
- Packaging

In large companies, a separate production department typically handles these activities. The publications organization simply hands off the final camera-ready copy or electronic files. In smaller organizations, the publications department is responsible for these activities.

This section provides only general information about printing and production processes. See Appendix D for sources of more thorough information on these subjects.

Deciding on a Strategy

Several factors influence the type of printing and packaging used for documentation.

- **Audience**. Is the documentation aimed at in-house engineers or commercial end users? This might determine your page layout or presentation. Under what conditions will your audience use the product? This might determine whether your books need to lie flat or whether you need to use a sturdier page weight or binding method.
- **Competitors**. How are similar products printed or packaged?
- **Distribution method**. If you sell directly to your customers, packaging can be minimal (for example, an envelope or corrugated box). If you are selling to resellers, you probably want a more professional presentation.
- **Cost**. Your operations or marketing departments will probably include the documentation production cost limit when they set a profit level for the product.

Printing Methods

While documents can be reproduced in various ways, the two main printing methods are offset printing and photocopying. If you need fewer than 1000 copies of your manuals, you probably want to use photocopying. For 1000 to 4000 copies, regular sheet-fed offset is usually appropriate. For over 4500 copies, you will probably need to use a printer with a web press (one that uses rolls of paper rather than sheets).

Offset Printing

Offset printing provides higher quality than photocopying and might be your only choice if you are using color in illustrations or text or including photographs. Note that if you are producing camera-ready copy on a 300-dots per inch (dpi) laser printer, offset printing will not increase the quality of the output.

Offset printing requires a larger print quantity to be cost effective. Ordering a larger quantity just to take advantage of the lower price is usually not a good strategy, though, because you might be left with many copies of outdated manuals. Costs for offset printing are also influenced by other factors, including the use of color, the size of the page (influencing how much trimming is needed), and the type of paper and ink used.

Photocopying

Photocopying produces lower-quality output than offset printing, but it is more cost effective for smaller quantities. Other costs for photocopying might include special handling if you are using an odd size of paper or special paper. Many photocopying machines today can provide rudimentary binding as well as photocopying.

Binding Methods

Several types of binding are generally available. The most common binding types are:

- Three-ring binders
- Wire-o
- Perfect
- Saddle-stitch

Consider the following factors when determining the binding method you use:

- Page size and number of pages
- Need for update insertions
- Frequency of users' access and the environment in which the book will be used
- Cost
- Customer preference

Three-Ring Binders

Three-ring binders hold standard 8.5-inch x 11-inch pages or other industry-standard page sizes. (For a price, you can also arrange for custom-size binders.) A big advantage to binders is that you can easily insert updates, change pages, and tabs. Covers can be slipped into plastic pockets in some binders on the front and spine, a feature that saves binder printing costs. However, three-ring binders take up a lot of room. Users often dislike them because these binders are bulky and awkward to handle, and because the rings can burst or rip pages.

Wire-O

Wire-o binding is much less expensive than three-ring binding, is smaller, and lies flatter. This binding offers much more variety in page size. However, updates are difficult to include and the wire prevents the book title from being printed on the spine. Wraparound covers are the workaround to this problem, but they are not very effective and add cost. Generally, users do not like wraparound covers and often cannot figure out how to use them.

Perfect

Perfect binding is less expensive than either three-ring or wire-o binding, especially in large quantities. A perfect-bound book usually includes the book title on its spine, making the book easily identifiable on a shelf. The chief complaint about perfect-bound books in the past was that they did not lie flat, but recently developed lay-flat or flex bindings have remedied this problem. You cannot insert updates or change pages into perfect-bound books. Also, large page counts sometimes mean that pages might fall out over time.

Saddle-Stitch

Saddle-stitch binding is possible only for page counts up to 96 pages. While this binding is very inexpensive, you cannot insert updates or change pages into saddle-stitched books, and they are too thin to have a spine.

Packaging

The type of packaging you use should be determined in large part by how you sell your products and what your competition provides. If you sell products directly to your customers, you might not need as elaborate a packaging scheme as if you were to sell products through an external commercial vendor, where your package competes with others.

Direct-to-customer packaging could be as simple as a padded envelope or corrugated box.

The type of *commercial* packaging you choose could be influenced by several factors:

- The packaging your competitors produce and, therefore, the packaging that customers expect.
- The number of different pieces delivered. For example, do you have several disks, several manuals, a quick reference card, and a warranty card? Or do you have a single disk and a single manual?
- Your budget.

If you are new to dealing with commercial packaging, you might want to go through your printer to find a reputable packaging source. You can also go through a broker, who puts together a whole production package, finding and dealing with printing and packaging vendors, for a fee.

When you find a packaging vendor, be sure to have the vendor produce prototypes of several packaging designs, and ask the pros and cons of each. You will probably have to provide the page counts for your manuals, and the number and type of other components in the package, before a realistic prototype can be produced.

Working With Outside Vendors

The best way to find a reputable printer or production broker is to ask people in your geographic area and industry. Ask printers or brokers about their experience with your type of product or about other jobs they have done for people in similar industries.

If your printing and packaging needs are relatively simple, you can probably use a printer who has less experience with your particular product area. However, you will be expected to provide the printer with camera-ready copy and all the information needed for the job.

If your needs are somewhat complex or you have little experience in this area, you will probably need to spend time finding a vendor who is right for you. Experienced printers can provide you with professional advice and samples. They can also explain the pros and cons of various printing methods, paper, ink, and so on. But you have to ask! Larger printers often have account representatives who can offer suggestions and get answers for you if the size of your account merits attention.

If you suspect your printing or packaging needs are very complex or you do not have either the expertise or the staff to investigate vendors, you might want to find a broker. Brokers quote a fee for your whole job and take on the responsibility of finding and dealing with vendors, procuring packaging samples, and so on.

Post-Production Considerations

After the documentation is delivered to production, your work is not done. You should have a plan in place to deal with last-minute product changes or inaccuracies in the documentation. Also, if the product documentation is likely to be revised, you should collect and maintain information that will help with the next version.

Handling Post-Production Revisions

Despite your best efforts, you might discover technical inaccuracies after the documentation is produced, either from omissions or from changes to the product. Therefore, allocations of monetary and staff resources to the project must continue even after the date the final documentation is delivered to production.

Typical ways to correct documentation inaccuracies include the following strategies:

- **Online files on the product disks**. These files can cover documentation inaccuracies and last-minute product revisions.

- **Replacement pages**. Errors in limited locations in printed manuals can be corrected through replacement pages that are inserted individually by users. These generally ship with the product and are accompanied by a card or insert listing all replacement pages.

- **Documentation update package**. A last-minute change to the product that has ramifications throughout the documentation might require too many change pages to make replacement pages feasible. In this case, you might want to include a documentation update package, which explains the exact changes that need to be made to specific pages, including the paragraph and line location and the information to be added or deleted. However, this solution should be a last resort.

Note – If your company sells directly to customers rather than through a third-party commercial distributor, you can issue change pages or update packages through your distribution channel or sales staff even after the product ships.

Make sure that customer support, marketing, localization, and sales personnel know about the inaccuracies and the steps taken to correct them.

Maintaining Project Continuity

Once a product has shipped, your first impulse might be to try to forget about it as soon as possible. However, your job will only be more difficult when you have to revise the documentation for the next version. Some of the information you might want to save or document about a project includes:

- The location of online documentation files. Delete irrelevant files such as earlier versions of text or graphics. You might want to establish a central archive where final files are kept.

- While the details are still fresh in your mind, conduct a *post-mortem meeting* with the documentation team and write down a brief project review. Document anything that might be helpful, for example:

    - Processes that didn't work as anticipated or could be modified to work better.

    - Controversies that arose. Even if they were resolved, having a record of each controversy could prove useful later.

    - Issues that affected the schedule and might recur during the next cycle.

    - Subject matter experts or other helpful project team members who were not official reviewers or project team members.

- Technical review comments from all official reviewers.

- Edits or review comments that you did not have time to incorporate for this version, but that should appear in a future version.

- Product information that you did not have time to incorporate for this version, but that should appear in a future version.

Checklists and Forms

This appendix provides samples of common publications forms and checklists. You might need to modify them to reflect your own company processes.

The following checklists and forms appear in this appendix:

Manuscript Tracking Chart

Document Title: _____

Project: _____

Writer: _____ No. of pages: _____

Edit Requested	Sent to Editor (1st review)	Returned to Writer (1st review)	Sent to Editor (2nd review)	Returned to Writer (2nd review)	Notes
Alpha					
Develop. edit					
Copy edit					
Proofread					
Release check					
Beta					
Develop. edit					
Copy edit					
Proofread					
Release check					
FCS					
Develop. edit					
Copy edit					
Proofread					
Release check					

Checked: ❏ Front matter   ❏ Back matter   ❏ Cross-references   ❏ Spelling

Dates of files to production:

Alpha _____   Beta _____   FCS _____   Print _____

Request for Editing Form

Document Title: _____

Writer: _____ Product code name: _____

Phone no.: _____ Email address: _____

Number of pages: _____ Date submitted: _____ Return by: _____

Target audience: _____

Type of edit requested: ❑ Developmental ❑ Copy ❑ Proofread

Development stage: ❑ Alpha ❑ Beta ❑ FCS

❑ Other: _____

Is this document part of a set? ❑ Yes ❑ No

Name of set: _____

Has this document been edited before? ❑ Yes ❑ No

Editor: _____ Date of previous edit: _____

Type of edit: _____

Were comments incorporated into this draft? ❑ Yes ❑ No

Do specific sections need particular attention? ❑ Yes ❑ No

If so, which ones? _____

Does the set have a style sheet? ❑ Yes ❑ No

If so, is it included for the editor? ❑ Yes ❑ No

Check for the following items before giving a book to the editor:

❑ Title page, credits page, TOC, LOF, LOT, and preface are current.

❑ Glossary and index are complete and current.

❑ Page numbers and footers are correct.

❑ Any blank pages are explained.

❑ Graphics are incorporated or content and placement are indicated.

❑ Cross-references are updated.

❑ Trademarked terms are marked appropriately on first reference in text.

❑ Spelling checker was run on all files.

Comments? _____

_____

_____

Artwork Request Form

Full manual title: _____

Full manual part number: _____

Requestor: _____ Phone no.: _____

Date due to writer (art delivered for proofing by midnight): _____

Document is: ❑ Beta   ❑ FCS   ❑ Other

Document created in: ❑ Frame   ❑ Other

No.	Figure caption to be used in this manual (and used in previous manuals, if different)	Existing Control No.	New/Rev. Control No.
			Column for Illustrator Use Only

Technical Review Cover Letter

TO: *Reviewer List*

FROM: *Writer Name*

SUBJECT: Technical Review of *Name of Book*

DATE: *Date*

The attached manuscript is the technical review version of *Name of Book*. Please review the entire manuscript, paying special attention to the notes and questions to reviewers. All open issues and unanswered questions must be resolved for this technical review to be complete.

I would appreciate your general comments as well as specific answers to the issues raised in the notes. Please give detailed and thorough responses. Also, please address the specific review responsibilities of your department.

[*Add any comments regarding specific issues or content.*]

Your review must be returned by 5 p.m. on *Date*. After reviewing your responses, I will discuss any discrepancies at the technical review sign-off meeting, which will be held on *Date* at *Time* in *Name* Conference Room.

Because the production schedule is tight, please make wording or style suggestions only if they affect the technical accuracy of the text.

Thank you very much for your attention to this document. Your comments are appreciated and contribute greatly to improving the quality of *Company Name* documentation.

Authorization to Produce Document

Book Title: _____

Book Part Number: _____

Writer: _____

Path: _____

❑ One clean copy of document given to Production Coordinator

❑ Authorizations signed off

❑ Permissions set for directory and above

❑ Directory cleared of backup and other extraneous files

Approvals

Editor: _____ Date: _____

Proofreader: _____ Date: _____

Writing Manager: _____ Date: _____

Comments? _____
_____
_____
_____

For Production Use Only

Transfer location: _____

PostScript files location: _____

Archive location: _____

Database: _____

PostScript files transmitted to: _____

Print Specification

Date:
Contact name
Contact phone no.

Company name
Company address
Company address
Fax number

Printing specification for: _____

Product description: _____

Documents to vendor (date): _____

Product ship date: _____

Quantity to print: _____

Manuals: (If the documentation set is small, fill in the table below. For larger jobs, attach a list of manuals, page counts, and the preferred binding method.)

Part Number	Title	Page Count	Binding

Format size: _____

Text stock: _____

Cover stock: _____

Cover art: _____

Tabs: _____

Cards: _____

Labels: _____

Special boxes or cartons: _____

Media: _____

Printing process: _____

Proofing requirements: _____
_____

Assembly instructions: _____
_____

General comments: _____
_____
_____

Please provide _____ with ___ check copies at time of first customer ship.

Return all original hand-off material to _____ at completion of job.

Correct Usage of Terms

The following table provides alternatives for terms that you should not use in technical documentation, and terms that you should avoid. The table also provides some guidance related to commonly confused words and terms. See also these sections in this book for related guidelines and examples:

- "Capitalization" on page 2
- "Hyphen" on page 23
- "Redundancies" on page 78
- "Abbreviations and Acronyms" on page 11
- "Units of Measurement" on page 13

TABLE C–1 Questionable Terms and Their Alternatives

Term	Usage
#	Do not use as an abbreviation for number. Use "no." instead.
above	Do not use to refer to the location of another piece of information. Instead, use "previous" or "preceding," or refer to the specific section title or figure number, for example.
affect	Verb meaning "to change or influence something." For example, "The style setting affects the appearance of the paragraph." See also "effect."
align to	Use "align with."
allows	Use only when discussing permission. For example, "Write access allows the user to modify the file." When discussing capabilities, use "enables" or rewrite the sentence. For example, "The Edit menu options enable you to modify the document" or "Use the Edit menu options to modify the document." Also applies to "lets" and "permits."
and/or	Do not use. If you mean "or," write "or." If you mean "and," write "and." If you mean that any or all of the things that are named might be affected, say so. For example, "Using the Edit menu, you can cut, paste, or cut and paste text or graphics."

TABLE C–1 Questionable Terms and Their Alternatives *(Continued)*

Term	Usage
appendices	Use "appendixes."
backward	Note lack of final "s."
baud rate	Often incorrectly assumed to indicate the number of bits per second (bps) transmitted, baud rate actually measures the number of events, or signal changes, that occur in one second. In most instances when "baud rate" is used, the correct term is "bps." For example, a so-called 9600-baud modem that encodes 4 bits per event actually operates at 2400 baud, but it transmits 9600 bits per second (2400x4 bits per event) and thus is correctly called a 9600-bps modem. Check your source material before using the term "baud rate."
below	Do not use to refer to the location of another piece of information. Instead, use "next" or "following," or refer to the specific section title or figure number, for example.
boot up	Use "boot."
bring the system down	Do not use. Write "cause the system to fail," "shut down the system," or "power off the system," depending on the meaning.
bring up	Do not use. Write "power up the system," "start the system," "turn on the machine," or "turn on the power to the system," or other text, depending on the meaning.
can	Use to indicate the power or the ability to do something. For example, "See if you can log in to the system." See also "may" and "might."
centigrade	Use "Celsius."
client	Use only when talking about the relationship with a server. Do not use to refer to a person.
client-server	Use when describing a relationship between a client and a server. For example, "This network is based on the client-server model."
.com; dot-com	Use .com when referring to the suffix itself.
	Also use .com in appropriate trademarked terms, or when your document requires no variations on the term ".com."
	Use dot-com when referring to companies ("dot-coms"), when using as a verb ("to dot-com," "dot-commed," "dot-comming"), or when the term is the first word in a sentence or heading.
comprise	Avoid using "comprise." Use "contain" or "include" instead. Do not use "comprised of" when you mean "composed of."
currently	Use only in a document that you know will be updated regularly, for example, in release notes. You can also use a specific date, for example, "August 2002."
data	Although in the pure Latin form this noun is plural, the most common industry usage is in the singular. For example, "The data is available."

TABLE C–1 Questionable Terms and Their Alternatives *(Continued)*

Term	Usage
deinstall	Use "uninstall."
-dependent	Avoid constructions such as "device-dependent" or "platform-dependent."
depress	You do not "depress" a key. Use "press."
design	Do not use. Do not write, for example, "XYZ is designed to search for files." If XYZ is designed to search, assume that it does. Write "XYZ searches for files."
desktop	Use only when you are referring to a specific piece of hardware. Otherwise, use "system" or "host."
die	Use "fail."
disappear	Do not use. A window does not "disappear." Use "dismiss" instead.
dot-com, .com	Use dot-com when referring to companies ("dot-coms"), when using as a verb ("to dot-com," "dot-commed," "dot-comming"), or when the term is the first word in a sentence or heading.
	Use .com when referring to the suffix itself.
	Also use .com in appropriate trademarked terms, or when your document requires no variations on the term ".com."
effect	Noun meaning a result or consequence. For example, "The style setting has an effect on the appearance of the paragraph." See also "affect."
e.g.	Use "for example."
ejector lever	Use "ejection lever."
electrical shock	Use "electric shock."
enable	See "allows."
-enabled	Avoid. Use text such as "works with" or "is compatible with" instead.
ensure that	Be sure to include the word "that" when introducing a restrictive clause.
enter the following command	To avoid confusion with the Enter key, do not use. Write "type the following command" instead.
etc.	Use more explicit text, which also solves problems with sentence-ending punctuation. For example, do not write "Mail Tool enables you to compose email messages, respond to email messages, etc." Instead, write "Mail Tool enables you to compose email messages, respond to email messages, and perform other mail administration tasks."
fixed disk	Use "disk drive."
floppy	Use "diskette."
floppy disk	Use "diskette."

TABLE C–1 Questionable Terms and Their Alternatives *(Continued)*

Term	Usage
floppy disk drive	Use "diskette drive."
floppy drive	Use "diskette drive."
geographical region	Use "geographic region."
graphics card	Use only when you are specifically referring to a graphics card. Otherwise, use "video display device."
hard disk, hard drive	Use "disk drive."
hit	Do not instruct a person to "hit" anything, including computer keys. Use "press."
hypertext, hypertext link	Use "link."
i.e.	Use "that is."
indices	Use "indexes."
information on	Use "information about."
in order to	Use "to."
instructions about	Use "instructions on."
in to, into	Use "in to" to denote direction with purpose, for example, "Log in to the system." Use "into" to indicate direction only. For example, "The engineer went into the lab."
invoke	Avoid. Use only if no other word accurately describes the action. Usually, you can substitute "run," "start," or "call."
its, it's	Without an apostrophe, "its" is the possessive form of the pronoun "it." For example, "The site describes the eMetrics program and its accompanying utilities."
	With an apostrophe, "it's" is an abbreviation for "it is." This construction should rarely be used as it is often incorrectly used without a clear reference for the pronoun. For example, "It's easy to install this product."
launch	Use "start."
left-hand side	Use "left side."
lets	See "allows."
log into	Use "log in to."
logoff, log off	Preferred usage is "logout" (noun, modifier) and "log out of" (verb).
logon, log on	Preferred usage is "login" (noun, modifier) and "log in to" (verb).
may	Use only when granting permission. For example, "You may use either uppercase or lowercase letters." Use "can" to indicate the power or ability to do something. Use "might" to indicate a possibility.
mice	Do not use. Use "mouse devices" to refer to more than one mouse.

TABLE C–1 Questionable Terms and Their Alternatives *(Continued)*

Term	Usage
might	Use to indicate a possibility. For example, "You might need to use another mouse." See also "can" and "may."
might want to	Do not try to read minds. Write "If you want to exit from the application, click Exit."
-most	Do not use with directional words such as "left" or "top." Use phrases such as "on the left" or "at the far left" instead.
non-preinstalled	Use "not preinstalled."
note that, notice	Use "note" for the noun, "notice" for the verb.
now	Use only in a document that you know will be updated regularly, for example, in release notes. You can also use a specific date, for example, "August 2002."
permits	See "allows."
Phillips screw, Phillips screwdriver, No. 2 Phillips screwdriver	Not "Phillips-head."
please	Do not use. You are not making a request, you are telling the reader to do something.
plug	For the verb form, use "connect" to avoid confusion except in the context of "plug and play."
pops up	Do not use. Use "appears" or "is displayed."
postinstall, preinstall	Write "install" unless you are describing a process that literally takes place before or directly after installation.
postpend	Means "attach to the end." Use "append" instead.
preceding	Use instead of "before" to refer to the location of an immediately prior piece of information.
presently	Use only in a document that you know will be updated regularly, for example, in release notes. You can also use a specific date, for example, "August 2002."
preventative	Use "preventive."
previous	Use instead of "before" to refer to the location of another piece of information mentioned earlier.
rear panel	Use "back panel."
recommend	Do not use. Just go ahead and recommend. For example, write "Back up all your files once each week," not, "It is recommended (or "We recommend") that you back up all your files once each week." In some less definitive instances, describe the circumstances in which backing up is recommended. For example, "Back up your xxx file whenever you modify it."

TABLE C–1 Questionable Terms and Their Alternatives *(Continued)*

Term	Usage
right click	To be safe, use "click mouse button 3." Some people reverse the "handedness" of their mouse devices.
right-hand side	Use "right side."
screen shot	Use "screen capture."
shut off	Use "power off."
simple	This term usually does not apply to technical information.
simply	This term usually does not apply to technical information.
-specific	Avoid using this imprecise term.
start up (verb)	Use "start."
system	Use to refer to software or a combination of hardware and software. For example, "file system" or "system software."
	Also use to refer to a computer and its peripherals. A system does not have to be connected to a network. Other terms that can be used for "system" are "host," "machine," and "computer." "Host" is typically used in network-related documentation. Use "machine" or "computer" when "system" is already being used to describe the software or combination of hardware and software.
	When possible, use more descriptive terms than the generic term "system," such as "mail server" or "remote system."
that	This word is often misused in nonrestrictive clauses instead of "which." Use "that" for restrictive clauses. For example:
	"I like mysteries that are suspenseful." (I only like those mysteries that are suspenseful.)
	"I like mysteries, which are suspenseful." (I like all mysteries, and mysteries have the attribute of being suspenseful.)
there are	Because "there are" is ambiguous, avoid using this phrase at the beginning of a sentence or clause.
there is	Because "there is" is ambiguous, avoid using this phrase at the beginning of a sentence or clause.
toward	Note lack of final "s."
trivial	Do not use. A cliche, this word does not mean "easy." It means "insignificant."
versus, vs.	Use "compared with."
via	Do not use. Use the more common equivalents "through," "by means of," "using," or "by way of."

TABLE C–1 Questionable Terms and Their Alternatives *(Continued)*

Term	Usage
whether or not	The words "or not" are usually unnecessary. This whole phrase can sometimes be replaced with "if."
which	This word is often misused in restrictive clauses instead of "that." Use "which" for nonrestrictive clauses. For example:
	"I like mysteries that are suspenseful." (I only like those mysteries that are suspenseful.)
	"I like mysteries, which are suspenseful." (I like all mysteries, and mysteries have the attribute of being suspenseful.)
wish	Use "want" rather than "wish."
workstation	Use "system" or "host" instead. Do not use "workstation" unless you are referring to a specific piece of hardware.

Recommended Reading

This appendix lists titles on general and technical writing and editing, as well as books primarily for technical writers in the computer industry.

Note – This list is for your reference only. You must seek permission from the publisher owning the copyrighted source material before reprinting any text that you select, either in book or electronic form.

This appendix covers the following categories:

- "Desktop Publishing and Document Design" on page 320
- "Editing Standards" on page 320
- "Graphics and Illustration" on page 321
- "HTML and XML" on page 322
- "Indexing" on page 322
- "Information Mapping" on page 323
- "Internationalization and Localization" on page 323
- "Legal Issues" on page 324
- "Online Help" on page 324
- "Online Writing Style" on page 325
- "Platform Style Guides" on page 326
- "Printing" on page 326
- "Project Management" on page 327
- "Reference Works" on page 328
- "Standard Generalized Markup Language (SGML)" on page 329
- "Typography" on page 330
- "Usability Testing" on page 330
- "User Interfaces" on page 330
- "Web and Internet Publishing" on page 332
- "Writing Standards" on page 333
- "Writing Standards for Technical Writing" on page 334

Desktop Publishing and Document Design

Devall, Sandra Lentz, and Esther Kibby. *Desktop Publishing StyleGuide.* 2d ed. Clifton, N.Y.: Delmar Learning, 1998.

Graham, Lisa. *Basics of Design: Layout and Typography for Beginners.* Clifton, N.Y.: Delmar Learning, 2001.

Lichty, Tom. *Design Principles for Desktop Publishers.* 2d ed. Belmont, Calif.: Wadsworth Publishing Co., 1994.

Schriver, Karen A. *Dynamics in Document Design: Creating Text for Readers.* New York: John Wiley & Sons, 1994.

Williams, Robin, and John Tollett. *Robin Williams Design Workshop.* Berkeley, Calif.: Peachpit Press, 2000.

Editing Standards

Einsohn, Amy. *Copyeditor's Handbook: A Guide for Book Publishing and Corporate Communications.* Berkeley, Calif.: University of California Press, 2000.

Gordon, Karen Elizabeth. *The Deluxe Transitive Vampire: The Ultimate Handbook of Grammar for the Innocent, the Eager, and the Doomed.* 1st ed. New York: Pantheon Books, 1993.

Gordon, Karen Elizabeth. *The New Well-Tempered Sentence: A Punctuation Handbook for the Innocent, the Eager, and the Doomed.* Revised and expanded. New York: Ticknor & Fields, 1993.

Judd, Karen. *Copyediting: A Practical Guide.* 3d ed. Los Altos, Calif.: Crisp Publications, 2001.

Ross-Larson, Bruce. *Edit Yourself: A Manual for Everyone Who Works With Words.* New York: W. W. Norton & Co., 1996.

Rude, Carolyn D. *Technical Editing.* 3d ed. New York: Longman, 2001.

Samson, Donald C., Jr. *Editing Technical Writing.* New York: Oxford University Press, 1993.

Stainton, Elsie Myers. *The Fine Art of Copyediting.* 2d ed. New York: Columbia University Press, 2001.

Tarutz, Judith A. *Technical Editing: The Practical Guide for Editors and Writers.* Cambridge, Mass.: Perseus Publishing, 1992.

Venolia, Jan. *Write Right! A Desktop Digest of Punctuation, Grammar, and Style.* 4th ed. Berkeley, Calif.: Ten Speed Press, 2001.

Venolia, Jan. *Rewrite Right! Your Guide to Perfectly Polished Prose.* 2d ed. Berkeley, Calif.: Ten Speed Press, 2000.

Graphics and Illustration

Bertoline, Gary R., and Eric Wiebe. *Technical Graphics Communication.* 3d ed. New York: McGraw-Hill Science/Engineering/Math, 2002.

Dreyfus, Henry. *Symbol Sourcebook: An Authoritative Guide to International Graphic Symbols.* New York: John Wiley & Sons, 1984.

Evans, Poppy. *Designer's Survival Manual: The Insider's Guide to Working With Illustrators, Photographers, Printers, Web Engineers, and More.* Cincinnati, Ohio: North Light Books, 2001.

Groff, Pamela. *Glossary of Graphic Communications.* 3d ed. Upper Saddle River, N.J.: Prentice Hall, 1998.

Horton, William. *The Icon Book: Visual Symbols for Computer Systems and Documentation.* New York: John Wiley & Sons, 1994.

Tufte, Edward R. *Envisioning Information.* Cheshire, Conn.: Graphics Press, 1990.

Tufte, Edward R. *The Visual Display of Quantitative Information.* 2d ed. Cheshire, Conn.: Graphics Press, 2001.

Tufte, Edward R. *Visual Explanations: Images and Quantities, Evidence and Narrative.* Cheshire, Conn.: Graphics Press, 1997.

Ware, Colin. *Information Visualization: Optimizing Design for Human Perception.* San Francisco: Morgan Kaufmann, 2001.

Williamson, Hugh Albert Fordyce. *Methods of Book Design: The Practice of an Industrial Craft.* 3d ed. New Haven, Conn.: Yale University Press, 1983.

HTML and XML

Burns, Joe. HTML Goodies Web site at `http://www.htmlgoodies.com/`.

Eckstein, Robert. *XML Pocket Reference.* 2d ed. Sebastopol, Calif.: O'Reilly & Associates, 2001.

Graham, Ian S. *The HTML 4.0 Sourcebook: A Complete Guide to HTML 4.0.* New York: John Wiley & Sons, 1998.

Harold, Elliotte Rusty, and W. Scott Means. *XML in a Nutshell.* 2d ed. Sebastopol, Calif.: O'Reilly & Associates, 2002.

Morris, Mary E.S., and John E. Simpson. *HTML for Fun and Profit.* 3d ed. Palo Alto, Calif.: Sun Microsystems Press, 1998.

Musciano, Chuck, and Bill Kennedy. *HTML & XHTML: The Definitive Guide.* 5th ed. Sebastopol, Calif.: O'Reilly & Associates, 2002.

Pfaffenberger, Bryan. *Web Publishing With XML in Six Easy Steps.* Boston: AP Professional, 1998.

Ray, Erik T., and Christopher R. Maden. *Learning XML.* Sebastopol, Calif.: O'Reilly & Associates, 2001.

Willard, Wendy. *HTML: A Beginner's Guide.* 2d ed. Emeryville, Calif.: McGraw-Hill/Osborne Media, 2002.

Indexing

Ament, Kurt. *Indexing: A Nuts-and-Bolts Guide for Technical Writers.* Norwich, N.Y.: William Andrew Publishing, 2001.

The American Society of Indexers Web site at `http://asindexing.org`.

Bonura, Larry. *The Art of Indexing.* New York: John Wiley & Sons, 1994.

Brenner, Diane, and Marilyn Rowland, eds. *Beyond Book Indexing: How to Get Started in Web Indexing, Embedded Indexing, and Other Computer-Based Media.* Medford, N.J.: Information Today, 2000.

Lathrop, Lori. *An Indexer's Guide to the Internet.* 2d ed. Medford, N.J.: Information Today, 1995.

Mulvany, Nancy C. *Indexing Books.* Chicago: University of Chicago Press, 1994.

Wellisch, Hans H. *Indexing From A to Z.* 2d ed. New York: H. W. Wilson, 1995.

Information Mapping

Horn, Robert E. *Mapping Hypertext: The Analysis, Organization, and Display of Knowledge for the Next Generation of On-line Text and Graphics.* Lexington, Mass.: Lexington Institute, 1990.

The Information Mapping® Method. Available at `http://www.infomap.com`.

Trubiano, John, and Gerard W. Paradis. *Demystifying ISO 9001:2000: Information Mapping's Guide to the ISO 9001 Standard, 2000 Version.* 2d ed. Upper Saddle River, N.J.: Prentice Hall, 2001.

Wycoff, Joyce. *Mindmapping: Your Personal Guide to Exploring Creativity and Problem-Solving.* New York: Berkley Books, 1991.

Internationalization and Localization

del Galdo, Elisa M., and Jakob Nielsen. *International User Interfaces.* New York: John Wiley & Sons, 1996.

Esselink, Bert. *A Practical Guide to Localization.* Philadelphia: John Benjamins Publishing, 2000.

Hoft, Nancy L. *International Technical Communication: How to Export Information About High Technology.* New York: John Wiley & Sons, 1995.

Taylor, Dave. *Global Software: Developing Applications for the International Market.* New York: Springer-Verlag, 1992.

Tuthill, Bill, and David Smallberg. *Creating Worldwide Software: Solaris International Developer's Guide.* 2d ed. Palo Alto, Calif.: Sun Microsystems Press, 1997.

Legal Issues

Bouchoux, Deborah E. *Protecting Your Company's Intellectual Property: A Practical Guide to Trademarks, Copyrights, Patents, and Trade Secrets.* New York: AMACOM, 2001.

Strong, William S. *The Copyright Book: A Practical Guide.* 5th ed. Cambridge, Mass.: MIT Press, 1999.

United States Copyright Office Web site at http://www.loc.gov/copyright/.

United States Patent and Trademark Office Web site at http://www.uspto.gov.

Online Help

Hedtke, John, and Brenda Huettner. *RoboHelp for the Web.* Includes CD-ROM. Plano, Texas: Wordware Publishing, 2002.

Help Technology Centre: Resources and Techniques for Help Systems. Available at http://mvps.org/htmlhelpcenter.

Klein, Jeannine M. E. *Building Enhanced HTML Help With DHTML and CSS.* Upper Saddle River, N.J.: Prentice Hall, 2000.

Wickham, Daina Pupons, Debra L. Mayhew, Teresa Stoll [et al.]. *Designing Effective Wizards: A Multidisciplinary Approach.* Includes CD-ROM. Upper Saddle River, N.J.: Prentice Hall, 2001.

Online Writing Style

Bricklin, Dan, and Trellix Corporation. *Good Documents: How to Write for the Intranet.* Available at `http://www.gooddocuments.com`. Concord, Mass.: Trellix Corporation, 1998, 1999.

Gahran, Amy. *Contentious: The Web-zine for Writers, Editors, and Others Who Create Content for Online Media.* Available at `http://www.contentious.com`. 1998–2002.

Hammerich, Irene, and Claire Harrison. *Developing Online Content: The Principles of Writing and Editing for the Web.* New York: John Wiley & Sons, 2001.

Kilian, Crawford. *Writing for the Web (Writers' Edition).* Bellingham, Wash.: Self-Counsel Press, 2000.

McGovern, Gerry, Rob Norton, and Catherine O'Dowd. *The Web Content Style Guide: An Essential Reference for Online Writers, Editors, and Managers.* Upper Saddle River, N.J.: Prentice Hall, 2001.

Nielsen, Jakob. "Writing for the Web." Useit.com. Available at `http://www.useit.com/papers/webwriting`.

Pfaffenberger, Bryan. *The Elements of Hypertext Style.* Boston: AP Professional, 1997.

Price, Jonathan, and Lisa Price. *Hot Text: Web Writing That Works.* Indianapolis, Ind.: New Riders Publishing, 2002.

Troffer, Alysson. "How to Write Effectively Online." Available at `http://homepage.mac.com/alysson/webfolio.html`.

Walker, Janice R., and Todd Taylor. *The Columbia Guide to Online Style.* New York: Columbia University Press, 1998.

Platform Style Guides

Apple Computer, Inc. *Macintosh Human Interface Guidelines*. Reading, Mass.: Addison-Wesley, 1992.

CDE Documentation Group. *Common Desktop Environment 1.0 Programmer's Guide*. Reading, Mass.: Addison-Wesley, 1995.

Commodore-Amiga, Inc. *Amiga User Interface Style Guide*. Reading, Mass.: Addison-Wesley, 1991.

Fountain, Anthony, and Paula Ferguson. *Motif Reference Manual: For Motif 2.1, Vol. 6*. 2d ed. Sebastopol, Calif.: O'Reilly & Associates, 2000.

Microsoft Corporation. *The Windows Interface: An Application Design Guide*. 2d ed. Redmond, Wash.: Microsoft Press, 1995.

Open Software Foundation. *OSF/Motif Style Guide: Revision 1.2 (for OSF/Motif Release 1.2)*. Upper Saddle River, N.J.: Prentice Hall PTR, 1993.

PalmSource. *Palm OS User Interface Guidelines*. Lincoln, Nebr.: iUniverse, 2002.

Sun Microsystems, Inc. *Java Look and Feel Design Guidelines*. 2d ed. Reading, Mass.: Addison-Wesley, 2001.

Sun Microsystems, Inc. *OPEN LOOK Graphical User Interface Application Style Guidelines*. Reading, Mass.: Addison-Wesley, 1989.

Sun Microsystems, Inc. *OPEN LOOK Graphical User Interface Functional Specification*. Reading, Mass.: Addison-Wesley, 1989.

Printing

Adams, J. Michael, and Penny Ann Dolin. *Printing Technology*. 5th ed. Clifton, N.Y.: Delmar Learning, 2001.

Beach, Mark, and Eric Kenly. *Getting It Printed: How to Work With Printers and Graphic Imaging Services to Assure Quality, Stay on Schedule and Control Costs*. 3d ed. Cincinnati, Ohio: North Light Books, 1998.

O'Quinn, Donnie. *Print Publishing: A Hayden Shop Manual*. 2d ed. Indianapolis, Ind.: Que, 2000.

Project Management

Brooks, Frederick P. *The Mythical Man-Month: Essays on Software Engineering.* Anniversary ed. Reading, Mass.: Addison-Wesley, 1995.

DeMarco, Tom. *Controlling Software Projects: Management, Measurement, Measurement & Estimation.* Upper Saddle River, N.J.: Prentice Hall PTR, 1998.

Faulconbridge, R. Ian, and Michael J. Ryan. *Managing Complex Technical Projects: A Systems Engineering Approach.* Norwood, Mass.: 2002.

Hackos, JoAnn T. *Managing Your Documentation Projects.* New York: John Wiley & Sons, 1994.

Humphrey, Watts S. *Introduction to the Team Software Process.* Reading, Mass.: Addison-Wesley, 1999.

Humphrey, Watts S. *Managing the Software Process.* Reading, Mass.: Addison-Wesley, 1989.

Kerzner, Harold. *Project Management: A Systems Approach to Planning, Scheduling, and Controlling.* 8th ed. New York: John Wiley & Sons, 1998.

Lewis, James P. *Project Planning, Scheduling & Control.* 3d ed. New York: McGraw-Hill Trade, 2000.

McConnell, Steve C. *Software Project Survival Guide.* Redmond, Wash.: Microsoft Press, 1998.

Murch, Richard. *Project Management: Best Practices for IT Professionals.* Upper Saddle River, N.J.: Prentice Hall PTR, 2000.

Nicholas, John M. *Project Management for Business and Technology: Principles and Practice.* Harlow, Essex, U.K.: Pearson Education, 2000.

Phillips, Joseph. *IT Project Management: On Track From Start to Finish.* Includes CD-ROM. Emeryville, Calif.: McGraw-Hill/Osborne Media, 2002.

Schwalbe, Kathy. *Information Technology Project Management.* 2d ed. Includes CD-ROM. Cambridge, MA.: Course Technology, a division of Thompson Learning, 2001.

Reference Works

The American Heritage Dictionary of the English Language. 4th ed. Boston: Houghton Mifflin Company, 1996.

The Chicago Manual of Style. 14th ed. Chicago: University of Chicago Press, 1993.

The Chicago Manual of Style FAQ. Available at `http://www.press.uchicago.edu/Misc/Chicago/cmosfaq/cmosfaq.html`.

ComputerUser High-Tech Dictionary. Available at `http://www.computeruser.com/resources/dictionary`.

FOLDOC: Free On-Line Dictionary of Computing. Available at `http://foldoc.doc.ic.ac.uk/foldoc`.

The Gregg Reference Manual. 9th ed. Woodland Hills, Calif.: Glencoe/McGraw-Hill, 2001.

IEEE 100: The Authoritative Dictionary of IEEE Standards Terms. 7th ed. New York: Institute of Electrical and Electronics Engineers, Inc., 2001.

McGraw-Hill Dictionary of Scientific and Technical Terms. 6th ed. New York: McGraw-Hill, 2002.

Merriam-Webster's Collegiate Dictionary. 10th ed. Springfield, Mass.: Merriam-Webster, 2001.

Merriam-Webster's Collegiate Thesaurus. Springfield, Mass.: Merriam-Webster, 1994.

Merriam Webster's Medical Desk Dictionary. 2d ed. Clifton, N.Y.: Delmar Learning, 2002.

Merriam-Webster Online. Available at `http://www.m-w.com`.

Microsoft Corporation. *The Microsoft Manual of Style for Technical Publications.* 3d ed. Redmond, Wash.: Microsoft Press, 2003. (Available September 2003.) The 2d edition is available for free download at `http://www.microsoft.com/mspress/education`.

Microsoft Corporation. *Microsoft Press Computer Dictionary.* 5th ed. Redmond, Wash.: Microsoft Press, 2002.

The New Hacker's Dictionary. 3d ed. Cambridge, Mass.: MIT Press, 1996.

The New York Public Library Writer's Guide to Style and Usage. 1st ed. New York: Harper Collins, 1994.

OneLook® Dictionary Search. Available at `http://www.onelook.com`.

Publications Manual of the American Psychological Association. 5th ed. Washington, D.C.: American Psychological Association, 2001.

Random House Webster's College Dictionary. New York: Random House, 2001.

Roget's II: The New Thesaurus. 3d ed. Boston: Houghton Mifflin Company, 1996.

The Synonym Finder. Completely revised by Laurence Urdang and Nancy LaRoche, eds. [et al.] New York: Time-Warner Books, 1986.

Webster's New World Computer Dictionary. 9th ed. New York: John Wiley & Sons, 2001.

Webster's Third New International Dictionary. Includes CD-ROM. Springfield, Mass.: Merriam-Webster, 2000.

Whatis?com: Definitions for Thousands of the Most Current IT-Related Words. Available at `http://whatis.techtarget.com`.

Words into Type. 3d ed. Upper Saddle River, N.J.: Prentice Hall, 1974.

Standard Generalized Markup Language (SGML)

Bryan, Martin. *SGML: An Author's Guide to the Standard Generalized Markup Language.* Wokingham, England; Reading, Mass.: Addison-Wesley, 1988.

Bryan, Martin. *SGML and HTML Explained.* 2d ed. Harlow, England; Reading, Mass.: Addison-Wesley Longman, 1997.

Goldfarb, Charles F., with Yuri Rubinsky *The SGML Handbook.* Oxford: Clarendon Press; Oxford and New York: Oxford University Press, 1990.

Maler, Eve, with Jeanne El Andaloussi. *Developing SGML DTDs: From Text to Model to Markup.* Upper Saddle River, N.J.: Prentice Hall PTR, 1995.

OASIS. Cover Pages standards Web site at `http://xml.coverpages.org/sgml.html`.

Van Herwijnen, Eric. *Practical SGML.* 2d ed. Boston: Kluwer Academic Publishers, 1994.

Walsh, Norman, and Leonard Muellner. *DocBook: The Definitive Guide.* Sebastopol, Calif.: O'Reilly & Associates, 1999.

Typography

Bringhurst, Robert. *Elements of Typographic Style*. 2d ed. Point Roberts, Wash.: Hartley & Marks, 1996.

Campbell, Alastair. *The Designer's Lexicon: The Illustrated Dictionary of Design, Printing and Computer Terms*. San Francisco: Chronicle Books, 2000.

Craig, James, and William Bevington. Susan E. Meyer, ed. *Designing With Type: A Basic Course in Typography*. 4th ed. New York: Watson-Guptill Publications, Inc., 1999.

Felici, James. *The Complete Manual of Typography*. Berkeley, Calif.: Peachpit Press, 2003.

Spiekermann, Erik, and E. M. Ginger. *Stop Stealing Sheep & Find Out How Type Works*. 2d ed. Mountain View, Calif.: Adobe Press, 2002.

Williams, Robin. *The Non-Designer's Design Book: Design and Typographic Principles for the Visual Novice*. Berkeley, Calif.: Peachpit Press, 1994.

Usability Testing

Barnum, Carol M. *Usability Testing and Research*. Reading, Mass.: Addison-Wesley Longman, 2001.

Dumas, Joseph S., and Janice C. Redish. *A Practical Guide to Usability Testing.* Bristol, U.K.: Intellect, 1999.

Rubin, Jeffrey. *Handbook of Usability Testing: How to Plan, Design, and Conduct Effective Tests*. New York: John Wiley & Sons, 1994.

User Interfaces

Beyer, Hugh, and Karen Holtzblatt. *Contextual Design: Defining Customer-Centered Systems*. San Francisco: Morgan Kaufmann, 1998.

Coe, Marlana. *Human Factors for Technical Communicators*. New York: John Wiley & Sons, 1996.

Cooper, Alan. *The Inmates Are Running the Asylum: Why High Tech Products Drive Us Crazy and How to Restore the Sanity*. Indianapolis, Ind.: Sams Publishing, 1999.

Cooper, Alan, and Robert M. Reimann. *About Face 2.0: The Essentials of User Interface Design*. New York: John Wiley & Sons, 2003.

Galitz, Wilbert O. *The Essential Guide to User Interface Design: An Introduction to GUI Design Principles and Techniques*. 2d ed. New York: John Wiley & Sons, 2002.

Hackoś, JoAnn T., and Janice C. Redish. *User and Task Analysis for Interface Design*. New York: John Wiley & Sons, 1998.

Hix, Deborah, and H. Rex Hartson. *Developing User Interfaces: Ensuring Usability Through Product & Process*. New York: John Wiley & Sons, 1993.

Isaacs, Ellen, and Alan Walendowski. *Designing from Both Sides of the Screen: How Designers and Engineers Can Collaborate to Build Cooperative Technology*. Indianapolis, Ind.: New Riders, 2001.

Johnson, Jeff. *GUI Bloopers: User-Interface Don'ts and Do's for Software Developers and Managers*. San Francisco: Morgan Kaufmann, 2000.

Laurel, Brenda, ed. *The Art of Human-Computer Interface Design*. Reading, Mass.: Addison-Wesley, 1990.

Laurel, Brenda. *Computers as Theatre*. Reading, Mass.: Addison-Wesley, 1993.

Mayhew, Deborah J. *Principles and Guidelines in Software User Interface Design*. Upper Saddle River, N.J.: Prentice Hall, 1997.

Mayhew, Deborah J. *The Usability Engineering Lifecycle: A Practitioner's Guide to User Interface Design*. San Francisco: Morgan Kaufman, 1999.

Nielsen, Jakob. *Usability Engineering*. San Francisco: Morgan Kaufmann, 1994.

Nielsen, Jakob. useit.com: Jakob Nielsen's site (Usability and Web Design). Available at `http://useit.com`.

Norman, Donald A. *The Design of Everyday Things*. New York: Basic Books, 2002.

Perlman, Gary. Suggested Readings in Human-Computer Interaction (HCI), User Interface (UI) Development, & Human Factors (HF). Available at `http://www.hcibib.org/readings.html`. Gary Perlman, 1993–2001.

Raskin, Jef. *The Humane Interface: New Directions for Designing Interactive Systems*. Harlow, Essex, U.K.: Pearson Education, 2000.

Society for Technical Communication Usability Web site. Available at `http://www.stcsig.org/usability/resources/index.html`.

Tognazzini, Bruce. *Tog on Interface*. Reading, Mass.: Addison-Wesley, 1992.

Vredenburg, Karel, Scott Isensee, and Carol Righi. *User-Centered Design: An Integrated Approach*. Harlow, Essex, U.K.: Pearson Education, 2001.

Web and Internet Publishing

Burdman, Jessica R. *Collaborative Web Development: Strategies and Best Practices for Web Teams.* Includes CD-ROM. Harlow, Essex, U.K.: Pearson Education, 2000.

Flanders, Vincent. *Son of Web Pages That Suck: Learn Good Design by Looking at Bad Design.* 2d ed. Includes CD-ROM. Alameda, Calif.: Sybex, 2002.

Garrett, Jesse James. *The Elements of User Experience: User-Centered Design for the Web.* Indianapolis, Ind.: New Riders Publishing, 2002.

Goto, Kelly, and Emily Cotler. *Web ReDesign: Workflow That Works.* Indianapolis, Ind.: New Riders Publishing, 2001.

Hackos, JoAnn T. *Content Management for Dynamic Web Delivery.* New York: John Wiley & Sons, 2002.

Hackos, JoAnn T., and Dawn M. Stevens. *Standards for Online Communication: Publishing Information for the Internet/World Wide Web/Help Systems/Corporate Intranets.* New York: John Wiley & Sons, 1997.

Krug, Steve. *Don't Make Me Think: A Common Sense Approach to Web Usability.* Indianapolis, Ind.: Que, 2000.

Lynch, Patrick J., and Sarah Horton. *Web Style Guide: Basic Design Principles for Creating Web Sites.* New Haven, Conn.: Yale University Press, 1999.

Morris, Mary E. S., and Randy J. Hinrichs. *Web Page Design: A Different Multimedia.* Palo Alto, Calif.: Sun Microsystems Press, 1996.

National Cancer Institute. *Research-Based Web Design and Usability Guidelines.* Available at http://usability.gov/guidelines.

Nielsen, Jakob. *Designing Web Usability: The Practice of Simplicity.* Indianapolis, Ind.: New Riders Publishing, 2000.

Nielsen, Jakob. *Multimedia and Hypertext: The Internet and Beyond.* Boston: AP Professional, 1995.

Nielsen, Jakob, and Marie Tahir. *Homepage Usability: 50 Websites Deconstructed.* Indianapolis, Ind.: New Riders Publishing, 2001.

Rosenfeld, Louis, and Peter Morville. *Information Architecture for the World Wide Web: Designing Large-Scale Web Sites.* 2d ed. Sebastopol, Calif.: O'Reilly & Associates, 2002.

Slatin, John M., and Sharron Rush. *Maximum Accessibility: Making Your Web Site More Usable for Everyone.* Reading, Mass.: Addison Wesley Professional, 2002.

Spool, Jared M., Tara Scanlon, Will Schroeder, et al. *Web Site Usability: A Designer's Guide*. San Francisco: Morgan Kaufmann, 1999.

Williams, Robin, and John Tollett. *The Non-Designer's Web Book: An Easy Guide to Creating, Designing, and Posting Your Own Web Site*. 2d ed. Berkeley, Calif.: Peachpit Press, 2000.

Wodtke, Christina. *Information Architecture: Blueprints for the Web*. Indianapolis, Ind.: New Riders Publishing, 2002.

Writing Standards

Barzun, Jacques. *Simple & Direct: A Rhetoric for Writers*. 4th ed. New York: Harper Collins, 2001.

Brooks, Brian S. *Working With Words*. 4th ed. New York: St. Martin's Press, 1999.

Dupre, Lyn. *Bugs in Writing: A Guide to Debugging Your Prose*. Rev. ed. Reading, Mass.: Addison-Wesley, 1998.

Ede, Lisa S. *Work in Progress: A Guide to Writing and Revising*, 4th ed. New York: St. Martin's Press, 1998.

Fiske, Robert Hartwell. *The Writer's Digest Dictionary of Concise Writing*. Cincinnati, Ohio: Writer's Digest Books, 1996.

Flesch, Rudolf, and A.H. Lass. *The Classic Guide to Better Writing*. 50th anniversary ed. New York: Harper Collins, 1996.

Lutz, William. *The New Doublespeak: Why No One Knows What Anyone's Saying Anymore*. 1st ed. New York: HarperCollins Publishers, 1996.

Strunk, William, Jr., and E. B. White. *Elements of Style*. 4th ed. New York: Macmillan, 1999.

Williams, Joseph M. *Style: Ten Lessons in Clarity and Grace*. 7th ed. New York: Longman, 2002.

Young, Matt. *The Technical Writer's Handbook: Writing With Style and Clarity*. Mill Valley, Calif.: University Science Books, 2002.

Writing Standards for Technical Writing

Alred, Gerald J., Charles T. Brusaw, and Walter E. Oliu. *Handbook of Technical Writing.* 7th ed. New York: St. Martin's Press, 2003.

Ament, Kurt. *Single Sourcing: Building Modular Documentation.* Park Ridge, N.J.: Noyes Publications, 2002.

Barker, Thomas T. *Writing Software Documentation: A Task-Oriented Approach.* 2d ed. Harlow, Essex, U.K.: Pearson Education, 2002.

Barnum, Carol M., and Saul Carliner. *Techniques for Technical Communicators.* Upper Saddle River, N.J.: Prentice Hall, 1992.

Bremer, Michael. *The User Manual Manual: How to Research, Write, Test, Edit and Produce a Software Manual.* Concord, Calif.: Untechnical Press, 1999.

Brogan, John A. *Clear Technical Writing.* New York: McGraw-Hill, 1973.

Burnett, Rebecca E. *Technical Communication.* 5th ed. Stamford, Conn.: Harcourt College Publishers, 2000.

Horton, William. *Designing and Writing Online Documentation: Hypermedia for Self-Supporting Products.* 2d ed. New York: John Wiley & Sons, 1994.

Mager, Robert Frank. *Preparing Instructional Objectives.* 3d ed. Atlanta, Ga.: Center for Effective Performance, 1997.

Perry, Carol Rosenblum. *The Fine Art of Technical Writing*, 1st ed. Hillsboro, Ore.: Blue Heron Publishing, 1991.

Price, Jonathan. *How to Communicate Technical Information: A Handbook of Software and Hardware Documentation.* Redwood City, Calif.: Benjamin/Cummings Publishing Co., 1993.

Sides, Charles H. *How to Write & Present Technical Information.* 3d ed. Phoenix, Ariz.: Oryx Press, 1998.

Simpson, Henry, and Steven M. Casey. *Developing Effective User Documentation: A Human-Factors Approach.* New York: McGraw-Hill, 1988.

Weiss, Edmond H. *How to Write Usable User Documentation.* 2d ed. Phoenix, Ariz.: Oryx Press, 1991.

Woolever, Kristen R., and Helen M. Loeb. *Writing for the Computer Industry.* Upper Saddle River, N.J.: Prentice Hall, 1998.

Index

lists (Continued)
    jump lists, 41
    jump lists, in online documents, 97
    of links, 108
    numbered, 40, 41
    in online documents, 102
    placement of, 36
    punctuating, 39
    sentence fragments in, 39
    unnumbered
        See bulleted lists
localization
    defined, 293
    overview, 293, 294
    recommended reading, 323
long procedures, dividing, 133
long URLs, 230
lowercase letters, plural of, 15

M

machine names, typographic conventions
    for, 58
managers, role of, 278
manuals
    chapter formats for, 176
    component descriptions, 174
    dividing into parts, 173
    document plan for, 171
    multiple-chapter, 173
    single-chapter
        components, 173
        examples of, 172
    types of hardware, 178
    types of software, 180
    typical structure of, 173
    when to index, 245
manufacturing department, documentation
    plan and, 285
marketing department
    documentation plan and, 285
    technical review and, 292
marks, editing, 195
maturity levels, of publications
    departments, 274, 275
"may," use of, 141, 314
measurement,, *See* units of measurement, 13

mechanics of writing
    defined, 2
    editing checklists for, 191, 193
menus
    formatting option names in text, 222, 227
    typographic conventions for, 227
    writing about, 227
messages, error, 47
metaphors, international audiences and, 138
metric system
    including measurements for all
        audiences, 13, 144
    using parentheses for equivalents to U.S.
        measures, 28
"might," use of, 141, 315
milestones, 283, 284
minus sign (-), 22
modifiers, compound, *See* compound
    modifiers, 8
mouse
    buttons, 223
    plural of, 223
    terminology, 223
multivolume sets
    global index for, 269
    style sheets and, 195

N

Need-to-Know proprietary label, 166
negative numbers, 22
news releases, copyrighting, 154
non-disclosure agreements, 281
Notes
    description of, 53
    guidelines for writing, 53
    indexing, 246, 251
noun clusters, international audiences and, 142
nouns
    possessive of, 14
    proper, capitalization and, 2
    using with trademarks, 160
nouns used with trademarked terms
    capitalization of, 160
    definition of, 156
    examples of, 160
    in place of trademarks, 160

organizing online documents
   considerations, 83
   by flow diagram, 88
   by hierarchy, 84
   by inverted pyramid, 85
   by table, 87
   by task, 91
organizing tasks
   using flow diagrams, 119, 122
   using jump lists, 119, 120
   using task maps, 119, 120
outside vendors, print production process
   and, 299
ownership
   copyright, 154
   trademark, 157

P

packaging, 297, 299
page breaks in indexes, 265
page design, online and printed
   documentation, 295
page ranges
   dashes in, 22
   global indexes and, 270
   indexes and, 243, 264
paragraph length, 69, 70
   in online documents, 94
parameters, typographic conventions for, 58
parentheses ()
   brackets and, 16
   glossary entries and, 237
   for metric equivalents to U.S. measures, 28
   plurals and, 27
   sentences and, 28
part divisions
   divider page for, 56, 177
   numbering style for, 8
   when to use, 173
participles
   correct use of, 5
   hyphenating, 24
partition names, typographic conventions
   for, 58
passive voice, 65
path names, typographic conventions for, 57

perfect binding, 298
period (.)
   abbreviations and acronyms and, 12
   dot, 28
   units of measurement and, 13
   when to use, 28, 125
personnel information, proprietary information
   in, 166
phone numbers, international audiences
   and, 137
photocopying, as print production method, 297
photographs
   copyrighting, 154
   using, 209
placing
   callouts, 214
   command syntax in steps, 130
   confirmation button instructions, 132
   footnotes and endnotes, 50
   glossaries, 177
   headings, 32
   illustrations, 211, 212
   index "See Also" references, 256
   index "See" references, 256
   links
      avoiding overlinking, 104
      at end of topic, 108
      to manage content, 107
      strategies, 102
      in text, 230
   lists, 36
   nouns used with trademarked terms, 160
   prerequisites for tasks, 118
   procedures, 124
   quotation marks, 29
   tables, 42
   third-party trademark symbols, 161
   trademark symbols, 157
   verbs in steps, 130
planning
   documentation, 286
   editing process, 288
   editing schedules, 194
   graphics design process, 289
   technical review process, 290
   using documentation plans, 284
   writing process, 287
platform style guides, 326

plurals
- of abbreviations, 12
- of acronyms, 12
- of "appendix", 312
- of "datum", 312
- in indexes, 264
- of lowercase letters, 15
- of mouse devices, 223
- of numbers, 15
- parentheses and, 27
- possessive of, 14
- of symbols, 15
- and trademarks, 159
- of units of measurement, 13
- of uppercase letters, 15

policies, legal
- copyright, 152

pop-up windows, *See* windows, 225

port names, typographic conventions for, 58

possessives
- forming, 14
- pronouns, 14
- and trademarks, 159

post-mortem, 301

post-production process, 300

pound sign (#), international audiences and, 144

preface
- description of, 175
- indexing, 245

prefixes, hyphenated, 24

prepositional phrases, placement of, 140

prepositions
- in headings, 3
- in index entries, 261
- for introducing URLs, 229
- list introductions and, 37

prerequisites for tasks, placement of, 118

presentation materials, proprietary information in, 166

prices, currency specified for, 144

print production process
- binding methods, 298, 299
- outside vendors, 299
- overview, 296, 297
- packaging, 297, 299
- printing methods, 297
- recommended reading, 326

print production process (Continued)
- strategy, 297

procedures
- alternative ways of presenting, 126
  - *See also* branching
- breaking up long, 123, 133
- combining basic, 133
- cross-references in, 124
- cross-referencing one set of shared steps, 132
- definition of, 116, 125
- documenting GUI and command-line, 126
- examples in, 118
- explanatory text for, 124
- glyph for single-step, 128
- heading structure for, 124
- headings for alternative interfaces, 126
- number of steps in, 123
- and overview information, 124
- placement of, 124, 125
- prerequisites for, 118
- proprietary information in, 119, 167
- refining, 132
- single-step
  - ensuring required steps in, 133
  - glyph instead of number for, 128
  - overuse of, 133
- using illustrations in hardware, 127
- verb placement in, 130
- within other procedures, 125
- writing, 117
- writing headings for, 125

product development department
- coordinating with publications department, 286, 291
- documentation plan and, 285
- technical review and, 291

product disks, correction files on, 300

product information, proprietary information in, 166

product labels, copyrighting, 154

product names
- and style sheets, 195
- and word count of steps, 128

product notes, 183
- proprietary information in, 165

product testing department, technical review and, 291

production brokers, 299, 300

S

"(s)," avoiding use of, 27
saddle-stitch binding, 299
scheduling
    online documentation, 295
    printed documentation, 282, 283
schematics, proprietary information in, 165
screen captures
    definition of, 207
    example of, 207
    guidelines for creating, 217
    as guideposts, 126
    international audiences and, 145
    proprietary information in, 119, 167, 168
    using in steps, 126
    when to use, 218
    writer's responsibility for, 289
screen reading, problems and solutions, 82
scrollbars, 226
second draft, 288
section mark (§), for table footnotes, 44
sections
    capitalization of headings, 3, 34
    capitalizing word "section", 3
    cross-references to, 48
    numbered, 34
security, guidelines, 165
"See" and "See Also" references
    in glossaries, 238
    in indexes, 253
    typographic conventions for in indexes, 256
semicolon (;)
    independent clauses and, 19
    in indexes, 256
    quotation marks and, 29
    when to use, 30
sentence structure
    and conjunctions, 67
    fragments in lists, 39
    and independent clauses, 67
    international audiences and, 143
    for lists, 36, 41
    in online documents, 93
    parallel structure, 68
    simplified, 66, 67
    for steps, 129
series, commas and, 19
service manuals, 179

service marks
    definition of, 156
    symbol (^{SM}), 157
        See also trademarks
sets of books
    documentation set plan for, 170
    indexing, 269
    style sheets and, 195
sexist language, avoiding, 75, 76
SGML (Standard Generalized Markup
    Language), recommended reading, 329
single-chapter manuals
    components of, 173
    examples of, 172
single letters, quotation marks around, 29
single quote ('), international audiences
    and, 144
single-step procedures
    ensuring required steps in, 133
    glyph instead of number for, 128
    overuse of, 133
slang, international audiences and, 138
slash (/)
    for fractions, 30
    international audiences and, 144
    multiple meanings of, 30
snapshots, *See* screen captures, 126
software
    Cautions and, 54
    code examples, 46, 118, 122
    code freeze, 287
    copyrighting, 154
    proprietary information in, 165
source code
    copyrighting, 154
    examples, 46
    proprietary information in, 165
source documents
    copyrighting, 154
    proprietary information in, 165, 166
spacing
    of callouts, 215
    of illustrations, 212
specifications, proprietary information in, 166
spelling, verifying
    checklists for, 191, 193
    for indexes, 263
    style sheets and, 195

tracking
cost savings, 276
delivery date changes, 284
time spent, 283
trade names, 156
trade secrets
definition of, 153
proprietary information in, 165
proprietary labels for, 153
trademark legends
definition of, 156
third-party attributions in, 161
and trademark symbols, 158
trademark symbols, 157
different for same term, 158
first occurrence of, 157, 158
most prominent use of, 157
placement of, 157
substituting text marks for, 157
and trademark legends, 156, 158
web pages and, 157, 158
where to use, 157
trademarks
abbreviations and, 11, 159
acronyms and, 11, 159
as adjectives, 159
also as trade names, 156
attributions, definition of, 156
avoiding shortening, 159
complete form of, 159
creating defined terms for, 160
definition of, 156
and fonts, 159
and hyphens, 159
See also nouns used with trademarked
terms
outside the United States., 156
and plural forms, 159
and possessive forms, 159
registered, 156
service marks, 156, 157
symbol (™), 157
symbol placement, 157
See also third-party trademarks
web pages and, 157
training documents, 184
transitions, checklist for, 191

translation
See also international audiences
recommended reading, 323
requirements for, 136
text expansion percentage, 136
translation expansion percentage, 148
typographic conventions, 56
for command-line user input, 59
in indexes, 243, 244, 256
for menus, 227
for text fields, 226
and trademarks, 159
for URLs, 228
for user input in GUIs, 226
when to use, 59
for window controls, 226
for window elements, 225
typography, recommended reading, 330

U

units of measurement
abbreviating, 13
fractions and, 9
for international audiences, 144
plurals of, 13
punctuating, 13
ranges of, 27
using numerals in, 8
unnumbered chapters, 176
unnumbered lists, *See* bulleted lists, 39
uppercase letters, plural of, 15
URLs
guidelines for, 109
long, 230
pronunciation of URL, 228
proprietary information in, 119, 168
in running text, 230
See also third-party Web sites; web pages
typographic conventions for, 228
usability testing
of online documents, 95
recommended reading, 330
usability testing department, technical review
and, 292